SOCIAL CITIZENSHIP IN AN AGE OF WELFARE REGIONALISM

This book presents a socio-legal examination of national and devolved-level developments in social protection in the UK, through the eyes of politicians and officials at the heart of this process.

Since its inception in 1998, devolution has altered the character of the UK welfare state, with dramatic change in the 10 years since 2010. A decade of austerity at national level has exposed diverging opinions of how governments in London, Edinburgh and Belfast view the social rights of citizenship. This political divide has implications for both social security law, as the devolved countries begin to flex their muscles in this key area for citizens' economic welfare, and the constitutional settlement.

The book reflects on the impact of austerity, the referendum on Scottish independence and subsequent changes to the devolution settlement, Northern Ireland's hesitant moves away from parity with Westminster in social protection, and the possible retreat from austerity during the COVID-19 pandemic.

The social union may or may not be weakening; its character is unquestionably changing, and the book lays bare the ideological and pragmatic considerations driving legal developments. TH Marshall's theory of citizenship provides the lens through which these processes are viewed, while itself being reinterpreted in light of the national government's increasing delegation of responsibility for social rights – whether to individuals, the voluntary sector or lower tiers of government.

Social Citizenship in an Age of Welfare Regionalism

The State of the Social Union

Mark Simpson

•HART•
OXFORD • LONDON • NEW YORK • NEW DELHI • SYDNEY

HART PUBLISHING

Bloomsbury Publishing Plc

Kemp House, Chawley Park, Cumnor Hill, Oxford, OX2 9PH, UK

1385 Broadway, New York, NY 10018, USA

29 Earlsfort Terrace, Dublin 2, Ireland

First published in Great Britain 2022

A catalogue record for this book is available from the British Library.

A catalogue record for this book is available from the Library of Congress.

Library of Congress Control Number: 2022932645

ISBN: HB: 978-1-50994-641-9
ePDF: 978-1-50994-643-3
ePub: 978-1-50994-642-6

Typeset by Compuscript Ltd, Shannon

ACKNOWLEDGEMENTS

Only one name appears on the cover of this book, but it would not have made it to publication without the contributions and support of many others. A large share of the credit must go to Gráinne McKeever, whose enthusiasm and critical friendship have been an inspiration since our paths first crossed in 2012. Also crucial to the success of the study were the 64 participants in the fieldwork. The generosity with which they shared their expertise, recollections and passion allowed me to gain insights into the developments the book describes that could not have been obtained any other way. From a practical point of view, the research would have been impossible without the funding and time to plan and execute the fieldwork and do an enormous amount of reading and writing. These came in the form of a Department of Employment and Learning PhD studentship, Socio-Legal Studies Association PhD fieldwork grant, British Academy-Leverhulme small research grant (SRG18R1\180575) and my research allocation and a semester's research leave from Ulster University. Too many other people to list have contributed to getting the work to this stage, but thanks are particularly due to Ann Marie Gray, Neville Harris, Derek Birrell, Mike Adler, Peter Dwyer, Ciara Fitzpatrick, Rory O'Connell, the non-academic staff at Ulster, everyone at Hart and of course Hannah Miller for the fantastic illustrations. Many of the ideas presented were first aired at conferences and workshops hosted or sponsored by the Socio-Legal Studies Association, Social Policy Association, Economic and Social Rights Academic Network, Society of Legal Scholars or Centre for Criminal Justice and Human Rights, or simply in conversation with colleagues or fellow postgraduate researchers at Ulster. If you took the time to ask questions about my paper, discuss my ideas, provide feedback on a draft, peer review a submission or co-author something with me, you have helped shape this work too. To the many others who have offered support, encouragement and opportunities along the way – you know who you are. Last, but by no means least, thanks to Nicola and Ossian for their patience and indulgence.

The cover and chapter illustrations were completed by Hannah Miller. More of Hannah's work can be viewed at www.hatiillustration.com/ and she tweets at @hatillustration.

CONTENTS

ABBREVIATIONS

AME	Annually managed expenditure
CDP	Child disability payment
CESA	Contributory employment and support allowance
CESCR	Committee on Economic, Social and Cultural Rights
CJTLS	Coronavirus jobs retention scheme
CRPD	Convention on the Rights of Persons with Disabilities
DHP	Discretionary housing payment
DLA	Disability living allowance
DSS	Department of Social Security
DUP	Democratic Unionist Party
DWP	Department for Work and Pensions
ECHR	European Convention on Human Rights (Convention for the Protection of Human Rights and Fundamental Freedoms)
ECtHR	European Court of Human Rights
EEA	European Economic Area
ESA	Employment and support allowance
ESC	European Social Charter
EU	European Union
HMRC	Her Majesty's Revenue and Customs
ICESCR	International Covenant on Economic, Social and Cultural Rights
IS	Income support
JCHR	Joint Committee on Human Rights
JSA	Jobseeker's allowances
LHA	Local Housing Allowance
NI	Northern Ireland

PIP	Personal independence payment
SCoSS	Scottish Commission on Social Security
SDLP	Social Democratic and Labour Party
SNP	Scottish National Party
SSAC	Social Security Advisory Committee
TFEU	Treaty on the Functioning of the European Union
UBI	Universal basic income
UC	Universal credit
UK	United Kingdom of Great Britain and Northern Ireland
UN	United Nations
UNCRC	United Nations Convention on the Rights of the Child
UUP	Ulster Unionist Party

LIST OF TABLES

TABLE OF CASES

TABLE OF STATUTES

TABLE OF STATUTORY INSTRUMENTS/RULES

TABLE OF INTERNATIONAL AGREEMENTS

1

Introduction: Social Citizenship in an Age of Welfare Regionalism

'Perhaps the most important item for the people of this country is the agreed parity in social services and in other matters which exists between ourselves [in Northern Ireland] and our kinsmen across the water [in Great Britain]. It has meant prosperity. It has meant the removal of fear and want from many homes.'[1]

'We should be concerned that [the numbers of children living in poverty] remain far too high and that driven by the UK Government's pernicious welfare reforms, the number

[1] B Brooke, HC (NI) Deb 2 March 1949 vol 33 col 37.

> of Scottish children living in poverty is expected to increase significantly … It highlights for me the constraints the current constitutional settlement places on our ability to deliver the step changes in tackling child poverty we aspire to.'[2]

Introduction

The social rights of citizenship are always in flux. The two quotations with which this chapter begins show two contrasting views on the United Kingdom (UK) as a social union, from different eras, countries and political perspectives. From the point of view of a Northern Ireland unionist, culturally, politically and religiously attached to Great Britain, located in one of the economically weaker regions of the UK and speaking during the 'trente glorieuses' in which welfare states were in the ascendancy internationally, the advantages of the union for living standards and public services are beyond question. For a Scottish nationalist, commenting more than 50 years later, committed to secession in any case, located in an economically stronger part of the UK and writing at a time when key parts of the welfare state were under severe financial pressure, the union appears to entrench poverty rather than acting as a bulwark against it.

Sturgeon's statement speaks to the extent to which the role of the state and of different parts of the state as a guarantor of social rights has been contested in the twenty-first century. Successive UK Governments in this period have shared a commitment to prioritise paid employment as the means of securing one's economic welfare while continuing to offer safety-net protection against poverty. Understandings of what poverty is, and the state's precise role in protecting against it, have been less consistent. Through financial crises, recessions and a pandemic, the social and economic context to which the welfare state must respond has also varied. Consequently, legal and policy measures to protect citizens against social risk have varied over time, often controversially. Change can also occur in the tier of government that – in law or in citizens' eyes – is responsible for ensuring a minimum level of economic welfare. Although the social union, embodied in the welfare state, has long had something of a regional character, this regional dimension has been accentuated in the post-1998 devolution era, in which questions of social rights are inextricably linked with constitutional questions. In the 2014 referendum on Scottish independence, competing claims of the social benefits of the union and of irreconcilable differences between UK and Scottish visions of social citizenship played a key role in the debate on the UK's continued existence as a union of four countries. The union survives, subject to renewed uncertainty in the wake of withdrawal from the European Union (EU), but the Scottish referendum forms part of a sequence of events in the 2010s that have brought greater

[2] N Sturgeon, 'Foreword from the Deputy First Minister' in Scottish Government, *Child Poverty Strategy for Scotland: Our Approach 2014–2017* (Edinburgh: Scottish Government, 2014) 3.

divergence in how social citizenship is defined and experienced in different parts of the UK. For the first time, substate institutions have had both the necessary powers and the political will to pursue a distinctive legislative and policy agenda in the key field of social security.

This book is concerned with the implications of these developments for social citizenship and the social union, understood to encompass both the sense of and mechanisms for solidarity between citizens from the various countries of the UK. Following an initial introduction to the concept of social citizenship, particularly its utility and relevance in a socio-legal and devolutionary context, it considers the extent to which changes to social protection at UK level fundamentally alter the character of the citizen's social rights. It explains how the devolved countries of Scotland and Northern Ireland have begun to diverge from the UK government in areas of social security under their control. It analyses the various contextual factors – legal, ideological, socio-economic, institutional and identity-based – that may drive or constrain divergence. It ultimately draws conclusions about whether it is still realistic to talk about a single UK social citizenship and about the implications of the process of regionalisation – however partial – for social citizenship theory. This introductory chapter introduces some of the key concepts that underpin the book: social citizenship, multi-level governance, the social union and welfare regionalism. The potential importance of the coronavirus pandemic for the future development of social citizenship is then highlighted. The chapter will also provide a brief introduction to the qualitative longitudinal research project on which the text draws and an overview of the subsequent chapters.

Social Citizenship

This being a book about social citizenship, it must start with a short introduction to the term, its origins and what it means.[3] Social citizenship has its origins as a strand of TH Marshall's theory of citizenship as sequentially conferring civil, political and social rights.[4] It is a contested concept, but at heart can be understood as shorthand for the state's obligation to 'fulfil normative expectations about how the basic requirements of … personal welfare and development can be met'.[5] Marshall views it as a 'guaranteed minimum' of income and services to be enjoyed by citizens as of right. The emergence of social citizenship marked a definitive break with the former Poor Law model, under which recipients of public support had to sacrifice their civil rights to the extent that they 'ceased to be citizens in any true

[3] Chapter 2 provides a fuller discussion of social citizenship theory.

[4] TH Marshall, 'Citizenship and social class' in TH Marshall and T Bottomore, *Citizenship and Social Class* (London: Pluto, 1992).

[5] N Harris, *Law in a Complex State: Complexity in the Law and Structure of Welfare* (Oxford: Hart, 2013) 4.

sense of the word'.[6] Access to these goods and services is not solely a question of income – healthcare and, to a large extent, education are provided free at the point of delivery in the UK, the latter featuring prominently across Marshall's writings. However, in the developed world, sufficient income generally is a prerequisite for access to means of subsistence or the goods, services and activities most members of society take for granted. To a large extent, then, an investigation of the state of social citizenship in the UK is an investigation of how the state ensures citizens have an adequate income for a minimum standard of living, particularly during periods when they are unable to access sufficient resources through the labour market.

The social rights of citizenship are closely related to the exercise of political rights. They can therefore vary depending on the political preferences of different societies at different times. For several decades following the Second World War, a broad consensus around the consolidation and development of modern welfare states prevailed across liberal democracies, albeit that the precise form of welfare state varied.[7] From the 1970s onwards, the nature of citizens' social entitlements and reciprocal obligations became more politically contested internationally, although movement towards a 'new consensus' has also been detected.[8] Relatively long standing pressures relating to economic globalisation, demographic change in the (post-)industrial world and a shift to the right in the prevailing political mood have been added to by the fallout from the post-2007 financial crisis.[9] These changes have been relatively well documented and there is an extensive body of literature comparing the welfare state models adopted by different states.[10] Until recently, less attention has been paid to the different choices about social rights that might be made *within* a state. In the UK, subnational differences of approach have long been a feature of social policy, but in the context of an apparently unassailable consensus around core principles, for example the delivery of healthcare largely free at the point of use. It is only in the last decade that this has applied to any significant extent to social security. This is important because social security is arguably the terrain on which the social rights of citizenship have been most contested and reshaped and the most important service in determining the standard of living citizens can enjoy when their earned income is low or they face specific, unavoidable costs that others may not. As tiers of government below the UK level assume competence for social security and exercise this competence

[6] Marshall, above n 4 at 15, 32.

[7] P Taylor-Gooby, *Reframing Social Citizenship* (Oxford: Oxford University Press, 2009).

[8] H Bochel and A Defty, 'MPs' attitudes to welfare: a new consensus?' (2007) 36(1) *Journal of Social Policy* 1; T Abou-Chadi and EM Immergut, 'Recalibrating social protection: electoral competition and the new partisan politics of the welfare state' (2019) 58(2) *European Journal of Political Research* 697.

[9] Taylor-Gooby, above n 7; A Nolan (ed), *Economic and Social Rights after the Global Financial Crisis* (Cambridge: Cambridge University Press, 2014).

[10] See G Esping-Andersen, *The Three Worlds of Welfare Capitalism* (Princeton: Princeton University Press, 1989); P Emmenegger, J Kvist, P Marx and K Petersen, 'Three worlds of welfare capitalism: the making of a classic' (2015) 25(1) *Journal of European Social Policy* 3.

to develop distinctive approaches, the 'guaranteed minimum' that social citizenship implies may come to differ between the four countries within the union. The central concern of this book is the extent to which devolved social citizenships are now emerging and the forces driving any such divergence.

Social Security and Multi-level Governance

The trend towards multi-level governance has been relatively long-running and pan-European. Sovereign states have transferred powers downward, to regional tiers of government (where states were not already federal in structure) and outward, to a supranational tier in the form of the EU.[11] The UK was home to the world's first 'perfect example of devolution' in the form of the Northern Ireland Parliament and its successor Assembly from 1921 to 1974.[12] An increasing range of country- and regional-level democratic institutions have been created since the enactment in 1998 of legislation re-establishing a Scottish Parliament and a Northern Ireland Assembly, while creating a Welsh Assembly. Turning briefly to the supranational tier, the UK was a member of the European Economic Community and EU from 1973 to 2020 and remains a member of the Council of Europe.

Devolution in the UK consists of an increasingly diverse, ever-evolving patchwork of institutional structures, functions, budgets and fiscal powers.[13] The most significant devolved institutions in terms of social citizenship are the Scottish Parliament, the Northern Ireland Assembly and the Senedd (Welsh Parliament). Each of these institutions holds primary legislative powers and extensive social policy competences – to the extent that they have been described as 'social policy parliaments'.[14] Differences in the law, policy and governance of key aspects of the welfare state predate legislative devolution in 1998–1999 and further differences have since emerged, although there are also examples of the maintenance of parity, convergence and policy learning.[15] Prior to 2010, social security was a rare area of social policy in which devolution had made little difference. In Scotland and

[11] L Hooghe, G Marks and A Schakel (eds) *Measuring Regional Authority* (2008) 18(2/3) Regional and Federal Studies, special issue; S Piattoni, 'Multi-level governance: a historical and conceptual analysis' (2009) 31(2) *Journal of European Integration* 163.

[12] 'An American professor' cited by JI Cook, 'Financial relations between the Exchequers of the United Kingdom and Northern Ireland' FH Newark, JI Cook, DAE Harkness, LGP Preer and DG Neill, *Devolution of Government: The Experiment in Northern* Ireland (London: George Allen and Unwin, 1953) 18.

[13] For an overview, see J Bradbury, *Constitutional Policy and Territorial Politics in the UK, Vol 1: Union and Devolution 1997–2007* (Bristol: Bristol University Press, 2021) and the forthcoming second volume.

[14] D Birrell, *The Impact of Devolution on Social Policy* (Bristol: Policy Press, 2009) 1.

[15] D Mackinnon, 'Devolution, state restructuring and policy divergence in the UK' (2015) 181(1) *The Geographical Journal* 47; A Paun, J Rutter and A Nicholl, *Devolution as a Policy Laboratory: Evidence Sharing and Learning between the UK's Four Governments* (London: Alliance for Useful Evidence, 2016).

Wales, this was simply because of the initial absence of devolved competences.[16] In Northern Ireland, despite full devolution of social protection since 1921, the convention that parity with Great Britain should be maintained meant that for 90 years its separately administered system delivered a near-identical set of benefits.[17] This has changed considerably since 2010, with Northern Ireland taking small but significant steps away from parity and Scotland beginning to build a devolved system following the revision of its devolution settlement in 2016.[18]

Wales continues to lack the necessary powers to build a genuine devolved system, but at the end of the last decade there were signs of increased political interest in changing this.[19] Devolution of a sort has become a feature of the English constitutional landscape, with the Greater London Authority established in 2000 belatedly joined by 10 combined authorities, eight of which are headed by 'metro mayors', and a 'devolution deal' in place between the UK Government and Cornwall Council.[20] To date, the powers of English regional institutions have largely been drawn up from local government rather than down from Whitehall and have focused mainly on housing, transport and economic development. However, there is provision for more or less any function of a public authority to be transferred to or delivered jointly with a combined authority, meaning these could come to play a greater role in the welfare state – Greater Manchester at least has seen some academic and policymaker debate about the future possibilities.[21] England and Wales do not feature prominently in the book as a result, but the developments in Scotland and Northern Ireland it analyses will carry important lessons for the potential development of subnational social citizenships there, or indeed outside the UK.

The EU's influence on social citizenship in its Member States has varied over time. Under the Treaty on the Functioning of the European Union (TFEU), Member State citizens are also EU citizens. The TFEU associates EU citizenship with specific civil and political rights, including freedom of movement and the opportunity to vote or stand in municipal and European elections in the state of residence.[22] The Treaty commitment to 'social progress … social justice and protection', action against 'social exclusion' and 'economic, social and territorial cohesion, and solidarity among Member States' forms a potential basis for an

[16] Scotland Act 1998 c 46 Sch 5, head F; Government of Wales Act 2006 c 32 Sch 5.

[17] M Simpson, 'Developing constitutional principles through firefighting: social security parity in Northern Ireland' (2015) 22(1) *Journal of Social Security Law* 31.

[18] Scotland Act 2016 c 11 Part 3.

[19] Equality, Local Government and Communities Committee, *Benefits in Wales: Options for better delivery* (Cardiff: National Assembly for Wales, 2019).

[20] Greater London Authority Act 1999 c 29; Local Democracy, Economic Development and Construction Act 2009 c 20 Part 6; HM Government, *Cornwall Devolution Deal* (London: Ministry of Housing, Communities and Local Government, 2016).

[21] Local Democracy, Economic Development and Construction Act 2009 c 20 s 105A; Greater Manchester Poverty Action, 'Devolved approaches to social security in the UK – lessons for Greater Manchester' (Manchester: GMPA, 2020). Available at: www.gmpovertyaction.org/devolved-approaches/.

[22] Treaty on the Functioning of the European Union, arts 20–25.

EU social citizenship,[23] but this has remained underdeveloped.[24] With 'welfare state walls' more fiercely defended by Member States than 'geographical boundaries' the EU has, at heart, remained an economic rather than a social union.[25] It has, though, been suggested that the new Pillar of Social Rights has potential to change this,[26] within which the development of a European unemployment insurance scheme would mark a step change in the extent of Union intervention in the provision made by Member States.[27] For the time being, though, 'hard limits on European social solidarity' remain.[28] Following the UK's withdrawal from the Union in 2020,[29] EU law continues to play a role in determining the circumstances under which its domestic system can be accessed by European Economic Area (EEA) nationals with settled status in the UK, or by EEA residents with sufficient connection to the UK.[30] Clearly, though, the UK will not be a participant in any European social security scheme that might emerge, therefore the EU cannot be described as a major force in determining the substance of social citizenship. This does not mean that the supranational or international tier is now irrelevant to social citizenship – the actual or potential influence of United Nations (UN) and Council of Europe human rights instruments on social rights in the UK will be considered in later chapters.

The Social Union and Welfare Regionalism

The UK is a state of unions. Its constituent countries came together at different times, in different circumstances and on different terms.[31] That this amalgam of territories and national identities has not always been stable is illustrated by Ireland's fractious spell in the union from 1801 until most of the island gained dominion status in 1922.[32] From then until the end of the twentieth century, Northern Ireland remained the only part of the UK with a high degree of legislative autonomy and the country where dissatisfaction with the union was most pronounced. In the

[23] Treaty on European Union, art 3.

[24] KA Polomarkakis, 'The European Pillar of Social Rights and the quest for EU social sustainability' (2020) 29(2) *Social and Legal Studies* 183, 189.

[25] C O'Brien, 'Real links, abstract rights and false alarms: the relationship between the ECJ's "real link" case law and national solidarity' (2008) 33(5) *European Law Review* 643, 645.

[26] Commission Communication establishing a European Pillar of Social Rights COM(2017) 250 final; Polomarkakis, above n 24.

[27] G McKeever and M Simpson, 'Worlds of welfare collide: Implementing a European unemployment benefit scheme in the UK' (2017) 19(1) *European Journal of Social Security* 21; see also M Beblavý, G Marconi and I Maselli, *A European Unemployment Benefit Scheme: The Rationale and the Challenges Ahead* (Luxembourg: Publications Office of the European Union, 2017).

[28] V Hooton, 'COVID-19, unemployment and social solidarity in EU law' (2021) 28(1) *Journal of Social Security Law* 16, 16.

[29] European Union (Withdrawal) Act 2018 c 16, s 1.

[30] European Union (Future Relationship) Act 2020 c 29, s 26.

[31] J Mitchell, *Devolution in the UK* (Manchester: Manchester University Press, 2009).

[32] Irish Free State (Agreement) Act 1922 c 4.

twenty-first century, Scotland, which has retained 'clear hallmarks of a nation' and 'a deep national self-consciousness' within the union, has arguably become the country whose place in the UK is most immediately in question, while recent polls have suggested increased support for Welsh independence.[33]

There have been multiple candidates for the title 'the glue that holds the UK together', including the EU, political parties and the monarchy,[34] but the idea of the state as a social union is a consistent contender. The term 'social union' can be interpreted in different ways, but here it is understood to refer to mutual solidarity between citizens thanks to common tax and welfare systems. The House of Lords Constitution Committee notes that, by this definition, 'social union' can be used interchangeably with the term 'welfare union'. Alternative interpretations, focused on family, community, linguistic and cultural ties, are synonymous with the term 'cultural union'.[35] This social or welfare union implies solidarity not only between individuals, but also between regions, with both fiscal and welfare measures serving to redistribute money towards a part of the country suffering either an economic shock or prolonged weakness. Returning to the Committee:

> The fundamental principle of the social union is the pooling of common funds at a UK level which are then expended on the basis of need, on a UK-wide basis. The social union is a manifestation of the solidarity that sees the people of the Union collectively support each other, no matter where in the UK they reside.[36]

From the UK, to the United States, to the EU, this sense of social solidarity has been identified as a crucial nation-building tool, binding individuals to the state and their fellow citizens and sustaining that sense of collectivity.[37] According to this analysis, the welfare state does is not just a vehicle for the social rights of citizenship, but plays a significant role in defining where an individual is a citizen of, by delimiting the community bonded by mutual solidarity. If the welfare state has played a role in binding citizens to states in the past, it can do so in the future. The premise of the 'welfare nationalism' thesis is that aspirations for the future of the welfare state can be closely linked to aspirations for the constitutional future of the state as a whole. Claimed variation in what citizens need from, or in

[33] Bradbury, above n 13; I Wells, 'Welsh independence: how worried should Ministers be?' (BBC News, 2 February 2021). Available at: www.bbc.co.uk/news/uk-wales-politics-55890643.

[34] V Bogdanor, 'Post-Brexit Britain may need a constitution – or face disintegration' (*Guardian*, 18 January 2019). Available at: www.theguardian.com/commentisfree/2019/jan/18/brexit-britain-constitution-disintegration-eu-uk-devolution-good-friday-agreement; J Hopkin, 'Party matters: devolution and party politics in Britain and Spain' (2009) 15(2) *Party Politics* 179; BS Turner, 'In defence of monarchy' (2012) 49 *Society* 84.

[35] Constitution Committee, *The Union and Devolution* (HL149, London: House of Lords, 2016) 18.

[36] Ibid, at 20.

[37] N McEwen, 'State welfare nationalism: the territorial impact of welfare state development in Scotland' (2002) 12(1) *Regional and Federal Studies* 66; M Keating, 'Social citizenship, solidarity and welfare in regionalised and plurinational states' (2009) 13(5) *Citizenship Studies* 501; CE Schall, 'Is the problem of European citizenship a problem of social citizenship? Social policy, federalism and democracy in the EU and United States' (2012) 82(1) *Sociological Inquiry* 123.

their ideological preferences for, a welfare state might be exploited, exaggerated or fabricated to promote the perception that fundamental regional differences exist that ought to be reflected in the devolution of more powers or independence.[38] If sufficient power is devolved and a fairly distinct welfare state emerges, then the sub-state region begins to take on the trappings of a nation state;[39] given sufficient fiscal autonomy, the boundaries of solidarity may begin to shrink to the regional level too. Conversely, welfare unionism might be expected to stress the advantages of the social union to all parts of the state to sustain support for the political union. Findings from the first wave of fieldwork on which this book draws called into question the notion that welfare and constitutional politics overlap as neatly as this. They point instead to an emerging welfare regionalism as both unionists and nationalists embrace the possibilities devolution offers to better support the economic welfare of citizens in their part of the UK.[40] The second wave of fieldwork was an opportunity to determine the persistence of such sentiments.

Enter Coronavirus

No account of the development of the social rights of citizenship in the twenty-first century could be complete without reference to the impact of the coronavirus outbreak that began in December 2019 and was declared a pandemic by the World Health Organisation in March 2020. States' responses to the pandemic spanned multiple areas of public policy, including a range of measures to support incomes. A full analysis of the UK's response even in this one field of policy goes beyond the scope of this book – other publications have begun this mammoth task.[41] The focus here will be on the changes offering the greatest insights into how the state views its obligations to ensure citizens' economic welfare. Even on this front, it is too early to say whether these developments mark a fundamental and lasting shift in the philosophy shaping social security law and policy.[42] Nonetheless, the contrast with the previous decade of austerity has been stark, with targeted

[38] G Mooney and L Poole, '"A land of milk and honey"? Social policy in Scotland after devolution' (2004) 24(4) *Critical Social Policy* 458; N McEwen, 'The territorial politics of social policy development in multilevel states' (2005) 15(4) *Regional and Federal Studies* 537.

[39] I McLean, J Gallagher and G Lodge, *Scotland's Choices: The Referendum and What Happens Afterwards* (Edinburgh: Edinburgh University Press, 2013).

[40] M Simpson, 'The social union after the coalition: devolution, divergence and convergence' (2017) 46(2) *Journal of Social Policy* 251; M Simpson, 'Renegotiating social citizenship in an age of devolution' (2017) 44(4) *Journal of Law and Society* 646.

[41] N Harris, C Fitzpatrick, J Meers and M Simpson, 'Coronavirus and social security entitlement in the UK' (2020) 27(2) *Journal of Social Security Law* 55; Special issue on COVID-19 (2021) 28(1) *Journal of Social Security Law*; D Cowan and A Mumford, *Pandemic Legalities: Wealth, Poverty and the Economic Recovery* (Bristol: Bristol University Press, 2021); R Patrick, M Power, K Garthwaite, G Page and K Pybus, *A Year Like No Other: Family Life on a Low Income in Covid-19* (Bristol: Policy Press, 2022).

[42] A Moreira and R Hick, 'COVID-19, the great recession and social policy: Is this time different?' (2021) 55(2) *Social Policy and Administration* 261.

increases to the level of certain social security benefits (universal credit and housing benefit for private tenants) and even more generous support to those kept in employment through the coronavirus jobs retention scheme. Yet in one respect there has been greater continuity of philosophy, if not in the actual policy measures adopted, when it comes to determining which groups are most deserving of assistance. Alongside a clear acknowledgement of the necessity of state action to support citizens' economic welfare in what has been both a public health crisis and an economic crisis sits a definite, though largely politically unacknowledged, privileging of people with current or recent ties to the paid labour market.

The coronavirus pandemic has been a major challenge for welfare states internationally,[43] but has also been hailed as a development on a par with the Spanish flu of 1918–1919, the Great Depression of the 1930s or the Second World War, with similar potential to reshape long term expectations of how states should support citizens.[44] A further effect of coronavirus has been as a case study of how the UK's system of devolved governance responds to a common crisis. Following an initial period of 'broad agreement' between governments on the necessary actions and an 'unusual level of coordination' between the various health services, differences in both infection control measures and economic interventions began to emerge at a fairly early stage.[45] At times this these differences of approach appeared to descend into competition and even recrimination, for example in the debate around devolved governments' competence to enforce travel restrictions limiting people's ability to cross the UK's internal borders.[46] However, the ultimate social security and constitutional implications of the pandemic will only become clear over time.

A Socio-legal Study of Social Citizenship

This book is the product of a study of social citizenship in the UK spanning close to a decade and straddling the disciplines of law and social policy. The Welfare Reform Act 2012 had received Royal Assent a few months before the research began. Changes associated with the Act have been and continue to be the focus of numerous investigations across the two disciplines. The devolutionary focus of this project was influenced by the backlash against the new Westminster model of social protection in Northern Ireland and Scotland, the fast-emerging,

[43] A Sprague, A Raub and J Heymann, 'Providing a foundation for decent work and adequate income during health and economic crises: constitutional approaches in 193 countries' (2020) 40(9/10) *International Journal of Sociology and Social Policy* 1087.

[44] New Statesman, 'The welfare conundrum' (2021) 150 (5603) *New Statesman* 3; S Glenister, 'How can we shape the way the country is run?' (2020) 85 *Socialist Lawyer* 5.

[45] A Paun, J Sargent and A Nice, *A Four-nation Exit Strategy: How the UK and Devolved Governments should Approach Coronavirus* (London: Institute for Government, 2020) 4, 5.

[46] C Matchett, 'Fact check: Labour peer's claim Scottish cross-border ban unlawful mostly false' (*The Scotsman*, 23 December 2020). Available at: www.scotsman.com/health/coronavirus/fact-check-labour-peers-claim-scottish-cross-border-ban-unlawful-mostly-false-3076779.

unprecedented political consensus that Northern Ireland should not automatically embrace the UK-level reforms and the contemporary debate on the merits of Scottish independence. It was clear that developments in both social security and constitutional law were largely being driven by political considerations, albeit that legal issues like human rights and the extent of devolved competences could themselves influence the positions taken by political actors or demarcate the politically possible. Marshall's theory of citizenship holds that social rights flow from the exercise of political rights yet can appear to have a blind spot as to what might happen to social rights once political rights come to be exercised at regional as well as national level – a question that was being answered in real time as the research progressed.

A full understanding of these important developments in social citizenship required deeper insights into the aspirations and motivations of the key actors driving – or aspiring to drive – the process than could be obtained through materials in the public domain. Politicians and their parties naturally adopted public positions on welfare reform and devolution, but seldom had the opportunity to articulate what deeper considerations on the social rights of citizenship, aspirations for the welfare state and ambitions for devolved government might underpin these views. Officials clearly had a wealth of knowledge about issues central to the study, but little scope to publicly express their own views. Qualitative interviews were therefore conducted with elected representatives and officials in both Scotland and Northern Ireland, on the basis of anonymity so as not to discourage interrogation of political parties' and government departments' or directorates' public positions.[47] By tapping into the expertise and insider knowledge of both groups, the first wave of fieldwork delivered unique insights into why the welfare state was developing in a certain way following devolution and the forces that might shape its future development. A longitudinal study was not envisaged at the outset, but the pace of development in both countries following the completion of wave one meant it would have been unthinkable to publish a book without returning to the field to gather reflections in the changed context.

Research participants were purposively recruited to cover the range of mainstream political opinion in each country, across both the left-right and unionist-nationalist spectrums. At least one member of every party represented in the Scottish Parliament and every party with two or more members in the Northern Ireland Assembly at the time of each wave took part. As far as possible, individual politicians were targeted on the basis of contemporary or recent committee, Ministerial or party spokesperson roles of relevance to the study. In Northern Ireland, this mainly meant individuals who had served on the Committee for Social Development, Committee for Communities or the ad-hoc committee established to assess the equality and human rights implications of the Welfare Reform Bill. In Scotland, most politicians interviewed had served on the Welfare Reform

[47] Semi-structured interviews were conducted, recorded and analysed in accordance with constructivist grounded theory practice – see K Charmaz, *Constructing Grounded Theory* (London: Sage, 2014).

Committee, Social Security Committee or Smith Commission. For the first wave of fieldwork, officials were recruited from departments or directorates with responsibility for social security, welfare more broadly (the Scottish Government's social security directorate did not yet exist), human rights, equality and finance. The second wave focused more narrowly on officials from departments, directorates or agencies with responsibility for social security, with occasional exceptions. Wave one, from late 2014 to spring 2015, involved 36 participants: 19 from Northern Ireland and 17 from Scotland. Of the 18 politicians across both jurisdictions, eight represented pro-union parties, nine represented nationalist or secessionist parties and one a party neutral on the constitutional issue. The remaining 18 participants were officials. Wave two, which stretched throughout much of 2020, involved 34 participants, six of whom had been interviewed during wave one. Eighteen were from Northern Ireland and 16 from Scotland. Of the 19 politicians, nine were unionists, eight were nationalists and two represented 'neutral' parties. The remaining 15 participants were officials.

An important question, both at the end of the doctoral study and in the preparation of the manuscript for this book, is where to establish a cut-off point. The interviews provide a snapshot of elite opinion at a given point in time; it is hard to imagine a more vivid illustration of the fact that developments continue after that point than the arrival of the coronavirus pandemic and significant social security response with the second wave still in progress. The narrative in these pages inevitably has an end point, but an arbitrary one driven by the fact that it is necessary to stop *somewhere*, otherwise nothing would ever be published. In this case, the publisher's deadline dictated that developments after October 2021 must await a future publication for analysis.

This section ends with a word on the nature of law. The author's scepticism towards natural law theories will become apparent, yet this is emphatically not a legal positivist work that views law as divorced from ethics or morality. Rather, the law is viewed as an 'instrument for achieving social justice'[48] through its role as governments' 'principal tool used … to deliver social and economic policy'.[49] Consequently, law emerges from and in turn helps shape a particular society and a particular political arena. Social justice is a contested concept. In this case, the society from which the law emerges is also contested; devolution has transformed the polity from which social policy and related fields of law emerge from a UK-wide one to a more regionalised one. Tamanaha argues that the 'mirror thesis' – which holds that law tends to reflect the needs, norms or demands of the society from which it emerges – breaks down when 'an overarching political authority enacts a uniform law that governs diverse populations', which may not share the

[48] DJ Galligan, 'Legal theory and empirical research' in P Cane and HM Kritzer (eds), *The Oxford Handbook of Empirical Legal Research* (Oxford: Oxford University Press, 2010) 983.

[49] M Partington, 'Empirical legal research and policy-making' in P Cane and HM Kritzer (eds), *The Oxford Handbook of Empirical Legal Research* (Oxford: Oxford University Press, 2010) 1003.

same norms or needs.[50] The findings presented provide insights into elite views on whether their respective countries want or need something different from their welfare state to the overarching authority in London, and the extent to which the constitutional settlement allows substate social security systems to hold a mirror to these differing visions of social justice.

Structure of the Book

The current state of social citizenship and the social union in the UK will be explored through a further nine chapters. Chapter 2 sets the theoretical scene for the book by introducing Marshall's theory of citizenship and its relationship with the alternative, human rights-focused perspective on the sources of social rights. Chapter 3 then focuses on multilevel governance and social citizenship – both its implications for Marshallian citizenship theory, which tends to be strongly associated with the nation state, and the opportunity that devolution presents for citizens' social rights to diverge in practice between the various UK countries. Chapter 4 sets out the key UK-level developments in social security during the twenty-first century and some of the key assumptions about social citizenship that underpin them – including continuity and change therein. The focus then shifts to the devolved level, with Chapter 5 providing an overview of the divergence from the UK model of social security that has occurred in Scotland and Northern Ireland to date. The second half of the book delves more deeply into the forces driving this divergence. Chapter 6 considers how perceptions of fairness, dignity and rights have underpinned developments in social security – as well as challenges to certain developments – at UK and devolved level. Chapter 7 looks to the devolved level specifically, building on the work of Béland and Lecours by examining the (potential) role of socio-economic, ideological and institutional factors as the foundations of emerging devolved social citizenships. The extent to which the developments described can be regarded as manifestations of welfare unionism, nationalism and/or regionalism – or of a clash between welfare unionist and nationalist positions – forms the focus of Chapter 8. Chapter 9 then provides an opportunity to take stock of how much progress has been made – normatively or empirically – towards the establishment of distinct Scottish and Northern Irish social citizenships, and where the process might next lead. Finally, Chapter 10 draws some conclusions about the state of the social union in the early 2020s – whether the UK is marked by a unifying vision of social citizenship and a single welfare state, or whether these have become definitively regionalised; the interconnectedness of welfare state and constitutional developments; and what Marshall's theory of citizenship and welfare regionalism can tell about each other.

[50] BZ Tamanaha, 'Law and society' in D Patterson (ed), *A Companion to Philosophy of Law and Legal Theory* (Hoboken: Wiley-Blackwell, 2010) 371.

2

A Socio-legal Perspective on Social Citizenship

Introduction

A socio-legal study of social citizenship must start by outlining what the author understands social citizenship to mean and the value this interdisciplinary approach can add given that Marshall's theory is sociological rather than legal. A legal perspective can enhance understanding of the social rights of citizenship through consideration of the human rights and constitutional context from which legal provisions to ensure a minimum standard of living emerge and that can inform expectations or set boundaries for their future evolution. At the same time, no analysis of the social rights of citizenship can be complete without understanding the visions of social justice that underpin governments' attempts to define or redefine these. Studies of citizenship can approach the concept in various ways, each of which influences the approach taken in this book to some degree. Citizenship is a legal status conferring rights and responsibilities. It is possible to explore empirically what those rights and responsibilities are, or to discuss normatively what they ought to be. This package of rights and responsibilities then shapes the lived experience of citizenship and the extent to which being a citizen is an active or passive status.[1] This book examines both empirical and normative perspectives on the legal status of citizenship, but the evolution of this legal status in turn affects how citizenship is practiced and experienced.

The next section gives an overview of Marshall's theory of citizenship. This narrative of the evolution of citizenship to confer first civil, then political and finally social rights forms the theoretical starting point for the book. What rights and responsibilities Marshall understood the social element of citizenship to confer, the people and institutions to whom those rights and responsibilities pertain and the extent to which twenty-first century social citizenship aligns with this view will be explored throughout the volume. The following section addresses the question of why a socio-legal exploration of the contemporary welfare state should choose citizenship as its theoretical grounding, rather than the more explicitly legal concept of human rights. Although citizenship and human rights have sometimes been presented as alternative sources of rights, it is suggested that the two are at least potentially complementary. This leads on to a section on the question of whether social rights are 'real', enforceable rights, in principle and in the context that the European Convention on Human Rights (ECHR), which is primarily concerned with civil and political rights, forms part of UK law, while treaties that focus on social rights do not.

Marshall's Theory of Citizenship: From Civil Rights to a 'Right to Welfare'

The concept of social citizenship is derived from TH Marshall's theory of citizenship, chiefly set out in his 1949 lecture on 'Citizenship and social class'. Marshall depicts citizenship as evolving alongside the development of capitalism and liberal democracy. The citizen first obtains civil rights, such as freedom of conscience, expression and contract and the right to property ownership and equality before

[1] M Lister, '"Marshall-ing" social and political citizenship: towards a unified conception of citizenship' (2005) 40(4) *Government and Opposition* 471; R Lister et al., *Gendering Citizenship in Western Europe: New Challenges for Citizenship Research in a Cross-national Context* (Bristol: Policy Press, 2007).

the law, these being necessary for the development of a market economy. Through the exercise of civil rights, the citizen can demand the political rights to vote and seek election. Having acquired the franchise, less well-off social groups, more exposed to social risks such as unemployment, sickness and poverty, can be expected to vote for representatives who promise an extension of social rights including healthcare, education and social protection. The social element of citizenship promises a minimum level of economic welfare. This social minimum may be located anywhere on a spectrum spanning:

> The whole range from the right to a modicum of economic welfare and security to the right to share to the full in the social heritage and to live the life of a civilised being according to the standards prevailing in the society.[2]

Once in place, the three elements of citizenship are as interdependent as the legs of a three-legged stool – remove one and the other two cannot stand.[3] Although the social element of citizenship emerges from the exercise of civil and political rights, the citizen's ability to enjoy his or her civil and political rights to the full may in turn be dependent on the exercise of social rights. The civil right to access justice may appear remote to someone lacking the legal capability to recognise that they have a justiciable problem – something associated with socio-economic disadvantage – or the means to procure legal representation.[4] Engagement with the political process may (but will not inevitably) be a lower priority, or less feasible, for someone preoccupied with accessing subsistence needs.[5]

The Marshallian theory of citizenship is a product of a particular time and place – post-Second World War Britain. Subsequent authors have questioned its continuing or global applicability. In particular, the teleological progression depicted in 'Citizenship and social class' has been critiqued as excessively anglo- and male-centric. It is undeniable that social rights have emerged in the absence of extensive rights to political engagement – including in imperial Germany, the prototypical welfare state, and the former socialist states of central and eastern Europe. Conversely, states can develop sophisticated systems of political rights despite persistent inequalities of civil rights, then fail to develop a comprehensive set of social rights.[6] Some authors respond that Marshall was aware that his account was of the development of citizenship in the UK specifically.[7] Marshall's second

[2] TH Marshall, 'Citizenship and social class'in TH Marshall and T Bottomore, *Citizenship and Social Class* (London: Pluto, 1992) 8.

[3] F Twine, *Citizenship and Social Rights: The Interdependence of Self and Society* (London: Sage, 1994) 104.

[4] G McKeever, M Simpson and C Fitzpatrick, *Destitution and Paths to Justice* (London: Legal Education Foundation/York: Joseph Rowntree Foundation, 2018).

[5] DS King and J Waldron, 'Citizenship, social citizenship and the defence of welfare provision' (1988) 18(4) *British Journal of Political Science* 415; M Lister, above n 1.

[6] G Delanty, *Citizenship in a Global Age: Society, Culture and Politics* (Milton Keynes: Open University Press, 2000).

[7] B Revi, 'TH Marshall and his critics: reappraising "social citizenship" in the twenty-first century' (2014) 18(3–4) *Citizenship Studies* 452.

claimed blind spot is for gender. Work, warfare and reproduction might have served as parallel routes to citizenship over the centuries,[8] but not always to the same citizenship. Women, whose contribution to many societies has traditionally been viewed through the narrow prism of their reproductive and caring roles, have not necessarily gained the three categories of citizenship rights at the same time, in the same order or to the same degree as men.[9] Women whose claim to citizenship is via the reproductive route have often had to rely on a male breadwinner (who in turn depended on a wife's unpaid domestic labour to enable him to focus on paid employment) or social assistance benefits – often lower value and more stigmatised than social insurance – for their economic welfare.[10] A third strand of the critique concerns the assertion that there are only three elements of citizenship. Multiple additional elements have been proposed, including domestic, cultural, ecological, global and intimate or reproductive citizenships.[11]

While none of these appraisals of Marshall is unimportant, questions about the accuracy or generalisability of his teleology of citizenship and the possibility that the citizenship stool might have more than three legs do not detract from the central point that modern citizenship *does* have a social element. This, at least, is not much disputed in the literature, although some authors have suggested that in North America the social element never fully developed or has been shorn off in recent decades.[12] There is ample space to debate the nature of the rights conferred and the responsibilities demanded of citizens in return and whether the reality of contemporary social citizenship can be reconciled with the Marshallian vision. Dean argues that Marshall was fundamentally mistaken to argue that the elements of citizenship emerge in sequence, rather that the civil, political and social rights it confers are continually contested and renegotiated.[13] It is unnecessary to dissect the historical accuracy of 'Citizenship and social class' to observe that such a process of renegotiation has been a feature of the period with which this book is concerned. Three possible challenges to the Marshallian view are of particular interest. First, the state clearly continues to underwrite a 'modicum of economic welfare' for those citizens who meet the required conditions. However, a 'right to share to the full' in society,[14] always of questionable relevance to the UK's liberal welfare state,

[8] BS Turner, 'The erosion of citizenship' (2001) 52(2) *British Journal of Sociology* 189.

[9] T Bottomore, 'Citizenship and social class, forty years on' in TH Marshall and T Bottomore, *Citizenship and Social Class* (London: Pluto, 1992); S Walby, 'Is citizenship gendered?' (1994) 28(2) *Sociology* 379; AM Rees, 'TH Marshall and the progress of citizenship' in M Bulmer and AM Rees (eds), *Citizenship Today: The Contemporary Relevance of TH Marshall* (London: Routledge, 1996) 11.

[10] C Pateman, *The Disorder of Women* (Cambridge: Polity Press, 1989); R Lister, *Citizenship: Feminist Perspectives* (Basingstoke: Palgrave Mamillan, 2003).

[11] Rees, above n 9; Delanty, above n 6; Turner, above n 8.

[12] JF Handler, *Social Citizenship and Workfare in the United States and Western Europe: The Paradox of Inclusion* (Cambridge: Cambridge University Press, 2004); D Hoxsey, 'Debating the ghost of Marshall: a critique of citizenship (2011) 15(6–7) *Citizenship Studies* 915.

[13] H Dean, 'A post-Marshallian conception of global social citizenship' in E Isin and P Nyers (eds), *The Routledge Handbook of Global Citizenship Studies* (Abingdon: Routledge, 2014).

[14] Marshall, above n 2 at 8.

appears a remote prospect following a decade of austerity marked by deep cuts to working age social security. Second, Marshall is frequently depicted as offering only a 'theory of entitlement' with 'little to say about duties and obligations'.[15] This raises the question of whether his perspective can be reconciled with intensifying demands that recipients of financial support from the state demonstrate 'good citizenship' in return, primarily through engagement with the paid labour market. Third, an account generally understood to locate citizenship at the level of the nation state (here the UK, although whether 'the nation' is represented by the UK or its constituent countries can be disputed) may struggle to accommodate a growing role for sub-state units in the definition, exercise and realisation of its associated rights – or to explain what citizenship means in a more globalised world. These questions about the contemporary relevance of Marshallian theory will be revisited over the subsequent chapters.

Sources of Rights: Why Citizenship?

It is not inevitable that an account of social rights under devolution should adopt citizenship as its theoretical driving force. In the legal discipline, discussion of what individuals can and should expect from the state often gravitate more naturally towards human rights than Marshall's sociological account. This book starts from the premise that legal accounts of the development of social rights need to take citizenship seriously, while accounts of social citizenship that omit a legal perspective are similarly incomplete. McKeever argues that 'a legal analysis can add value to the discourse on social citizenship';[16] research on administrative justice as the route to the realisation of social rights has made a significant contribution on this front.[17] To complete the picture, it is also necessary to consider the role of human rights in defining the social rights of citizenship and of constitutional law in assigning responsibility for defining and realising those rights and delimiting who can access them. These matters will be explored in subsequent chapters. This section focuses on the high-level complementarity of citizenship and human rights perspectives in the context of legal discourses on social rights.

[15] Turner, above n 8 at 191 – note that Turner does not necessarily endorse this assessment of Marshall.

[16] G McKeever, 'Accessing social citizenship' (PhD thesis, University of Ulster, 2013) 38.

[17] See, for example, J Baldwin, R Young and N Wikeley, *Judging Social Security: The Adjudication of Claims for Benefit in Britain* (Oxford: Clarendon Press, 1992); M Adler, 'Decision-making and appeals in social security: in need of reform?' (1997) 68(4) *Political Quarterly* 388; G McKeever, 'Improving decision making in employment and support allowance' (2014) 21(1) *Journal of Social Security Law* 13; N Harris, 'Complexity in the law and administration of social security: is it really a problem?' (2015) 37(2) *Journal of Social Welfare and Family Law* 209; J Tomlinson, 'Remodelling social security appeals (again): the advent of online tribunals' (2018) 25(2) *Journal of Social Security Law* 84.

The welfare state, Marshallian citizenship theory and the modern system of human rights protection are all creatures of the post-Second World War period. The Universal Declaration of Human Rights, adopted in 1948, recognises the 'economic, social and cultural rights indispensable for [human] dignity' (article 22), including specific rights relating to social security, work, an adequate standard of living, parenthood, childhood and education. The same year saw the UK enact the National Assistance Act 1948, putting a fairly comprehensive (albeit in part discretionary) system of social assistance in place of the punitive Victorian Poor Law. For Marshall, this was the final, essential piece in the jigsaw of rights that form the social element of citizenship.[18] In human rights law, social and economic rights sit alongside cultural, political and civil rights. Marshall's citizenship triad explicitly includes only civil, political and social elements, but the social element seems to encompass cultural rights, including as it does 'the right to share to the full in the social heritage'.

Despite this evident crossover, Tambakaki claims the tensions between the two perspectives – human rights as legally defined, universal and global, citizenship rights as politically negotiated, particular and national – are all but irreconcilable. Liberal democracy can act as the promoter and protector of human rights or citizenship, but not both. Rights may flow from the status of being human or from membership of a political community, but not both.[19] Other authors suggest social rights are by nature unsuitable for casting as human rights or are merely declaratory, with the implication that only the state can really confer social rights. Both perspectives seem to set up a false dichotomy between citizenship and human rights. Assertions of the inherent non-justiciability of social rights are increasingly difficult to sustain (see below), while claims that human rights are natural, universal and indivisible seem founded on idealism rather than empiricism. Enjoyment of internationally recognised human rights in practice may depend on their adoption as rights of citizenship, or at least their reflection in domestic law, policy and practice, at the level of the nation state. At the same time, the standards accepted through accession to human rights treaties have an obvious role to play in establishing the minimum level of (in this context) social protection the state ought to provide and assessing whether the state is meeting the standards it has set for itself through ratification. This is reflected in Lister's construction of human rights as a rallying point for active citizenship and democratic mobilisation, which assumes that the two concepts can be and are complementary.[20]

It is undeniable that classical citizenships operated in an exclusionary manner, with the status of citizen and its attendant rights reserved to male property owners who took part in politics and military service.[21] In the modern age, more inclusive

[18] Marshall, above n 2.
[19] P Tambakaki, *Human rights or Citizenship?* (Abingdon: Birkbeck Law Press, 2010) 15.
[20] R Lister, 'Power not pity: poverty and human rights' (2013) 7(2) *Ethics and Social Welfare* 109.
[21] Delanty, above n 6.

language has at times obscured a citizenship package that in practice continued to exclude large sections of society from full membership of the community and substantive enjoyment of citizenship rights.[22] Citizenship remains closely tied to nationality, so that non-nationals can be (though are not inevitably) excluded from some or all of its rights, while even more socio-economically vulnerable nationals find their 'rights' look increasingly conditional.[23] At face value, human rights might be expected to eschew the exclusionary elements of citizenship in favour of a common set of rights for all. If human rights are God-given or otherwise innate then, unless some people are deemed closer to the divine image than others, it seems that rights must also be universal, indivisible and perhaps unchanging. On the other hand, if rights are simply the product of negotiation between geopolitical actors, then the possibility that international law consists of a menu of possible rights that states may or may not embrace, and whose interpretation is context-dependent, must be considered.

Human rights discourse frequently tends, explicitly or implicitly, towards a natural rights perspective. People are constructed as having 'inherent dignity' and 'equal and inalienable rights'.[24] Often, although not always, the claimed basis for these equal and inalienable rights is that people (or men) are created equal, with their rights flowing from a creator – and their creation in the creator's image.[25] Such an assumption that governments and societies do not bestow rights, but are formed to 'secure' the enjoyment of rights people already hold by divine grace,[26] is self-evidently problematic from a secular perspective, or to those, like Finnis, who hold that it is presumptuous for humans to claim to know what rights the creator intended them to have.[27] An appeal to a religious basis for rights is unlikely to convince adherents to other religious traditions, far less non-believers,[28] or those who feel that the record of religious institutions in defending, advocating and perpetrating rights violations means they lack authority on the subject.[29] Whether any model of natural rights can be sustained without recourse to theistic arguments is a matter for debate; there are those who argue that it is possible to identify a set of fundamental moral principles and recognised basic needs that seem to transcend cultures, societies and belief systems, possibly explicable by the

[22] R Lister, above n 10; M Lister, above n 1.

[23] C Fitzpatrick, G McKeever and M Simpson, 'Conditionality, discretion and TH Marshall's "right to welfare"' (2019) 41(4) *Journal of Social Welfare and Family Law* 445.

[24] Universal Declaration of Human Rights, preamble.

[25] J Hanvey, 'Dignity, person and *imago trinitatis*' in C McCrudden (ed), *Understanding Human Dignity* (Oxford: Oxford University Press, 2013); J Soskice, 'Human dignity and the image of God' in C McCrudden (ed), *Understanding Human Dignity* (Oxford: Oxford University Press, 2013).

[26] Declaration of Independence (US 1776); T Paine, *Rights of Man* (Harmondsworth: Penguin, 1971) 90.

[27] J Finnis, *Natural Law and Natural Rights* (Oxford: Clarendon Press, 1980).

[28] S Dellavalle, 'From *imago dei* to mutual recognition: the evolution of the concept of human dignity in the light of the defence of religious freedom' in C McCrudden (ed), *Understanding Human Dignity* (Oxford: Oxford University Press, 2013).

[29] B Schlink, 'The concept of human dignity: current uses, future discourse' in C McCrudden (ed), *Understanding Human Dignity* (Oxford: Oxford University Press, 2013).

evolutionary advantages to the species of altruistic behaviour.[30] Further, it is by no means a given that those who hold to theistic explanations of the foundation of rights would categorise a minimum level of economic welfare as a right.[31] Lord Ellenborough does not state whether his assertion that there is a 'law of humanity, which is anterior to all positive laws'[32] has any religious basis, and according to Finnis's perspective he does not need to.

It being impossible to definitively conclude that rights are divinely ordained or otherwise inherent, the alternative explanation is that they represent socially negotiated statements of those things a society, polity or international community agrees merit protection.[33] From this perspective, the argument that rights are universal and unchanging is harder to sustain. Perhaps Parliaments, courts and international bodies can aspire to do no more than set out their 'best guess *at that moment*' as to what constitute a person's most fundamental needs, with reference to whatever religious or secular philosophy dominates at the time.[34] Arendt goes further suggesting that, even in the post-Second World War period, 'no one seem[ed] able to define with any assurance what … general human rights, as distinguished from the rights of citizens, really are'.[35] Which human needs gain recognition as rights at international level may ultimately be an amalgam of the various rights enjoyed by the citizens of the states that take part in negotiations. Analyses of the emergence of the Universal Declaration of Human Rights show that the foundational document of the international law system of rights protection was as much the product of negotiation, horse-trading and the use of ambiguous terms to generate consensus among ideologically opposed delegates as any national declaration of rights.[36]

Even when a 'right' gains international recognition, it does not necessarily follow that it will be, or is intended to be, enjoyed to the same extent and in the same way across societies. Human rights discourse is peppered with references

[30] DG Ritchie, *Natural Rights: A Criticism of Some Political and Ethical Conceptions* (London: Allen & Unwin, 1924); R Dawkins, *The God Delusion* (New York: Bantam, 2006); D Hollenbach, 'Human dignity: experience and history, practical reason and faith' in C McCrudden (ed), *Understanding Human Dignity* (Oxford: Oxford University Press, 2013).

[31] S Moyn, 'The secret history of constitutional dignity'in C McCrudden (ed), *Understanding Human Dignity* (Oxford: Oxford University Press, 2013).

[32] *R v Inhabitants of Eastbourne* (1803) 4 East 103, 107 (Lord Ellenborough).

[33] H Dean, 'The translation of needs into rights: reconceptualising social citizenship as a global phenomenon' (2013) 22(S1) *International Journal of Social Welfare* S32.

[34] C Gearty, 'Socio-economic rights, basic needs and human dignity: a perspective from law's front line' in C McCrudden (ed), *Understanding Human Dignity* (Oxford: Oxford University Press, 2013) 168; see also O Chadwick, *The Secularisation of the European Mind in the 19th Century* (Cambridge: Cambridge University Press, 1975).

[35] H Arendt, *The Origins of Totalitarianism* (London: George Allen and Unwin, 1967) 293.

[36] C McCrudden, 'In pursuit of human dignity: an introduction to current debates' in C McCrudden (ed), *Understanding Human Dignity* (Oxford: Oxford University Press, 2013); DA Jones, 'Is dignity language useful in bioethical discussion of assisted suicide and abortion?' in C McCrudden (ed), *Understanding Human Dignity* (Oxford: Oxford University Press, 2013); K Boyle, *Economic and Social Rights Law: Incorporation, Justiciability and Principles of Adjudication* (Abingdon: Routledge, 2020).

to margins of appreciation, minimum cores, progressive realisation, living instruments and judicial deference. Whichever term is used, the inference that rights have a particular meaning in the here and now, and that the executive and legislature in each state have a key role to play in establishing that meaning, is seldom far away. This is abundantly clear in the case of social rights. As the European Court of Human Rights (ECtHR) observes:

> A wide margin is usually allowed to the State under the Convention when it comes to general measures of economic or social strategy … Because of their direct knowledge of their society and its needs, the national authorities are in principle better placed than the international judge to appreciate what is in the public interest on social or economic grounds, and the Court will generally respect the legislature's policy choice unless it is 'manifestly without reasonable foundation'.[37]

The European Social Charter (ESC) is explicit about the non-universality of some of the rights it confers. Articles 12 (the right to social security), 13 (the right to social assistance), 18 (the right to economic migration) and 19 (migrant workers' right to protection) confer rights upon the nationals of contracting states, not people in general. Even within the group of beneficiaries, the provision in Article 13(4) that the right to social assistance applies 'on an equal footing' to nationals of the host state and lawfully present nationals of other contracting states is, in practice, applied more selectively than its wording suggests, with temporarily resident non-nationals only entitled to *emergency* assistance or, in some cases, repatriation.[38] Human rights protections, some of them at least, begin to look like recent conceptions of 'nested' or 'tiered' citizenship, whereby various categories of people within a state boundary enjoy different subsets of the rights available to full citizens depending on their country of origin, immigration status, the circumstances of their arrival in the host state and their relationship with the labour market.[39] Tambakaki's summary of the chief argument in favour of citizenship as the foundation of social rights seems apt: 'Since we still live in a world of nation states … it is always state citizenries that frame and define the content of human rights, not the other way round'.[40]

It is certainly the premise of this book that the enjoyment of rights in practice depends on state action, therefore the state is in a position to determine who has the right to hold those rights. As Arendt and others who experienced statelessness in the 1930s and 1940s discovered: 'The Rights of Man … had been defined as "inalienable" because they were supposed to be independent of all governments;

[37] *Stec v UK* (Admissibility) (65730/01) [2005] 41 EHRR SE18 at [52].

[38] European Committee of Social Rights, *Conclusions XV-1 – United Kingdom – article 13-4* (1997–98); Committee of Independent Experts, *Conclusions VII – United Kingdom – article 13-4* (1978–79).

[39] T Faist, 'Social citizenship in the European Union: nested membership' (2001) 39(1) *Journal of Common Market Studies* 37; L Hooghe and G Marks, *Multi-level Governance and European Integration* (Rowman and Littlefield, 2001); W Maas, 'Migrants, states, and EU citizenship's unfulfilled promise' (2008) 12(6) *Citizenship Studies* 583.

[40] Tambakaki, above n 19 at 2.

but it turned out that the moment human beings lacked their own government … no authority was left to protect them.'[41] It would, however, be an exaggeration to claim that the flow of ideas is unidirectional. Even if human rights are viewed as the product of a search for international consensus on what the rights of citizenship ought to be, international endorsement lends them a normative and moral weight that cannot be lightly dismissed. Once a state has indicated its acceptance of a set of internationally agreed standards by ratifying the relevant treaty, it can legitimately be criticised for any subsequent failure to live up to those standards. A legal pathway to accountability may or may not be available, but a reasoned, authoritative and sufficiently high-profile conclusion that the state is not complying with its commitments can sting politically. This is evident from the UK Government's defensive reaction to a critical report by the UN Special Rapporteur on Extreme Poverty and Human Rights.[42]

Lister argues that human rights have been increasingly deployed as a means of asserting social rights as and because citizenship has appeared to become a less effective means of doing so.[43] In the post-Second World War 'trente glorieuses', when social rights were generally on the rise in the liberal capitalist democracies, welfare rights were not usually understood in legalistic terms, nor was such an understanding really necessary.[44] The expansion of social provision could appear inexorable, giving rise to a 'sense … that the welfare state is inevitable'.[45] The era of neoliberal globalisation led many to question whether citizenship *could* any longer serve as the vehicle for the realisation of social rights.[46] At the same time, perhaps as a result, the ascendancy of a 'more conservative' politics led to increased scepticism about both the affordability and effectiveness of social transfers as a solution to poverty.[47] If the forces that lined up against the rights of citizenship, notably its social rights, were global in nature, the 'sovereign' state powerless to resist, people's very identities 'postnational', 'denationalised' or grounded in the 'global city',[48] then the response must also be global, or at least supranational.[49] The age of Brexit and 'America first'[50] may or may not herald the resurgence of

[41] Arendt, above n 35 at 291.

[42] P Walker, 'Amber Rudd condemns UN poverty report in combative return to frontline politics' (*Guardian*, 19 November 2018). Available at: www.theguardian.com/politics/2018/nov/19/amber-rudd-un-poverty-report-return-frontline-politics.

[43] R Lister, above n 20.

[44] DT Prosser, 'Poverty, ideology and legality: supplementary benefit appeals tribunals and their predecessors' (1977) 4 *British Journal of Law and Society* 39.

[45] LM Mead, 'Citizenship and social policy: TH Marshall and poverty' (1997) 14(2) *Social Philosophy and Policy* 197, 198.

[46] J Shaw and I Stiks (eds), *Citizenship Rights* (Farnham: Ashgate, 2013).

[47] Mead, above n 45.

[48] S Sassen, 'The repositioning of citizenship: emergent subjects and spaces for politics' (2002) 46 *Berkeley Journal of Sociology* 13, 16.

[49] Z Bauman, 'Freedom from, in and through the state: TH Marshall's trinity of rights revisited' (2005) 44 *Theoria* 13.

[50] DJ Trump, 'Inaugural address' (Washington DC, 20 January 2017).

the nation state, but recent accounts of the difficulty of realising social rights in the context of a global economic crisis and ideology of austerity continue to ring true.[51] Even if it is accepted that the pre-eminence of the nation state is diminished, it does not follow that citizenship is redundant. Citizenship may simply be recast in a multi-layered, tiered or nested form, with rights negotiated at multiple levels – a process that manifests within as well as between states.[52] A common set of human rights obligations has potential to act as a centripetal force, spurring different tiers of government with responsibility for social security towards shared objectives. But varying degrees of political commitment to human rights also have potential to act as a centrifugal force, driving or being used to justify steps towards divergence in citizens' social rights.

Treating human rights and citizenship as complementary or alternative routes to the same end in the way that Lister suggests is only possible if their ultimate objectives are sufficiently similar. It is easy to pick out ways in which both routes lead to the same destination in terms of social rights, admittedly helped by the ambiguities inherent in each. Marshall's statement that the social rights of citizenship can consist of anything from 'a modicum of economic welfare and security to the right to share to the full in the social heritage and to live the life of a civilised being according to the standards prevailing' has potential to cover a wide range of living standards.[53] This might be viewed as a contradiction in terms or as a spectrum within whose limits the social provision on offer to citizens, and on what terms, may legitimately vary between states and over time.[54] The two Marshallian terms map fairly neatly onto differing sociological conceptions of poverty. A modicum of economic welfare is easily understood as freedom from absolute poverty (inability to afford life's basic necessities), with the ability to live according to prevailing standards of a civilised life equating to freedom from relative poverty (inability to access what are generally recognised as 'normal' goods, services and activities).[55] In human rights terms, the guarantee of a modicum of economic welfare might be described as a minimum core obligation, perhaps in line with the core obligations of the right to social security as protected by Article 9 ICESCR: access to 'at least essential health care, basic shelter and housing, water and sanitation, foodstuffs, and the most basic forms of education'.[56] Enabling every

[51] A Nolan, R O'Connell and C Harvey (eds), *Human rights and Public Finance: Budgets and the Promotion of Economic and Social Rights* (Oxford: Hart, 2013); A Nolan (ed), *Economic and Social Rights after the Global Financial Crisis* (Cambridge: Cambridge University Press, 2014).

[52] Dean, above n 33.

[53] Marshall, above n 2 at 8.

[54] P Dwyer, *Understanding Social Citizenship: Themes and Perspectives for Policy and Practice* (Bristol: Policy Press, 2010); different welfare services may tend towards the maximalist (in the UK, healthcare) or minimalist (social security) end of the spectrum – M Powell, 'The hidden history of social citizenship' (2002) 6(3) *Citizenship Studies* 229.

[55] R Lister, 'Defining poverty' in *Poverty* (Cambridge: Polity Press, 2021).

[56] Committee on Economic, Social and Cultural Rights, 'General comment no 19: the right to social security' (E/C.12/GC/19, Geneva: United Nations, 2008) para 59.

member to live the life of a civilised being might then be described as the goal of 'full realisation'.[57]

An increasingly credible meeting point for human rights and citizenship as vehicles for social rights is dignity. As a legal concept, dignity is strongly associated with human rights, but to paint it purely in legal terms does not do justice to its transdisciplinary roots and deployment.[58] That is not to say it has always been a natural companion to citizenship. The term 'dignity' does not appear in the index to any of Marshall's published works. While it has been a recurring theme in Lister's work, long alive to the potential crossover between human rights and citizenship,[59] as recently as 2010 Dwyer could write a textbook on social citizenship without discussion of dignity.[60] That such an omission would verge on unthinkable now is due in part to developments in Scotland since 2016. However, Lister highlights several twenty-first-century studies in which dignity and the related concept of respect emerge as core elements of citizenship from the perspective of people with experience of poverty.[61]

Like Marshall's citizenship, dignity is a malleable and contested concept, variously constructed as the objective of all human rights, a right in itself or a mere 'placeholder', a grand but ultimately hollow buzzword around which the ideologically divergent framers of the Universal Declaration of Human Rights (UDHR) could rally.[62] Nonetheless, from the UDHR onward, dignity has been closely associated with social rights in particular, albeit in different ways by different authors. Boyle regards dignity as requiring the realisation of a minimum core of social rights.[63] McCrudden's definition is potentially more expansive, with dignity requiring the prohibition of inhuman or degrading treatment and humiliation, the conditions for self-fulfillment and autonomy, protection of group identify and culture and the conditions for the satisfaction of essential needs.[64] Examining dignity in the context of social security specifically, Patrick and Simpson identify a distributional dimension – sufficient income to enjoy a minimum standard of living; a relational dimension – so that individuals are treated with respect in their interactions with the social security system; and an intrinsic dimension – enabling claimants to retain a sense of self-worth.[65] These definitions can imply

[57] Committee on Economic, Social and Cultural Rights, 'General comment no 3: the nature of states parties' obligations' (E/1991/23, Geneva: United Nations, 1991).

[58] C McCrudden (ed), *Understanding Human Dignity* (Oxford: Oxford University Press, 2013).

[59] R Lister, *The Exclusive Society: Citizenship and the Poor* (London: Child Poverty Action Group, 1990); R Lister, 'To count for nothing: poverty beyond the statistics' (2015) 3 *Journal of the British Academy* 139.

[60] Dwyer, above n 54.

[61] R Lister, *Poverty* (Cambridge: Polity Press, 2021).

[62] C O'Mahony, 'There is no such thing as a right to dignity' (2012) 10(2) *International Journal of Constitutional Law* 551.

[63] Boyle, above n 36.

[64] C McCrudden, 'Human dignity and judicial interpretation of human rights' (2008) 19(4) *European Journal of International Law* 655.

[65] R Patrick and M Simpson, 'Conceptualising dignity in the context of social security: bottom-up and top-down perspectives' (2020) 54(3) *Social Policy and Administration* 475.

various things about the standards a social security system must meet to preserve dignity, but how it can do so will be discussed more fully in forthcoming chapters. One point of overlap between citizenship and dignity bears highlighting. Marshall saw the extension of the status of 'citizen' to a progressively wider share of the population as inextricably linked with the evolution of the associated rights.[66] Similarly, one goal of the Rights of Man/human rights project from the French Revolution onwards has been to enable everyone to enjoy the dignity that was once the preserve of the aristocracy. In each case, rights and status that were once the preserve of the few have been democratised.

Ultimately, human rights, citizenship, dignity and poverty studies provide different vocabularies for talking about social rights but tend towards similar objectives. Citizenship is the theoretical reference point for this book, but the human rights provisions endorsed by the UK through ratification and, in some cases, incorporation into domestic law inform what the social rights of citizenship are, or what they ought to be to ensure dignity is protected. The next section of this chapter briefly examines the debate on the extent to which social rights should be regarded as enforceable, legal rights on a par with civil and political rights.

On the Nature and Enforceability of Social Rights

The interdependence of categories of rights is recognised from both citizenship and human rights perspectives. Lord Hoffmann notes:

> Human rights are the rights essential to the life and dignity of the individual in a democratic society … I think it is well arguable that human rights include the right to a minimum standard of living, without which many of the other rights would be a mockery.[67]

A similar analysis can be found from the dawn of the United Nations human rights regime to more recent discussions of what humans require to enjoy dignity, autonomy and social participation.[68] However, rhetoric about the indivisibility and equal status of rights sits uneasily alongside the separation of social and economic rights from civil and political rights in the key international legal instruments for their protection – in the UN regime, the Covenants on Civil and Political Rights and on Economic, Social and Cultural Rights; in the Council of Europe system, the European Convention on Human Rights and the European Social Charter. The literature addressing the status of social rights is broader and richer than can be covered here, but a few key observations follow.

[66] Marshall, above n 2.
[67] *Matthews v Ministry of Defence* [2003] UKHL 4 at [26] (Lord Hoffmann).
[68] See Boyle, above n 36; McCrudden, above n 64; McCrudden, above n 58.

Boyle argues convincingly that the bifurcation of rights in international law was never intended to imply a hierarchy.[69] Nonetheless, the perception of a hierarchy clearly arose – and perceptions can easily become reality. Claims that social rights represent not only a second (Marshall would presumably argue third) generation but also a second tier of rights typically centre on the view that their realisation is especially dependent on the availability and (re)distribution of resources within a society. The critique runs that the resource-intensive nature of social entitlements, the need for appropriate administrative structures and their vagueness means they inhabit the terrain of political decision-making on social and economic policy, thus enshrinement as 'rights' may make unrealistic demands on limited resources or excessively constrain democratic decision-making on priorities for public spending. Some states might simply be more able than others to provide particular standards of housing, healthcare, education or income, or electorates might choose different standards.[70] This critique neglects both the interdependence of rights highlighted by Lord Hoffmann and the reality that it is not only social rights that depend on positive, potentially costly actions by the state for their realisation.[71]

On one level, it is now well established that social rights are not by nature less amenable to protection in law or judicial enforcement.[72] Certainly Boyle considers that "the idea that [economic and social rights] are non-justiciable has now been debunked, in theory and in practice'.[73] Judgments in the last decade or so in Germany and Belgium mean it is no longer necessary to look outside Europe for real-life examples.[74] Even the ECtHR, charged with oversight of a treaty whose principal focus is on civil and political rights, recognises no qualitative difference and 'no watertight division' between these and social and economic rights.[75] Clément's 2018 article on social justice and 'rights inflation'[76] shows the persistence

[69] Boyle, above n 36.

[70] For discussion, see J King, *Judging Social Rights* (Cambridge: Cambridge University Press, 2012); H Alviar García, K Klare and LA Williams (eds), *Social and Economic Rights in Theory and Practice: Critical Inquiries* (Abingdon: Routledge, 2015).

[71] S Fredman, *Human Rights Transformed: Positive Rights and Positive Duties* (Oxford: Oxford University Press, 2008); Special issue: Positive obligations and the European Court of Human Rights (2010) 61(3) *Northern Ireland Legal Quarterly.*

[72] See M Langford (ed), *Social Rights Jurisprudence: Emerging Trends in International and Comparative Law* (Cambridge: Cambridge University Press, 2008).

[73] Boyle, above n 36 at 73.

[74] BVerfG 1 BvL 1/09, Judgment of 9 February 2010; *Cleon v la Commisson communautaire française* [2011] Conseil d'État, section du contentieux administratif, arrêt no 215.309 du 23 septembre 2011; BVerfG 1 BvL 10/10, Judgment of 18 July 2012; BVerfG 1 BvL 7/16, Judgment of 5 November 2019; for discussion, see IT Winkler and C Mahler, 'Interpreting the right to a dignified minimum existence: a new era in German socio-economic rights jurisprudence?' (2013) 13(2) *Human Rights Law Review* 388; I Hachez, 'Le standstill, ou comment les juges ont permis de mieux protéger les droits fondamentaux en limitant des possibilités de recul' (Justice en ligne, 12 February 2016). Available at www.justice-en-ligne.be/article821.html.

[75] *Airey v Ireland* (A/32) [1979–80] EHRR 305 at [26].

[76] D Clément, 'Human rights or social justice? The problem of rights inflation' (2018) 22(2) *International Journal of Human Rights* 155.

of what seems more like a classical liberal definition of rights, with little space for social rights. However, if some states remain reluctant to allow justiciability, this is a matter of individual political and legal culture – speaking to the need for human rights to become citizenship rights to be effectively enjoyed – rather than an inherent defect in social rights.[77] It is also worth noting that justiciability is not the be-all and end-all of human rights realisation. Effective enjoyment of a social right is most effectively delivered when that right is embedded in the political culture of the state.[78] Justiciability can provide a useful tool for pushing the political arms of government in this direction, but in the main it is down to the legislature and executive, not the vagaries of who has the time, motivation and resources to bring a judicial review, to ensure social rights are widely enjoyed.[79]

With that in mind, for the purposes of this book the focus must be on the political culture and the status of social rights in the UK specifically. In this context, a hierarchy of rights definitely does exist. Human rights in the UK 'are conceptually framed in a way that excludes the operation and enforceability of [economic and social rights] … domestic human rights structures marginalise ESR to the sidelines'.[80] Incorporation into domestic law of the ECHR but not the ESC means there are obstacles to resorting to the courts in defence of social rights. Litigants must shoehorn claims of unlawful denial or erosion of social entitlements into ECHR rights, notably the rights to peaceful enjoyment of one's possessions and to respect for family life, or equality and anti-discrimination law. Nonetheless, challenges to elements of social policy have been heard and on occasion succeeded in passing the high bar of proving that a discriminatory measure was manifestly without reasonable foundation.[81]

This leads to some final observations on the relationship between human rights and citizenship rights. Returning to Boyle, 'rights are legally binding and justiciable if the application of the law renders them so'.[82] If citizenship is viewed empirically, as a legal status, then those human rights that are incorporated into national law form part of the set of rights that citizenship confers. If citizenship is viewed normatively, as an ideal, then all human rights endorsed by the state through accession to the relevant international agreements form part of the package of rights citizens ought to enjoy, regardless of whether they do so in practice. Conversely, a right laid down in international law can be regarded as incorporated

[77] G van Bueren, 'Including the excluded: the case for an economic, social and cultural Human Rights Act' (2002) *Aut Public Law* 456; King, above n 70.

[78] C Gearty, 'Against judicial enforcement' in C Gearty and V Mantouvalou, *Debating Social Rights* (Oxford: Hart, 2011); Boyle, above n 36; M Simpson, G McKeever and C Fitzpatrick, 'Legal protection against destitution in the UK: restoring a right to a subsistence minimum' (under review).

[79] V Mantouvalou, 'In support of legalisation' in C Gearty and V Mantouvalou, *Debating Social Rights* (Oxford: Hart, 2011).

[80] Boyle, above n 36 at 1.

[81] M Simpson, 'Social rights, child rights, discrimination and devolution: untangling the web' (2018) 40(1) *Journal of Social Welfare and Family Law* 3.

[82] Boyle, above n 36.

if its requirements are consciously reflected in sectoral legislation (for example, if social security law reflects the requirements of the right to social security and the right to an adequate standard of living), even in the absence of explicit incorporation of the international legal provision into domestic legislation.[83] The lived experience of citizenship exists in the space between the rights the state endorses in principle, those it in fact enshrines in national law, the sectoral measures adopted to operationalise rights (in the form of legislation, policy and the establishment of the necessary structures and processes for service delivery) and the citizen's ability to enjoy and if necessary enforce his or her rights in practice.

Conclusion

This chapter has provided an overview of Marshall's theory of the evolution of citizenship to include civil, political and social elements. These overlap with most of the main fields of human rights law: civil, political and socio-economic rights. For the purposes of this chapter, the two 'sources' of rights are assumed to be complementary, with human rights both informing what rights citizens have, or ought to have, and depending, to at least some extent, on their adoption as rights of citizenship for their realisation. While the view that social rights are ill-suited in principle to justiciability is rejected, there are obstacles to the legal enforcement in the UK of more than the most basic social entitlements. The focus therefore falls on the legislature and executive to ensure the enjoyment of the rights the state has in principle undertaken to guarantee. How these branches of the state have approached the task, and the response of the courts when called to adjudicate on how they have done so, will be examined as the focus of the book moves from an introduction of Marshall's theory of citizenship to consideration of what social citizenship actually means in the contemporary UK. First, Chapter 3 looks more closely at the role of sub-state tiers of government in defining, conferring and guaranteeing social citizenship rights.

[83] Ibid.

3

Social Citizenship and Multi-level Governance

Introduction

The UK has traditionally adhered to a very centralised notion of citizenship,[1] but this does not mean the rights of citizenship are solely determined by UK-level institutions of government. The Scottish Parliament and Senedd Cymru have conferred the political right to vote in elections upon individuals too young to vote in UK general elections, while EU membership extended voting rights in

[1] D Bubeck, 'Democratic, gender-neutral citizenship' in JP Gardner, *Citizenship: The White Paper* (London: British Institute of International and Comparative Law, 1999); see, for example, Scotland Act 1998 c 46 Sch 5, Head B.

local and European elections to some non-nationals.[2] Devolution places considerable responsibility for the social rights of citizenship in the hands of regional institutions,[3] allowing social citizenship to acquire a regional character in a way that sits uncomfortably alongside mainstream interpretations of Marshallian theory as situating responsibility for defining and realising the citizen's rights with the national government. The extent to which this process has resulted in the emergence of fully fledged sub-state social citizenships has, though, been limited by shared adherence to key social policy tenets and, until recently, the lack of devolved competence for (Scotland and Wales) or divergence (Northern Ireland) in social security. This is now changing.

Assessing the implications for Marshallian theory of the regionalisation of political citizenship and possible regionalisation of social citizenship under devolution involves a measure of speculation. It is possible to conclude that he, like other liberal citizenship theorists, thought about localism or regionalism only as relics of a bygone era.[4] No contemporary account of social citizenship can make such an assumption. This chapter first introduces the challenges multi-level governance poses to conceptions of unitary, national citizenship and, potentially, to Marshallian theory. It then outlines the role of devolved governments and legislatures in securing citizens' social rights – primarily in the field of social security – within the UK's devolution settlement. It briefly considers the extent to which a sub-state hand on the policy levers has in fact resulted in the emergence of different approaches to social security at devolved level, a question that will be revisited in subsequent chapters.

Social Citizenship and Multi-level Governance

'Territorial politics', according to Wincott, 'provides a partially hidden subtext to Marshall's analysis' of citizenship.[5] Readers might be forgiven for concluding that if territoriality is a feature of Marshall's work, it is for the most part very well hidden. However, Wincott argues that the citizenship described must be geographically demarcated. In the evolution of citizenship, Marshall observes a repeated phenomenon of the 'separation' of individuals from local judicial, political and welfare institutions and their 'fusion' with national institutions.[6]

[2] Consolidated version of the Treaty on the Functioning of the European Union [2012] OJ C326/1, art 20(2); Scottish Elections (Reduction of Voting Age) Act 2015 asp 7; Senedd and Elections (Wales) Act 2020 anaw 1 s 10.

[3] L Moreno, 'Multilevel citizens, new social risks, and regional welfare' in AM Suszycki and IP Karolewski (eds), *Citizenship and identity in the welfare state* (Baden-Baden: Nomos, 2013).

[4] D Heater, *What is citizenship?* (Cambridge: Polity Press, 1999).

[5] D Wincott, 'Citizenship in time and space: observations on TH Marshall's *Citizenship and social class*' in SL Greer (ed), *Devolution and Social Citizenship in the UK* (Bristol: Policy Press, 2009) 39.

[6] TH Marshall, 'Citizenship and social class' in TH Marshall and T Bottomore, *Citizenship and Social Class* (London: Pluto Press, 1992) 9.

Wincott views the political interventions to construct a modern welfare state and secure near-full (male) employment in the post-Second World War period as a further step in this process. Whether Marshall would have viewed developments in these terms is unclear, but the statement that by 1949 'Marshall must have found it easy to take national integration for granted' rings true,[7] not least because of the absence of a single reference to Northern Ireland's devolved status in his published works.[8]

National integration cannot be taken for granted today. The 2021 election to the Scottish Parliament saw parties committed to a referendum on secession from the UK before 2026 (the Scottish National Party and Scottish Greens) win a majority of votes and seats. Northern Ireland's place in the UK has been contested for longer, often violently, and has, for some, been weakened by withdrawal from the European Union.[9] Even absent the break-up of the UK, the question of where someone is a citizen of is now harder to answer than Marshall may have assumed. Government, or governance, takes place at different levels and various tiers of government play a role in defining the rights of citizenship. A sense of English, Scottish, Welsh, Northern Irish, Irish and/or European identity can coexist more or less comfortably with a UK or British identity. More localised identities, or identities based on roots *outside* the UK, further complicate the picture.[10] This pattern is repeated in other countries, so that across Europe 'nested', 'tiered' or 'layered' citizenships are becoming the norm.[11] To the extent that these tiered citizenships are reflected in representative institutions, they have potential to affect the source and nature of citizens' rights.

Devolution unquestionably has implications for the citizen's political rights. Not only is there now an opportunity for democratic participation at a level between the national and the local, but the nature of that participation varies. This may be because Parliament established different rules for the electoral game in different parts of the UK, with various forms of proportional representation now used for most elections outside England, or because the devolved legislatures themselves changed the rules, as with the Scottish Parliament and Senedd's extension of voting rights to 16- and 17-year-olds. This regionalisation of political citizenship was a deliberate decision, but whether the UK Government intended

[7] Wincott, above n 5 at 40.

[8] Mann suggests that Northern Ireland 'would not fit well into [Marshall's] theory' – M Mann, 'Ruling class strategies and citizenship' in M Bulmer and AM Rees (eds), *Citizenship Today: The Contemporary Relevance of TH Marshall* (London: UCL Press, 1996) 126.

[9] C Gormley-Heenan and A Aughey, 'Northern Ireland and Brexit: three effects on "the border in the mind"' (2017) 19(3) *British Journal of Politics and International Relations* 497.

[10] Opinium, 'UK: national identity in Britain' (Opinium, 9 March 2020). Available at: www.opinium.com/resource-center/national-identity-in-britain/.

[11] Heater, above n 4 at 123, 126; T Faist, 'Social citizenship in the European Union: nested membership' (2001) 39(1) *Journal of Common Market Studies* 37.

or anticipated an impact on public policy is another matter.[12] An irony of the phase of devolution launched in 1998–1999[13] is that its architects appear to have assumed they could meet demands for some regionalisation of political citizenship without significant, widespread policy divergence. The Labour party had shown varying degrees of interest in devolution from the Wilson Government's establishment of the Royal Commission on the Constitution in 1969.[14] Evans suggests, though, that its 'temporary evangelical zeal' for the project under Tony Blair's leadership was motivated primarily by vote-seeking, with no real appetite for the 'radical assault' on the primacy of England, Parliament and the prime minister that true federalism would imply.[15] New political communities were established, but under the assumption that they would remain interdependent, integrated and with limited policy divergence within a still relatively centralised state. Devolved institutions might handle 'allocation', but the big decisions on 'redistribution' would be national.[16] Labour may have assumed that devolution would make little difference to the nature of public services or conceptions of citizenship, but the settlement 'created no guarantees of this' while creating the conditions for such differences to emerge – a process, Trench suggests, which was well underway by 2009 and has accelerated since.[17]

The motives of the architects of devolution, as portrayed by Evans and Trench, seem predicated on the 'devolution paradox' that citizens may demand the 'ownership' of the political process and the 'proximity and responsiveness of decision-making' that regional government allows, while clinging to the 'equity and solidarity' that state-wide uniformity of public services embodies.[18] From a Marshallian point of view, it can be argued that the vision of reducing the 'skyscraper' of inequality to a 'bungalow' might be hindered by significant regional differences in services, social transfers or taxation. However, if Marshall the idealist held to a national vision for citizenship, Marshall the empiricist was clear that

[12] M Evans, 'New Labour and the rise of the new constitutionalism' in M Beech and S Lee (eds), *Ten Years of New Labour* (Basingstoke: Palgrave Macmillan, 2008) 79.

[13] Legislative devolution operated in Northern Ireland from 1921 to 1974, while administrative devolution operated in Scotland, Wales and Northern Ireland prior to the establishment of the new legislatures in 1998 and 1999. For a more detailed overview of the settlement, with an emphasis on devolved social policy functions, see D Birrell and AM Gray, 'The devolved administrations and welfare delivery' in *Delivering Social Welfare: Governance and Service Provision in the UK* (Bristol: Policy Press, 2017).

[14] See Royal Commission on the Constitution, *Report of the Commission* (Cmnd 5460, London: HMSO, 1973).

[15] Evans, above n 12 at 72, 68.

[16] R Simeon, 'Federalism and social justice: thinking through the tangle' in SL Greer, *Territory, Democracy and Justice: Regionalism and Federalism in Western Democracies* (Basingstoke: Palgrave Macmillan, 2006) 25.

[17] A Trench, 'Un-joined-up government: intergovernmental relations and citizenship rights' in SL Greer (ed), *Devolution and Social Citizenship in the UK* (Bristol: Policy Press, 2009) 132.

[18] A Henderson, C Jeffery, D Wincott and R Wyn Jones, 'Reflections on the "devolution paradox": a comparative examination of multilevel citizenship' (2013) 47(3) *Regional and Federal Studies* 303.

the social rights of citizenship emerge and develop through the exercise of political rights.[19] Returning to Wincott, 'if legitimate inequality is socio-politically negotiated, what happens when some groups in society do not accept that a given pattern of stratification *is*, in fact, legitimate'?[20] Contestation of the dominant view of legitimate inequality, or of what 'guaranteed minimum' the welfare state ought to provide its citizens,[21] need not be geographically concentrated, but if it becomes ingrained within the politics of a particular region, with a strong sense of identity and its own representative institutions, it has the potential to become another factor that marks that region out as distinct to the state as a whole. As shall be seen, the extent to which the dominant view of social justice in Scotland differs to the dominant view in the UK (or England) is much debated. Such differences as exist may manifest in the various arms of the welfare state under devolved control, to the extent that the constitutional settlement and any political or economic constraints allow or produce pressure for the transfer of the competences needed for a distinct substate approach to emerge.

Devolution or federalism, then, has potential to result in divergence across multiple areas of public policy, but since the devolved legislatures are to a large extent 'social policy parliaments' the scope for an impact on the citizen's social rights is particularly great.[22] Various studies have considered whether decentralisation has a consistent impact on welfare states. Banting identifies a basic tension in that 'the promise of social citizenship is the equality of treatment of citizens [while] the promise of federalism is regional diversity in public policies'.[23] Recent decades have seen a retreat from assumptions that regionalism is associated with 'welfare-state disintegration'.[24] The once-conventional argument goes that costly, redistributive areas of social policy – social security in particular – are best controlled by central government, with its greater resources. Regionalisation brings an inherent risk of migration of claimants in search of more generous benefits, or of a 'race to the bottom' between regions in order to avoid this, while diminishing the role of social transfers as an economic stabiliser and means of interregional redistribution.[25] These risks may be exacerbated when devolution

[19] M Simpson, 'Renegotiating social citizenship in the age of devolution' (2017) 44(4) *Journal of Law and Society* 646, 667.

[20] Wincott, above n 5 at 50.

[21] Marshall, above n 6 at 32.

[22] D Birrell, *The Impact of Devolution on Social Policy* (Bristol: Policy Press, 2009) 1.

[23] KG Banting, 'Social citizenship and federalism: is a federal welfare state a contradiction in terms?' in SL Greer (ed), *Territory, Democracy and Justice: Regionalism and Federalism in Western Democracies* (Basingstoke: Palgrave Macmillan, 2006) 44.

[24] D Béland and A Lecours, 'Does nationalism trigger welfare-state disintegration? Social policy and territorial mobilization in Belgium and Canada' (2010) 28(3) *Environment and Planning C: Government and Policy* 420.

[25] KC Wheare, *Federal Government* (Westport, CT: Greenwood Press, 1963); PE Peterson, *The Price of Federalism* (Washington DC: Brookings Institution, 1995); T Iversen, 'Democracy and capitalism' in FG Castles, S Leibfried, J Lewis, H Obinger and C Pierson (eds), *The Oxford Handbook of the Welfare State* (Oxford: Oxford University Press, 2010); G Lodge and A Trench, 'Devo more and welfare: devolving benefits and policy for a stronger union' (London: IPPR, 2014).

or federalism is associated with substate nationalisms, which by definition 'tend to oppose state-wide solidarity'. Literature in recent decades is clear that such an effect is far from inevitable. 'Territorial … disintegration' in welfare provision is possible, but powerful 'institutional obstacles' often limit its extent.[26] Where fragmentation does occur, this may take the form of a 'race to the bottom' – but this has mainly been observed in non-European, English-speaking federations and has not been particularly evident in Europe.[27] Béland and Lecours argue that 'competitive nation-building' between the federal and Québécois governments has put *upward* pressure on welfare provision.[28] Similar competition can be observed in Spain, where the autonomous communities led the way in establishing social assistance programmes, which had previously been absent.[29] Overall, though, Banting sees relative welfare state uniformity as the norm even where political institutions are regionalised.[30] Belgium and Germany are examples of states where devolution and federalism have produced comparatively little welfare state divergence, although with greater pressure for divergence in Belgium.[31] Despite the general absence of a 'race to the bottom' tendency, resentment at transfers from richer to poorer regions exists within European countries and cannot be ruled out in the UK.[32]

In the context of multi-level governance, supranational as well as subnational tiers of government may assume or seek a role in defining the social rights of citizenship. The European Union has performed such a role in the UK, challenging gender-based discrimination in the welfare state[33] and establishing (and varying) the circumstances in which non-nationals exercising their free movement rights can access welfare services in a host state. This process first encroached upon but

[26] Béland and Lecours, above n 24 at 420–421.

[27] Simeon, above n 16.

[28] Béland and Lecours, above n 24 at 421.

[29] M Laparra and M Aguilar, 'Social exclusion and minimum income programmes in Spain' in M Rhodes (ed), *Southern European Welfare States: Between Crisis and Reform* (London: Frank Cass, 1997); B Suárez Corujo, 'Devolution and decentralisation in social security: the situation in Spain' in G Vonk and P Schoukens (eds), *Devolution and Decentralisation in Social Security: A European Comparative Perspective* (The Hague: Eleven, 2019).

[30] Banting, above n 23.

[31] Béland and Lecours, above n 24 at 421; J de Weyer and P Schoukens, 'Devolution and decentralisation in social security: the situation in Belgium' in G Vonk and P Schoukens (eds), *Devolution and Decentralisation in Social Security: A European Comparative Perspective* (The Hague: Eleven, 2019); S Rixen, 'Devolution and decentralisation in social security: the situation in Germany' in G Vonk and P Schoukens (eds), *Devolution and Decentralisation in Social Security: A European Comparative Perspective* (The Hague: Eleven, 2019).

[32] C Jeffery, 'German federalism from cooperation to competition' in M Umbach (ed), *German Federalism: Past, Present and Future* (Palgrave, 2002); J Subirats, 'Multi-level governance and multi-level discontent: the triumph and tensions of the Spanish model' in SL Greer (ed), *Territory, Democracy and Justice: Regionalism and Federalism in Western Democracies* (Palgrave Macmillan, 2006); D Béland and A Lecours, *Nationalism and Social Policy: The Politics of Territorial Solidarity* (Oxford University Press, 2008); J Harris, 'Could Wales leave the United Kingdom?' (*Guardian*, 1 February 2012). Available at: www.theguardian.com/uk/2012/feb/01/could-wales-leave-united-kingdom.

[33] Case C-262/88 *Douglas Harvey Barber v Guardian Royal Exchange Assurance Group* [1990] ECR I-1889.

ultimately affirmed the Member State's 'right to bound' its sphere of solidarity.[34] At present, the EU is showing renewed signs of desire to be an engine of social justice through its new 'pillar of social rights'.[35] From a UK perspective, although there will be residual effects of EU membership for individuals with an existing right to export a social security entitlement or with settled status in the UK, the post-Brexit trajectory of Union influence on social citizenship is likely to be downward. The UK remains part of other supranational structures, notably the Council of Europe and UN systems of human rights protection. These form part of the normative context from which the citizen's social rights emerge, but do not exert the same force domestically as EU law once did. Ratification of a human rights instrument may require reporting on, or allow external assessment of, progress towards its goals, but does not bind the UK to its provisions as a matter of domestic law, unless Parliament or one of the devolved legislatures so chooses.

The Welfare State in the UK's Devolution Settlement

Internationally, regional tiers of government tend to be important actors in the field of social policy, but not, on paper at least, in social security. This, though, is in the context of a stricter division between 'social security' and 'social assistance' in most European states than is the case in the UK,[36] albeit that the dividing line between the two can be decidedly 'blurred'.[37] Whereas social insurance has 'remained immune from the forces of devolution and territorial decentralisation',[38] social assistance is a regional, local or shared responsibility in at least 50 per cent

[34] Contrast the judgment in Case C-184/99 *Grzelczyk v Centre Public d'Aide Sociale d'Ottignies Louvain la Neuve* [2002] ECR I-1693 with the subsequent judgments in Case C-333/13 *Dano v Jobcenter Leipzig* [2015] 1 CMLR 48 and Case C-67/14 *Jobcentre Berlin Neukölln v Alimanovic* [2016] 1 CMLR 29; for commentary, see M Ferrera, *The Boundaries of Welfare: European Integration and the New Spatial Politics of Social Protection* (Oxford: Oxford University Press, 2005); M Wind, 'Post-national citizenship in Europe: the EU as a welfare rights generator?' (2009) 15 *Columbia Journal of European Law* 239; M Ferrera, 'Solidarity in Europe after the crisis' (2014) 21(2) *Constellations* 222; R Bebayev, 'Re-shaping the paradigm of social solidarity in the EU: on the UK's welfare reforms and pre- and post-EU referendum developments' (2016) 18(4) *European Journal of Social Security* 356; V Hooton, 'COVID-19, unemployment and social solidarity in EU law' (2021) 28(1) *Journal of Social Security Law* 16.

[35] Commission Communication establishing a European Pillar of Social Rights COM(2017) 250 final; KA Polomarkakis, 'The European Pillar of Social Rights and the quest for EU social sustainability' (2020) 29(2) *Social and Legal Studies* 183.

[36] Social security may be defined as a specific scheme (which may be universal in its scope) offering protection, on a contributory or non-contributory basis, against specified social risks, such as 'sickness, disablement, maternity, family, unemployment, old age, death, widowhood, vocational accidents and illnesses'. Social assistance consists of payments for the relief of 'individual need', however caused and regardless of employment status or scheme membership – Committee of Independent Experts, *Conclusions XIII-4* (Strasbourg: Council of Europe, 1996) 34.

[37] Suárez Corujo, above n 29 at 188.

[38] P Schoukens and G Vonk, 'The state of devolution and decentralisation in social security, a comparative European analysis: an introduction' in G Vonk and P Schoukens (eds), *Devolution and Devolution and Decentralisation in Social Security: A European Comparative Perspective* (The Hague: Eleven, 2019) 19.

of the 31 European countries covered by the Mutual Information System on Social Protection (MISSOC).[39] The UK is moving towards a greater role for devolved tiers of government in social protection. In Northern Ireland, this could potentially extend to any area of social security or social assistance, although in practice devolved-level interventions have thus far been highly selective. In Scotland, devolved competences focus on non-contributory social security benefits offering protection against specified social risks, with a broader power to top up any UK benefit allowing targeted additions to social assistance. This section sets out the changing place of the welfare state, and of social security in particular, in the devolution settlement.

The UK's devolution settlement is highly asymmetrical.[40] Areas with some form of devolved government structures vary in their geographic extent, extending to one of the UK's constituent countries (Scotland, Wales or Northern Ireland), a metropolitan area (the English combined authorities) or a county (Cornwall). Large swathes of England have no devolved arrangements at the time of writing. Devolved institutions take different forms, use different electoral systems and differ in their powers and areas of competence. The Northern Ireland Assembly and Scottish Parliament have primary legislative powers; the Welsh Assembly originally did not, but its latest incarnation, the Senedd, does. The Northern Ireland Executive operates like the UK Government in miniature, with Ministers presiding over legally distinct departments, while the Scottish and Welsh Governments each act as a single entity. There is no legislative devolution within England: the UK Parliament is also the English Parliament and the UK Government the government of England.[41] From the outset, then, the constitutional settlement places boundaries on the extent to which devolution *can* affect citizens' social rights, but the location of these boundaries varies.

Northern Ireland since 1921, Scotland since 1999 and Wales since 2017 operate a reserved powers model of devolution. This means that all matters are within the competence of the devolved legislature unless reserved to the UK Parliament (or, in Northern Ireland, excepted from being devolved) by the constitutional legislation.[42] Most major areas of social policy are devolved, but there are

[39] See www.missoc.org/missoc-database/; for country case studies, see G Vonk and P Schoukens (eds), *Devolution and Decentralisation in Social Security: A European Comparative Perspective* (The Hague: Eleven, 2019).

[40] For a detailed, although somewhat dated, examination of the asymmetries of the devolution settlements for Scotland, Wales and Northern Ireland, see D Birrell, *Comparing Devolved Governance* (Basingstoke: Palgrave Macmillan, 2012).

[41] Due to the asymmetric devolution of powers, the UK Parliament and Government may act for England alone, or for any combination of the four countries within the UK. For discussion of the complications associated with Parliament's position as legislature for both England and the UK, see D Gover and M Kenny, 'Answering the West Lothian Question? A critical assessment of "English votes for English laws" in the UK Parliament' (2018) 71(4) *Parliamentary Affairs* 760.

[42] Scotland Act 1998 c 46 ss 29–30; Northern Ireland Act 1998 c 47 ss 4, 6; Government of Wales Act 2006 c 32 ss 94–95, 108A–109; reserved matters may be devolved by Order in Council, whereas matters listed as 'excepted' in the Northern Ireland Act could only be devolved by primary legislation.

differences in which functions are reserved. Westminster controls social security and welfare foods, child support, employment, legal aid, some regulatory aspects of healthcare, alcohol licensing and key areas of family law in Wales.[43] Despite the general reservation of social security, devolved competences include discretionary assistance and council tax reduction, which are treated as local government rather than social security functions in England. Reserved matters in Scotland include child support, employment and similar aspects of healthcare regulation. Social security and welfare foods were originally reserved, but important changes in this area occurred in 2016. Devolved competences now include disability, industrial injuries, carer and housing benefits, discretionary assistance, welfare foods and assistance with maternity, funeral or cold-weather heating costs, as well as the power to top up reserved benefits. Other areas of social security remain reserved.[44] Spicker notes that this new model of shared competence for social security creates 'scope for conflict' between tiers of government,[45] but in practice the same potential exists in Northern Ireland despite (on paper) a cleaner division of competences. Northern Ireland has the most extensive non-fiscal devolved powers. The only reserved areas of social policy are the national minimum wage and regulatory functions relating to healthcare and occupational or personal pension schemes.[46] However, the formally devolved status of social security and child support must be read in conjunction with the non-devolution of national insurance rates and the provision that:

> The Secretary of State and the Northern Ireland Minister having responsibility for social security … shall from time to time consult one another with a view to securing that, to the extent agreed between them, the legislation … provides single systems of social security, child support and pensions for the United Kingdom.[47]

This is the latest legislative incarnation of a longstanding arrangement that has had a profound influence on social security provision in Northern Ireland. In practice, the 'agreement' between the two Ministers has almost always been that Northern Ireland's separately administered social security system should be a mirror image of Great Britain's. This was accepted practice to the extent that a 1971 Act provided for the making of social security legislation by Order – the Northern Ireland Parliament effectively legislating away its own scrutiny role.[48] In the event, the suspension of legislative devolution in 1974 meant the vast majority of 'primary' legislation for Northern Ireland was made in this way for the next quarter of a century, regardless of policy area.[49] On the restoration of the Assembly in 1998,

[43] Government of Wales Act 2006 c 32 sch 7A.

[44] Scotland Act 1998 c 46 sch 5 – see, in particular, head F.

[45] P Spicker, 'The devolution of social security benefits in Scotland: the Smith Commission' (2015) 23(1) *Journal of Poverty and Social Justice* 17, 17.

[46] Northern Ireland Act 1998 c 47 sch 3.

[47] Northern Ireland Act 1998 c 47 s 87; sch 2.

[48] Social Services (Parity) Act (Northern Ireland) 1971 c 21.

[49] Northern Ireland Act 1974 c 28 sch 1.

social security Bills typically used the accelerated passage procedure, skipping scrutiny by committee, but this practice became increasingly controversial and was ultimately abandoned.[50]

Why social security was devolved to Northern Ireland in 1998, but not to Scotland or Wales, does not appear to have been officially explained. In practice, the explanation appears to be simply that successive Northern Irish devolution settlements have largely maintained the very extensive transfer of competences envisaged by the Government of Ireland Acts 1914 and 1920.[51] With the social insurance system in its infancy and the Victorian Poor Law yet to give way to a modern system of social assistance, it seems that the architects of these Acts simply did not see social protection as a significant enough area of policy to reserve.[52] Parliamentarians quickly lined up to declare this an error.[53] This and the lack of divergence in social protection between Great Britain and Northern Ireland in the subsequent decades may hint at why a different approach was taken when establishing the Scottish and Welsh legislatures, but does not explain why Northern Ireland continued to be treated differently, given that the range of devolved competences has, to some extent, evolved over time. The move to devolve social security competences – albeit accounting for just 15 per cent of pre-2016 expenditure on benefits[54] – to Scotland is easier to explain. Here, the devolution of new fiscal and 'welfare' powers was central to UK political leaders' 'vow' to enhance the role of the Scottish Parliament if voters rejected independence in the 2014 referendum.[55]

The Welsh devolution settlement has been particularly dynamic but, until relatively recently, demand for the transfer of any significant social security competences to Cardiff was virtually absent.[56] This may be changing following a National Assembly inquiry which resulted in a call for partial social security devolution, alongside improvements to the small financial support programmes under devolved control and a more interventionist approach to promoting take-up of reserved benefits.[57] The report envisages flexibility in universal credit

[50] Committee for Social Development, Pensions Bill deb 8 November 2007; Committee for Social Development, Pensions Bill: accelerated passage deb 8 September 2011.

[51] Government of Ireland Act 1914 c 90; Government of Ireland Act 1920 c 67.

[52] M Simpson, 'Developing constitutional principles through firefighting: social security parity in Northern Ireland (2015) 22(1) *Journal of Social Security Law* 31.

[53] D Reid, HC deb 9 Mar 1926 vol 192 col 2174; Earl of Plymouth, HL deb 23 March 1926 vol 63 col 747; J Craig, HC deb 1 Mar 1929 vol 225 col 2360; Lord Templemore, HL deb 17 Mar 1936 vol 100 col 4.

[54] Scottish Government, *A new future for social security: consultation on social security in Scotland* (Edinburgh: Scottish Government, 2016).

[55] D Clegg, 'David Cameron, Ed Miliband and Nick Clegg sign joint historic promise which guarantees more devolved powers for Scotland and protection of NHS if we vote No' (Daily Record, 15 September 2014). Available at: www.dailyrecord.co.uk/news/politics/david-cameron-ed-miliband-nick-4265992.

[56] Commission on Devolution in Wales, *Empowerment and responsibility: legislative powers to strengthen Wales* (Cardiff: Commission on Devolution in Wales, 2013).

[57] Equality, Local Government and Communities Committee, *Benefits in Wales: options for better delivery* (Cardiff: National Assembly for Wales, 2019).

payment arrangements as well as devolution of various housing-related benefits, incapacity and disability assessments, attendance allowance, the sanctions regime, assistance with winter fuel, maternity and funeral expenses, and the power to top up reserved benefits or create new benefits. The Welsh Government accepted recommendations around the unified administration of currently devolved benefits and agreed to explore the possibility of greater flexibility around universal credit payment patterns with the UK Government, but said any serious consideration of further-reaching reform could only take place after there has been time to reflect on the medium-term effects of the coronavirus pandemic on the UK system.[58] Some literature is now beginning to emerge on what considerations should inform decisions on which social security powers should be targeted for transfer.[59]

Devolution in England remains in its infancy and the various combined authorities hold relatively limited powers, largely drawn up from local government rather than down from central government. Since 2016 there has been provision for the transfer of functions from any public authority to a combined authority by Order, but since legislative functions are non-transferrable any devolution of social security within England would be purely administrative in nature, allowing for operational differences but no radical departures from the Westminster policy agenda. That is not to say there would be no impact on how social security is delivered and experienced. To date, though, the only concerted attempt to explore the possibilities English devolution offers in this area has been in Greater Manchester,[60] where the mayor has called for the transfer of some social security and employment support functions.[61] Even if the logic behind English devolution is to 'co-opt and engage local stakeholders in the flexible delivery of Whitehall priorities',[62] the recent histories of Scotland and Wales show that if regional institutions can find their voice and catch the imagination of their communities, the process can take on a life of its own. Devolution in all parts of the UK remains 'a process not an event',[63] one whose endpoint is unknown.

[58] Welsh Government, 'Benefits in Wales: options for better delivery – Welsh Government response' (Cardiff: Welsh Government, 2019); Hannah Blythyn MS, Letter to John Griffiths AM, 20 May 2020.

[59] Bevan Foundation, *Making Welfare Work for Wales: should benefits for people of working age be devolved?* (Merthyr Tydfil: Bevan Foundation, 2016); E Taylor-Collins and D Bristow, *Administering social security in Wales: evidence on potential reforms* (Cardiff: Wales Centre for Public Policy, 2020).

[60] Greater Manchester Poverty Action, 'Devolved approaches to social security in the UK – lessons for Greater Manchester' (Manchester: GMPA, 2020). Available at: www.gmpovertyaction.org/devolved-approaches/.

[61] A Bounds, 'Andy Burnham sees more devolution as "best answer" to Brexit' (*Financial Times*, 9 May 2018) Available at: www.ft.com/content/7a6aa9c0-52ce-11e8-b3ee-41e0209208ec.

[62] J Denham, 'A nation divided? The identities, politics and governance of England' (Open Democracy, 16 August 2018). Available at: www.opendemocracy.net/en/opendemocracyuk/nation-divided-identities-politics-and-governance-of-england/.

[63] R Davies, cited by D Torrance, *'A process not an event': Devolution in Wales, 1998–2020* (CBP8318, London: House of Commons, 2020).

Towards Devolved Approaches to Social Security

The dynamic nature of the devolution settlement and its potential to evolve in ways that its original architects may not have foreseen, and that UK-level actors struggle to control, is well illustrated by the increasing assertiveness of devolved government in social security. Prior to 2012 it was scarcely credible to talk about a devolved approach to social security. Competence was only devolved to Northern Ireland, which had historically adhered closely to the convention of parity with Great Britain. In the early period of devolution after 1921, Unionist governments wished to avoid obstacles to future reintegration into a unitary UK,[64] maintain similar levels of social provision and standards of living among citizens from whatever region,[65] and prevent mass flight to Great Britain in search of better services and higher benefits.[66] Northern Ireland's relatively weak economic and fiscal position meant equivalence of social protection was only possible thanks to a 'temporary' arrangement agreed in 1926 – that persists to the present day. Under the agreement, the UK Government ensures the relative balances of the national insurance funds for Northern Ireland and Great Britain match their share of the total population and pays for non-contributory benefits outside the block grant, except to the extent that these are more generous in Northern Ireland.[67] Divergence occurred over time in many areas of policy, whether through innovation, like the unified administration of health and social care, or inertia, such as the retention of academic selection for secondary education while Great Britain largely moved to a comprehensive system.[68] In social security, parity retained a strong hold for 90 years.[69] Despite occasional differences of approach – on family allowance payments to larger families, residence tests, the recovery of debts to public authorities, the operation of the appeals process and support with local taxes – social security devolution has been described as an 'anomaly' that served no real purpose.[70]

[64] L Lundy, 'Parity, parrotry or plagiarism? Legislating for the unemployed poor in Northern Ireland 1838–1995' in N Dawson, D Greer and P Ingram (eds), *One Hundred and Fifty Years of Irish Law* (Belfast: SLS Legal Publications, 1996).

[65] J Craig, HC Deb (NI) 7 May 1925 vol 6 col 468.

[66] M Samuel, HC Deb 1 March 1929 vol 225 cols 2347, 2374.

[67] Unemployment Insurance (Northern Ireland Agreement) Act 1926 c 4; Unemployment Insurance (Northern Ireland Agreement) Act 1929 c 18; Northern Ireland Act 1998 c 47 s 87.

[68] H Andrew, 'The organisation of secondary education' (Circular 10/65, London: Department of Education and Science, 1965); Health and Personal Social Services (Northern Ireland) Order 1972 No 1265 (NI 14) art 4; see also D Birrell and A Murie, 'Ideology, conflict and social policy' (1975) 4(3) *Journal of Social Policy* 243.

[69] Simpson, above n 52.

[70] D Birrell and D Heenan, 'Devolution and social security: the anomaly of Northern Ireland' (2010) 18 *Journal of Poverty and Social Justice* 281; J Bradshaw, Social security parity in Northern Ireland (Belfast: Policy Research Institute, 1989).

This has changed in the twenty-first century. A previous Minister for Social Development argued that the 'politics of parity' should not deter devolved policy-makers from engaging with the 'politics of poverty' or exploring ways to 'stretch parity … to avoid, reduce, ease or lessen the impact of welfare cuts' emanating from Westminster. At this point the Minister remained cautious, warning of the risk that the established funding model for social security in Northern Ireland might be 'put on the table' if parity were stretched too far.[71] Legislative divergence became a more serious possibility, and to a limited extent a reality, following the Welfare Reform Act 2012. However, the difficulties that remain inherent in taking distinctive policy decisions are illustrated by the tortuous, three-year legislative process this involved (see Chapter 5). This could only be resolved through a temporary transfer of social security competences to Westminster, enabling the extension of the 2012 and 2016 reforms to Northern Ireland by Order while allowing for some devolved level mitigation measures.[72] Despite broad consensus around the need to protect claimants from certain cuts and to cushion the financial blow that the reform of disability benefits represented to some, without agreement on the detail of divergence it proved politically challenging to find a middle way between adopting the UK-level reforms wholesale and rejecting them outright. The first option would have been costly to many claimants, the second costly to the devolved budget; either would likely have carried a political cost for the Executive parties. Steps away from parity have thus far been cautious, but, on another level, the change has been profound – the presumption of parity has been swept away even as its practice largely continues.

Scotland's journey towards a devolved approach to social security had a different starting point. The Calman Commission's 2009 report was extremely cautious in its consideration of a role for devolved government in social security. Despite acknowledging a link between certain benefits and core devolved functions, the Commission concluded that virtually all important benefits should remain reserved. Contributory benefits *could* not be devolved because of the difficulty in apportioning the national insurance fund between the UK and Scotland. Means-tested income replacement benefits *should* not be devolved because of the need to ensure 'broadly common social citizenship' and the risk of 'benefit tourism'. While other benefits might appear more suitable for devolution in principle, in practice their interconnectedness with the main income replacement benefits meant the Scottish Government's role should effectively be limited to that of a consultee on their operation in Scotland. Only the discretionary social fund was considered suitable for devolution.[73] Two years later, the Scottish Parliament nonetheless signalled its belief that the time was right for devolved institutions to play a role in social protection by voting down parts of a legislative consent

[71] A Attwood, NIA deb 23 Nov 2011 vol 58 no 2 p 65.

[72] Northern Ireland (Welfare Reform) Act 2015 c 34; Welfare Reform (Northern Ireland) Order 2015 SI No 2006 (NI 1) 70; Welfare Reform and Work (Northern Ireland) Order 2016 SI No 999 (NI 1).

[73] Commission on Scottish Devolution, *Serving Scotland better: Scotland and the United Kingdom in the 21st century* (Edinburgh: Commission on Scottish Devolution, 2009) 200.

memorandum that would have allowed the UK Parliament to make consequential amendments to matters under devolved control flowing from the Welfare Reform Act 2012.[74] This was the first time a legislative consent memorandum had not been approved in full.[75] The same motion led to the establishment of a parliamentary Welfare Reform Committee to report (invariably critically) on the implementation of the 2012 Act in Scotland.

With the question of whether social justice could be better advanced within the union or in an independent Scotland an important issue in campaigning ahead of the 2014 referendum,[76] the final impetus for social security devolution appears to have come from the evaporation of what had once appeared a healthy pro-union majority as polling day approached. A late opinion poll showing a slender majority in favour of independence[77] was followed by a flurry of promises from unionist political leaders that additional powers, including some responsibility for 'welfare', would be devolved in the event that Scotland remained part of the UK.[78] The post-referendum Smith Commission recommended devolved control of universal credit payment patterns, housing-related benefits, disability and industrial injuries benefits and employment support, as well as powers to create new benefits and top up reserved benefits.[79] The Smith recommendations were accepted by the UK Government and legislated for by the UK Parliament in an attempt to achieve an 'enduring settlement' for Scotland within the UK.[80] By this stage, previously devolved powers, some exercised by local rather than regional government, were already being used to support people affected by some UK-level measures.[81]

Scottish circumstances were potentially more favourable for divergence in the new areas of devolved competence given the absence of an entrenched commitment to parity. They were potentially less favourable in that the country lacked established structures for the delivery of benefits. Given the extent to which

[74] SP deb 22 Dec 2011, session 4 col 5097.

[75] Welfare Reform Committee, *Stage 1 report on the Welfare Reform (Further Provision) (Scotland) Bill* (SP125, Edinburgh: Scottish Parliament, 2012).

[76] G Mooney and G Scott, 'The 2014 Scottish independence debate: questions of social welfare and social justice' (2015) 23(1) *Journal of Poverty and Social Justice* 5.

[77] W Dahlgreen, 'Yes campaign lead at 2 in Scottish referendum' (YouGov blog, 6 September 2014) Available at: https://yougov.co.uk/topics/politics/articles-reports/2014/09/06/latest-scottish-referendum-poll-yes-lead.

[78] BBC News, 'Scottish independence: Brown sets out more powers timetable' (BBC News, 8 September 2014) Available at: www.bbc.co.uk/news/uk-scotland-scotland-politics-29115556; Clegg, above n 55; D Cameron, 'Scottish independence referendum: statement by prime minister' (London: Scotland Office, 2014). Available at: www.gov.uk/government/news/scottish-independence-referendum-statement-by-the-prime-minister.

[79] Smith Commission, *Report of the Smith Commission for further devolution of powers to the Scottish Parliament* (Edinburgh: Smith Commission, 2014).

[80] HM Government, *Scotland in the United Kingdom: an enduring settlement* (Cm 8990, Edinburgh: Scotland Office, 2015); Scotland Act 2016 c 11 part 3.

[81] Welfare Funds (Scotland) Act 2015 asp 5; K Berry, *Discretionary housing payments* (SPICe briefing 14/17, Edinburgh: Scottish Parliament, 2014); this approach required a legislative change to remove a cap on DHP expenditure – Discretionary Housing Payments (Limit on Total Expenditure) Revocation (Scotland) Order 2014 SSI No 298.

'conflict over the welfare state … contributed to Scottish … campaigns for devolution and a nationalist tinge to welfare politics there',[82] it was always likely that the Government would want to be seen to take a different approach to England and Wales. This would also be in keeping with post-1999 developments in other fields of social policy.[83] As in Northern Ireland, this could reflect devolved-level innovation or 'refusal to pursue some of the UK government's more radical policy initiatives'.[84] This was particularly evident in health and social care, where the restoration of the NHS's role as a service provider (as opposed to commissioner) and introduction of free personal care for older people produced 'a different genus of health system' from England.[85] However, Holyrood does not have an entirely free hand in healthcare, being bound by a Great Britain-wide statutory commitment to deliver most core services free at the point of use,[86] and it may not have a free hand within devolved areas of social security. The devolved system will be years in the making: the first new benefits were direct replacements for payments from the regulated social fund, small top-ups to reserved benefits or new payments to specific groups. The far larger task of replacing the UK disability benefits (disability living allowance, personal independence payment and attendance allowance) was ongoing as this text was being completed. Arguably the most significant steps up to that point were the establishment of policymaking and delivery structures within government (the social security directorate and Social Security Scotland) and the Parliament's unanimous adoption of a framework Act putting in place a set of guiding principles for devolved social security, a charter composed of commitments for the operationalisation of the principles and new accountability mechanisms.[87]

Thus far, Wales has made much less progress towards what could reasonably be called a devolved approach to social security. As noted, the Senedd's social security competences are analogous to an English local authority rather than the Scottish Parliament or Northern Ireland Assembly.[88] Hints of future pressure for change

[82] SL Greer and M Mätzke, 'Introduction: devolution and citizenship rights', SL Greer (ed), *Devolution and Social Citizenship in the UK* (Bristol: Policy Press, 2009) 9.

[83] G Mooney and L Poole, '"A land of milk and honey"? Social policy in Scotland after devolution' (2004) 24(4) *Critical Social Policy* 458.

[84] N McEwen, 'The territorial politics of social policy development in multilevel states' (2005) 15(4) *Regional and Federal Studies* 537, 542.

[85] SL Greer, 'The territorial bases of health policymaking in the UK after devolution' (2005) 15(4) *Regional and Federal Studies* 501, 506; N Timmins, *The four UK health systems: learning from each other* (London: King's Fund, 2013); G Bevan, M Karanikolos, J Exley, E Nolte, S Connolly and N Mays, *The four health systems of the United Kingdom: how do they compare?* (London: Health Foundation/Nuffield Trust, 2014).

[86] National Health Service Act 2006 c 41 s 1; National Health Service (Scotland) Act 1947 c 27 s 1; National Health Service (Wales) Act 2006 c 42 s 1.

[87] Social Security (Scotland) Act 2018 asp 9.

[88] These responsibilities have increased since 2010, perhaps reflecting a concerted effort to transfer 'blame' for social security cuts from central to local government – see J Meers, 'Discretion as blame avoidance: passing the buck to local authorities in "welfare reform"' (2019) 27(1) *Journal of Poverty and Social Justice* 41.

on this front are emerging and it is noteworthy that something called a 'Welsh benefits system' seems set to enter existence, the Government having accepted the Equality, Local Government and Communities Committee's recommendation to establish one. This will differ from the Scottish or Northern Irish systems, being simply an exercise in unifying administration of the small areas of means-tested support for which Wales is already responsible. However, the new nomenclature can perhaps be taken as a signal of intent for the future. This sense is reinforced by the Government's commitment to 'develop options to reduce costs for families and boost incomes … where Welsh Government can make a difference' and the Committee's call for it to follow the Scottish example in developing a set of coproduced principles to guide the design and delivery of devolved benefits.[89]

Conclusion

Whether or not Marshall's theory of citizenship was devised with an eye to the implications of multi-level governance – the evidence suggests not – it is clear that devolution has implications for social citizenship. The UK government remains the most important actor in determining what provision is made for the economic welfare of citizens and others in the UK, but it is no longer the only significant voice. It would be reasonable to question the point of devolving political power if it did not make a difference to citizens' lives in the devolved countries or lead to experimentation with different policy solutions to both distinct and shared challenges facing the polity – even if that is what the architects of devolution in 1998 had in mind. Those implications, and the factors that both drive and limit the scope for a reshaping of the citizen's social rights at devolved level, will be explored in later chapters. First, though, unless it is presumed that devolved social security policymaking reflects a purely welfare nationalist pursuit of divergence for its own sake, it is necessary to take a closer look at the evolution of social citizenship rights at UK level.

[89] Welsh Government, above n 58 at 1; Equality, Local Government and Communities Committee, above n 57.

4

Twenty-first-century Welfare and the UK Model of Social Citizenship

Introduction

The social element of citizenship confers a right to a minimum standard of living, but what this minimum standard consists of can vary between states and over time. This book assesses the extent to which the guaranteed minimum is also coming to vary within the UK. The first step towards this is to examine the recent evolution of social citizenship at UK level. This is necessary because devolved social citizenships are emerging through divergence from the UK model, with which they still have much in common, and because devolved-level policymakers tend to define their approach through comparison with, or in opposition to, that of the UK Government. This chapter provides an overview of successive governments' efforts to build a twenty-first century welfare state that matches what they feel society needs or desires. These changing visions are particularly embodied in changes to the generosity of and behavioural conditions associated with the receipt of social security benefits, but how support is targeted and administered is also relevant. This empirical description of the evolution of social citizenship sits alongside a normative discussion of what, according to Marshallian theory, the social rights of citizenship *ought* to look like. A final section briefly considers the implications of the coronavirus pandemic for social citizenship.

The Legislative Development of the Twenty-first-century Welfare State

Changing views of the extent of the state's obligation to ensure citizens enjoy a minimum standard of living are likely to manifest in changes to social security law, policy and practice, although it should not be assumed that rhetoric automatically translates into far-reaching reform.[1] Proposals are almost routinely described as 'the most radical reform since William Beveridge',[2] but in reality each tends to build incrementally on the last.[3] As Marshall states: 'When we find men proclaiming a revolution every few years, and … it is always the same revolution, we may be sure that what is happening is a continuous evolutionary movement.'[4] This has continued in the twenty-first century, which has seen incremental change to the architecture of the social security system under governments of different political composition. 'New' benefits perform broadly the same function as their predecessors, with differences in targeting, administration, behavioural conditionality or generosity. Some trends have transcended governments, such as increasingly disciplinary approaches to the 'activation' of working-age claimants and the long-term erosion of the contributory principle. There have been greater differences in the generosity of support provided. The following subsections provide a thematic overview of key legislative developments in social security since 1997.

[1] P Pierson, *Dismantling the Welfare State? Regan, Thatcher and the Politics of Retrenchment* (Cambridge: Cambridge University Press, 1994); S McKay and K Rowlingson, 'Social security and welfare reform' in M Powell (ed), *Modernising the Welfare State: The Blair Legacy* (Bristol: Policy Press, 2008).

[2] J Purnell, 'We need a welfare state that secures Beveridge's legacy' (*Financial Times*, 2 March 2012). Available at: www.ft.com/content/6c8aa290-639e-11e1-b85b-00144feabdc0.

[3] G McKeever, 'Scrutinising social security law and protecting social rights: Lord Kerr and the benefit cap' in B Dickson and C McCormick (eds), *The Judicial Mind: A Festschrift for Lord Kerr of Tonaghmore* (Oxford: Hart, 2022).

[4] TH Marshall, 'The welfare state and the affluent society', *Class, Citizenship and Social Development* (New York: Doubleday, 1964).

Trajectories in Generosity

The New Labour era saw a clear, if largely unsung, trend towards higher benefit levels, particularly those targeted at low-income households with dependent children.[5] Interventions were often designed to incentivise labour market engagement as well as increasing incomes. The first significant reform was the introduction of working families' tax credit.[6] Like its predecessor, family credit, this provided an income supplement to low-earning households with dependent children, if at least one adult was employed for at least 16 hours per week. Greater generosity was achieved through a higher headline rate for parents of younger children, a higher earnings threshold before the award began to be reduced, a reduced taper once earnings exceeded the threshold and increased support with childcare costs.[7] Its replacement with child tax credit and working tax credit[8] brought further increases in entitlement for most recipients, due to a lower effective taper rate for the lowest earners, higher awards for babies under one and the extension of support to low-income households without children.[9] Labour's final social security Act before leaving office in 2010 empowered the Secretary of State to uprate awards in April 2010 even in the absence of price inflation.[10] An exception to this largely upward trend was a change to housing benefit to enable the setting of the maximum local housing allowance for private tenants at a level below their actual rent.[11]

Following the change of government in 2010, social security became a key area for spending cuts.[12] This began with a change of indexation for benefit and tax credit uprating, immediately slowing the year-on-year growth of awards, and a lower ceiling on housing benefit awards to private tenants.[13] The Welfare Reform Act 2012 brought the reduction of housing benefit awards to under-occupying social tenants,[14] abolition of the discretionary social fund and council tax benefit,[15] and a new cap on household benefit entitlement, set with reference to average earnings.[16] Cuts flowing from the 2012 Act were unquestionably significant,

[5] R Lister, 'Doing good by stealth: the politics of poverty and inequality under New Labour' (2001) 8(2) *New Economy* 65; M Mullard and R Swaray, 'New Labour legacy: comparing the Labour governments of Blair and Brown to Labour governments since 1945' (2010) 81(4) *Political Quarterly* 511.

[6] Tax Credits Act 1999 c 10 s 1.

[7] A Dilnot and J McCrae, 'Family credit and the working families' tax credit' (BN3, London: Institute for Fiscal Studies, 1999).

[8] Tax Credits Act 2002 c 21 ss 8–12.

[9] M Brewer, 'The new tax credits' (BN35, London: Institute for Fiscal Studies, 2003).

[10] Welfare Reform Act 2009 c 24 s 23.

[11] Welfare Reform Act 2007 c 5 s 30.

[12] See N Ellison, 'The coalition government, public spending and social policy' in H Bochel and M Powell (eds), *The Coalition Government and Social Policy: Restructuring the Welfare State* (Bristol: Policy Press, 2016).

[13] Housing Benefit (Amendment) Regulations 2010 SI No 2835 reg 2; Rent Officers (Housing Benefit Functions) Amendment Order 2010 SI No 2836 arts 2, 4; Housing Benefit (Amendment) Regulations 2011 SI No 1736 reg 2.

[14] Welfare Reform Act 2012 c 5 s 69.

[15] Ibid, ss 33, 70.

[16] Ibid, s 96.

particularly the benefit cap as it broke the long-established link between social security awards and need (as measured with reference to household composition and housing costs).[17] However, they were arguably of secondary importance to the Act's primary purpose of restructuring social assistance and disability benefits. The social security provisions of its 2016 successor were almost exclusively concerned with reducing entitlement. The link between the benefit cap and average earnings was broken, with the cap now set with reference to a (lower) statutory limit.[18] A range of benefits and tax credits were frozen at their 2015–2016 level until April 2020.[19] Child tax credit and the child element of universal credit became payable in respect of additional children born after April 2017 only if the household already contained no more than one qualifying child – a further breach of the former principle of benefit awards responding to need.[20] Higher payments (compared with jobseekers) to claimants of incapacity-related benefits able to take part in work-related activity were abolished.[21]

Again, there were exceptions to the trend. Disability benefits were exempt from the four-year freeze and their recipients – and those with the highest awards of incapacity-related benefits – are exempt from the benefit cap.[22] Universal credit is intended to increase support for low-earning in-work claimants compared to the legacy system, although the extent to which this is achieved depends on household composition and has varied over time.[23] In-work claimants with sufficient earnings, or new claimants with sufficient earnings in their last year of employment, are also exempt from the cap.[24]

Trajectories in Behavioural Conditionality

Intensification of claimant conditionality has transcended governments. New Labour swiftly introduced mandatory work-focused interviews for claimants of some income-replacement benefits[25] and compulsory employment support programmes for certain claimant groups – the young and long-term unemployed – alongside voluntary schemes for others.[26] Mandatory programmes for claimants of lower

[17] D Hirsch, 'After a decade of austerity, does the UK have an income safety net worth its name?' in J Rees, M Pomati and E Heins (eds), *Social Policy Review 32* (Bristol: Policy Press, 2020); McKeever, above n 3.

[18] Welfare Reform and Work Act 2016 c 7 s 8.

[19] ibid, ss 11, 12.

[20] ibid, c 7 ss 13, 14.

[21] ibid, ss 15, 16.

[22] Benefit Cap (Housing Benefit) Regulations 2012 SI No 2994 reg 2; Universal Credit Regulations 2013 SI No 376 regs 79, 83.

[23] J Browne, A Hood and R Joyce, 'The (changing) effects of universal credit' in C Emmerson, P Johnson and R Joyce (eds), *IFS Green Budget 2016* (London: Institute for Fiscal Studies, 2016).

[24] Benefit Cap (Housing Benefit) Regulations 2012 SI No 2994 reg 2; Universal Credit Regulations 2013 SI No 376 reg 82.

[25] Welfare Reform and Pensions Act 1999 c 30 s 57.

[26] ibid, s 60; D Finn, 'Employment policy' in N Ellison and C Pierson (eds), *Developments in British Social Policy* (London: Macmillan, 2003).

level incapacity-related benefits were central to the new employment and support allowance launched in 2008.[27] The final Act under Labour brought the introduction of mandatory unpaid work placements, styled '"work for your benefit" schemes'.[28] The Conservative–Liberal Democrat coalition would introduce a short Act to enable their continued operation after the underpinning Regulations were held to be *ultra vires*.[29] The 2009 Act also provided for the classification of out-of-work lone parents as jobseekers from their youngest child's seventh birthday (this previously happened at 16),[30] for income support claimants other than lone parents of a child under three to be required to take part in work-related activity[31] and for new sanctions for non-attendance at a Jobcentre interview.[32] Provision was also made for the relaxation of conditionality on grounds of domestic violence, recognition of health and childcare availability as defences for non-compliance with benefit conditions and the consideration of child wellbeing when devising jobseeker's agreements.[33]

A further intensification of conditionality occurred under the coalition and Conservatives after 2010. Universal credit includes a claimant commitment setting out the claimant's responsibilities in terms of jobseeking and work-related activities. Unlike the former jobseeker's agreement, individuals who are *not* required to be available for paid work and those already in low-paid employment must sign a claimant commitment. Conditionality can be tailored to the claimant's circumstances and claimants can move between conditionality groups without changing benefit.[34] The previous special rules on lone parent conditionality now extend to the main caregiver within a joint-claim couple with children and the point at which availability for employment is expected has been brought forward to the youngest child's third birthday; lesser forms of conditionality apply from the first birthday.[35] Non-compliance with the claimant commitment is punishable by a tiered system of sanctions, as shown in the table below. Increased use of sanctions in practice was at least as significant as the legislative change. A record 9.5 per cent of jobseeker's allowance claimants had their benefit stopped in a single quarter of 2008, but this was dwarfed by subsequent spikes of 15 per cent in 2010 and more than 20 per cent in 2013 before the sanctioning rate dropped back to just below 5 per cent per quarter by 2017.[36]

[27] Welfare Reform Act 2007 c 5 ss 13–15.

[28] Welfare Reform Act 2009 c 5 s 1.

[29] Jobseekers Act 2013 c 17 s 1; *R (on the application of Reilly) v Secretary of State for Work and Pensions* [2013] EWCA Civ 66; *R (on the application of Reilly) v Secretary of State for Work and Pensions* [2013] UKSC 68.

[30] Welfare Reform Act 2009 c 5 s 3.

[31] ibid, s 2.

[32] Ibid, s 33.

[33] ibid, c 24 ss 29–31; Welfare Reform Act 2012 c 5 ss 116–120.

[34] Welfare Reform Act 2012 c 5 part 2.

[35] ibid, ss 19–22; Welfare Reform and Work Act 2016 c 7 s 17.

[36] D Webster, 'Tackling Britain's misleading benefit sanctions statistics' (Welfare Conditionality, 21 April 2016). Available at: www.welfareconditionality.ac.uk/2016/04/tackling-britains-misleading-benefit-sanctions-statistics/; D Webster, Written evidence (ANC0019) to the Work and Pensions Committee Benefit Sanctions inquiry (London: House of Commons, 2018).

Table 4.1 Universal credit sanctions from October 2012[37]

Sanction level	Lowest	Lower	Intermediate	Higher
Failure	Failure to punctually attend work-focused interview, when subject to no other conditions	Failure to: attend adviser interview; attend employment or training programme; comply with a jobseeker direction	Not being available for work; not actively seeking work	Leaving a job voluntarily; losing a job through misconduct; failure to apply for/accept a suitable job or participate in mandatory activity
First failure	Until compliance restored	4 weeks	4 weeks	13 weeks
Second failure	Until compliance restored	4 weeks	13 weeks	26 weeks
Third failure	Until compliance restored	13 weeks	13 weeks	156 weeks (now 26 weeks)[38]
Sanction prior to October 2012	No equivalent	1, 2, 4 or 26 weeks	Until compliance restored	1–26 weeks

Claimants have increasingly become subject to non-work-related behavioural conditionality. This has included the disqualification from benefit of persons convicted, penalised or cautioned for social security fraud,[39] as well as the creation of new fraud-related offences.[40] Provision has been made for disqualification from benefit due to non-compliance with a community order,[41] eviction due to anti-social behaviour[42] or violence against social security staff.[43] For a period, legislation allowed mandatory questioning, testing and treatment for claimants whose employment prospects were thought to have been affected by drug or alcohol misuse.[44]

[37] Universal Credit Regulations 2013 SI No 376 regs 101–105.
[38] Jobseeker's Allowance and Universal Credit (Higher-Level Sanctions) (Amendment) Regulations 2019 SI No 1357.
[39] Social Security Fraud Act 2001 c 11 s 7; Welfare Reform Act 2009 c 24 s 24.
[40] Social Security Fraud Act 2001 c 11 s 16.
[41] Child Support, Pensions and Social Security Act 2000 c 19 s 62, repealed by Welfare Reform Act 2009 c 24 s 26.
[42] Welfare Reform Act 2007 c 5 s 31.
[43] Welfare Reform Act 2009 c 24 s 25.
[44] ibid, s11, repealed by Welfare Reform Act 2012 c 5 s 60.

Trajectories in Targeting

The importance of the contributory principle in working-age benefits has continued to decline,[45] with the duration of entitlement to contribution-based incapacity-related benefits reduced on three occasions in the twenty-first century.[46] Entitlement to contributory benefits now lasts only six months for jobseekers and one year for claimants of incapacity-related benefits. This will have brought a corresponding increase in reliance on means-tested benefits, with some claimants from higher-earning households losing their entitlement. A degree of means testing has also been introduced to child benefit, previously a universal payment to families with dependent children, with payments to households in which an individual earns £50,000 per year or more now recovered through the income tax system.[47]

Selectivity in the allocation of additional support based on disability or incapacity has also increased. New capability assessments for claimants of incapacity-related benefits have been designed in part to identify those who could be in paid work.[48] In the most recent round of reforms, those who are recognised to have limited capability for work, but are able to take part in work-related activity, lost their additional payment compared with jobseekers.[49] Targeting of disability benefits has also been reformed, with the replacement of disability living allowance for working age claimants with personal independence payment bringing a reduction in the number of bands for awards and revision of some of the criteria against which entitlement is assessed.[50]

Trajectories in Administration and Service Delivery

It is harder to identify a clear trend in social security administration, but some themes can be identified. One is the move towards a mixed economy of welfare, increasing the role of private actors in the delivery of functions like medical and work capability assessments or employment support.[51] Local government has taken on an enhanced role, particularly in England, through the creation of replacement schemes for the discretionary social fund and council tax benefit, and increased use of discretionary housing payments to make up shortfalls in housing-related benefits.[52] This followed short-lived, unimplemented legislative provision

[45] Social Security Committee, *The contributory principle* (HC51-I, London: House of Commons, 2000).

[46] Welfare Reform and Pensions Act 1999 c 30 s 62; Welfare Reform Act 2009 c 24 s 13; Welfare Reform Act 2012 c 5 s 51.

[47] Finance Act 2012 c 14 s 8.

[48] Welfare Reform and Pensions Act 1999 c 30 s 61; Welfare Reform Act 2007 c 5 ss 8, 9.

[49] Welfare Reform and Work Act 2016 c 7 ss 15, 16.

[50] Welfare Reform Act 2012 c 5 ss 77–81.

[51] Welfare Reform Act 2007 c 5 s16; Welfare Reform Act 2009 c 24 s 32.

[52] J Meers, 'Discretion as blame avoidance: passing the buck in welfare reform' (2019) 27(1) *Journal of Poverty and Social Justice* 41.

for the replacement of crisis and budgeting loans with 'social loans' from non-state sources.[53] Increasingly, the voluntary sector has become the welfare provider of last resort.[54]

Within central government, the period has seen some reassignment of responsibility for income maintenance. The tax credits introduced between 1999 and 2002 have been administered by the Treasury, whereas predecessor benefits, such as family credit, were delivered by the Department of Social Security.[55] Consolidation of means-tested out-of-work benefits came onto the agenda in the latter years of the New Labour era.[56] Universal credit is now bringing together most forms of working age social assistance,[57] transferring functions from the Treasury back to the Department for Work and Pensions (as the DSS was rebranded in 2001) as tax credits are phased out. Another administrative consequence of universal credit is the shift to a digital-by-default application and claim management system. A final change to note is the introduction of mandatory (internal) reconsideration of a disputed decision about a benefit award before the claimant can appeal to the first-tier tribunal.[58]

Retirement Benefits

Trajectories in the main retirement benefits can be summed up more succinctly, with three trends transcending governments in the twenty-first century. First, in contrast with working-age benefits, an increase in generosity. Under New Labour, this focused on low-income pensioners, who benefitted from the new state pension credit. Guarantee credit sets a minimum income floor for UK residents of pensionable age, while savings credit aims to reduce any disincentive to save privately for retirement by applying a taper to the reduction of pension credit income where a household has some income from savings or other pension plans.[59] After 2010, the emphasis shifted to the level of contributory retirement pensions. The non-statutory 'triple lock' ensures that the basic and new state pensions increase annually by the higher of price inflation, earnings growth or 2.5 per cent.[60] As a result, by October 2021, the new state pension for individuals

[53] Welfare Reform Act 2009 c 24 ss 16, 17.

[54] C Fitzpatrick, G McKeever and M Simpson, 'Conditionality, discretion and TH Marshall's right to welfare' (2019) 41(4) *Journal of Social Welfare and Family Law* 445.

[55] Tax Credits Act 1999 c 10 s 2.

[56] D Freud, *Reducing Dependency, Increasing Opportunity: Options for the Future of Welfare to Work* (London: Department for Work and Pensions, 2007); Economic Dependency Working Group, *Dynamic Benefits: Towards Welfare that Works* (London: Centre for Social Justice, 2009).

[57] Welfare Reform Act 2012 c 5 part 1.

[58] Ibid, s 102.

[59] State Pension Credit Act 2002 c 16 ss 1–3.

[60] See D Thurley and R McInnes, *State Pension Triple Lock* (CBP-07812, London: House of Commons, 2021).

with a complete contributions record was slightly higher than guarantee credit and 140 per cent higher than the universal credit personal allowance for a single claimant. This means that the insurance principle continues to play a more important role in retirement benefits than in working-age benefits.

The second trend concerns the rise of a mixed economy of welfare. The state has operated various additional pension schemes to enable people making more than the minimum level of national insurance contributions to build an earnings-related top-up to their basic pension.[61] Over time, these placed progressively greater emphasis on encouraging higher earners to 'contract out' of the additional state pension and invest in an occupational or personal pension, while preserving some additional earnings-related entitlement for lower earners. The coalition Government abolished the distinction between the basic and additional pension, introducing a new, contribution-based state pension with a higher maximum award than its predecessor.[62] Erosion of the additional state pension has been accompanied by measures to promote and ultimately require provision of occupational or similar pensions for most employees,[63] culminating with automatic enrolment of employees into an occupational or stakeholder pension.[64]

The third major trend is the raising of pensionable age. Equalisation of pensionable age for men and women at 65 years was legislated for in 1995,[65] then accelerated.[66] Subsequent increases to pensionable age for all have also been accelerated since the initial legislation.[67] Ultimately, anyone born from April 1978 will become eligible for state pension at 68 years old.

Implications for Social Citizenship

As the twenty-first century has seen a mixture of continuity and change in terms of legal and policy developments in UK social security, so there is a mixture of continuity and change in the underpinning conceptions of social citizenship. Unifying themes include a drive to ensure fairness and reciprocity and a paternalistic effort to encourage or require individuals to act in their own best interests. Changes of government have brought greater change to the dominant conception of poverty – and the state's responsibility for preventing or alleviating poverty – and to the prominence of concerns about the financial sustainability of the welfare state. This section focuses on how evolving social citizenship ideologies can explain changes

[61] National Insurance Act 1959; Social Security Pensions Act 1975 c 60 s 6; Social Security Act 1986 c 50 s 18; Child Support, Pensions and Social Security Act 2000 c 19 ss 30–33.

[62] Pensions Act 2014 c 19 part 1.

[63] Welfare Reform and Pensions Act 1999 c 30 part 1.

[64] Pensions Act 2008 c 30 ss 2–8, 67; National Employment Savings Trust Order 2010 SI No 917; Pensions Act 2011 c 19 part 2; Pensions Act 2014 c 19 ss 37–40.

[65] Pensions Act 1995 c 26 s 126.

[66] Pensions Act 2011 c 19 s 1.

[67] Pensions Act 2007 c 22 s 13; Pensions Act 2011 c 19 s 1.

to the generosity of social security and the reciprocal duties demanded of claimants. These respectively affect the ability of social security to guarantee at least a modicum of economic welfare and the extent to which it acts as a largely unconditional safety net. The focus is on working age benefits. Retirement benefits are excluded from the discussion. The quite different trajectory of legal and policy developments shows that elites view the social citizenship of older people in a different light to that of working-age people. Furthermore, there is currently nothing to indicate that any devolved country is considering a distinctive approach While administrative justice issues have affected some people's ability to enjoy their social rights in practice,[68] the section largely concentrates on the nature in principle of those rights and corresponding duties.

Generosity of Social Security Benefits and Underlying Conceptions of Poverty

Marshall's most-quoted definition of the social element of citizenship describes it as encompassing:

> The whole range from the right to a modicum of economic welfare and security to the right to share to the full in the social heritage and to live the life of a civilised being according to the standards prevailing in the society.[69]

The 1942 Beveridge report and the post-Second World War legislation influenced by its proposals for social protection and healthcare confirmed that society has a collective responsibility to ensure citizens can access at least a subsistence income and minimum essential services.[70] This contrasted with the former Poor Law, which was often as concerned with deterring the poor from seeking support as it was with providing it.[71] The UK social security system is generally associated with the liberal welfare state model, which tends towards the guarantee of a subsistence minimum rather than the social inclusion associated with the more ambitious end of the Marshallian spectrum.[72] Nonetheless, there has been variation over time in

[68] Work and Pensions Committee *Decision Making and Appeals in the Benefits System* (HC313, London: House of Commons, 2010); R Thomas, 'Administrative justice, better decision making and organisational learning' (2015) *Jan Public Law* 111; D Cowan, A Dymond, S Halliday and C Hunter, 'Reconsidering mandatory reconsideration' (2017) *Public Law* 215.

[69] TH Marshall, 'Citizenship and social class' in TH Marshall and T Bottomore, *Citizenship and Social Class* (London: Pluto, 1992) 8.

[70] W Beveridge, *Social insurance and Allied Services* (Cmd 6404, London: HMSO, 1942); National Insurance Act 1946 c 67; National Health Service Act 1946 c 81; National Assistance Act 1948 c 29; see TH Marshall, *Social Policy in the Twentieth Century* (London: Hutchinson, 1975).

[71] TH Marshall, 'The right to welfare' in *The Right to Welfare and Other Essays* (London: Heinemann, 1981); J Offer, '"Desert," "need," the social theory of the Poor Law report of 1834 and John Stuart Mill' (1989) 9(1) *International Journal of Sociology and Social Policy* 63, 66.

[72] G Esping-Andersen, *The Three Worlds of Welfare Capitalism* (Princeton: Princeton University Press, 1990); FG Castles and D Mitchell, 'Worlds of welfare and families of nations' in FG Castles (ed), *Families of Nations: Patterns of Public Policy in Western Democracies* (Aldershot: Dartmouth, 1993).

how this responsibility is understood and in the social security measures put in place to discharge it.[73]

This variation has been associated with changing views about the nature of poverty. Lister emphasises that the 'definition [of poverty] has to be understood as a political as well as a social scientific act'.[74] In the twenty-first century UK, it has also been a legal act; for much longer it has been an act with legal consequences. Absolute definitions construct poverty as an inability to access the means of physical survival – to enjoy even a modicum of economic welfare. Relative definitions of poverty ask whether an individual or family has 'resources … so seriously below … the average' that they are 'excluded from ordinary living patterns, customs and activities'.[75] In either case, poverty can be defined in terms of income or deprivation – that is, with reference to how much money a household has coming in, or what it can afford.

Conservative governments of the 1980s and 1990s have been associated with the view that poverty was no longer an issue for the UK, a position that would ultimately jar with growing public concern.[76] New Labour's 1997 election victory brought a 'paradigm shift',[77] with poverty placed at the centre of the government's agenda by a pledge to eradicate child poverty within a generation.[78] This commitment, which focused anti-poverty measures on the unambiguously 'deserving' poor and preventing intergenerational cycles of poverty,[79] would be placed on a statutory footing by the Child Poverty Act 2010. The Act attempted to reconcile absolute and relative, income- and deprivation-based conceptions of poverty, setting targets for its near-elimination by four definitions.[80] In practice, though, the political emphasis fell heavily on relative low income.[81] Cash transfers were not the only tool used in pursuit of the child poverty targets – much reliance was placed on increasing maternal employment.[82] However, Joyce observes that

[73] R Lowe, *The Welfare State in Britain Since 1945* (London: Macmillan, 1999).

[74] R Lister, *Poverty* (Cambridge: Polity Press, 2021) 14.

[75] P Townsend, *Poverty in the United Kingdom* (London: Penguin, 1979) 31.

[76] D Piachaud, 'The new right and New Labour' in R Walker (ed), *Ending Child Poverty: Popular Welfare for the 21st Century?* (Bristol: Policy Press, 1999); D Piachaud and H Sutherland, 'Child poverty in Britain and the New Labour government' (2001) 30(1) *Journal of Social Policy* 95.

[77] McKay and Rowlingson, above n 57 at 57.

[78] T Blair, 'Beveridge revisited: a welfare state for the 21st century' in R Walker (ed), *Ending Child Poverty: Popular Welfare for the 21st Century?* (Bristol: Policy Press, 1999) 17; R Lister, 'Children (but not women) first: New Labour, child welfare and gender' 2006 26(2) *Critical Social Policy* 315.

[79] Department for Social Security, *Opportunity for All: Tackling Poverty and Social Exclusion* (Cm 4445, London: DSS, 1999) 5; see also S Machin, 'Childhood disadvantage and intergenerational transmissions of economic status' in Centre for Analysis of Social Exclusion, *Persistent Poverty and Lifetime Inequality: The Evidence* (Occasional paper no 10, London: HM Treasury, 1999).

[80] Child Poverty Act 2010 c 9 ss 3–6.

[81] D Piachaud and H Sutherland, 'Child poverty in Britain and the New Labour government' (2001) 30(1) *Journal of Social Policy* 95.

[82] B Featherstone, 'Why gender matters in child welfare and protection' (2006) 26(2) *Critical Social Policy* 294; Lister, above n 78.

'the years in which entitlements ... rose relative to the poverty line coincide almost perfectly with the years in which child poverty fell'.[83]

The 2010 Act secured cross-party support in Parliament. However, signs soon emerged that the coalition government elected that year had a different understanding of the nature and causes of, and the solutions to, poverty. Its 'new approach' combined increased emphasis on those furthest below statutory poverty lines with a sharper focus on non-income indicators and causes of poverty.[84] This new paradigm shift was confirmed in 2016, when the 2010 Act was amended to remove poverty reduction targets and renamed the Life Chances Act 2010.[85] The prevalence of relative low income, absolute low income, combined low income/material deprivation, persistent poverty and severe poverty continues to be measured in the absence of targets to reduce their extent,[86] alongside statutory reporting on worklessness and educational attainment.[87]

These amendments are telling. Although Labour and Conservative-led governments have shared the view that paid employment represents the 'best route out of poverty'[88] post-2010 administrations have presented non-employment, rather than lack of financial resources, as the defining characteristic of both material and moral poverty. A focus on employment rather than social transfers is justified pragmatically, as treating the 'cause' of poverty rather than the 'symptoms' and morally, ensuring 'those who take a full-time job' are rewarded financially in absolute terms and relative to those who do not.[89] Although the coalition also stressed the need to rebuild the public finances following financial crisis and the claimed profligacy of its Labour predecessors, this does not in itself explain why working age social security specifically was identified as a key target for austerity measures.[90] The accompanying rhetoric of fairness and individual responsibility shows that reforms were also driven by a particular social citizenship ideology. Social security continues to underwrite a modicum of economic welfare, albeit one whose level diminished throughout the 2010s, for those who strive for self-sufficiency, or are excused from doing so. The opportunity to share to the full in the social heritage and live the life of a civilised being is effectively reserved for those who engage in (sufficiently well-)paid work. In part this is because the low

[83] R Joyce, 'Child poverty in Britain: recent trends and future prospects' (W15/07, London: IFS, 2014) 10.

[84] HM Government, *A New Approach to Child Poverty: Tackling the Causes of Disadvantage and Transforming Families' Lives* (Cm 8061, London: DWP, 2011); Department for Work and Pensions, *Measuring Child Poverty: A Consultation on Better Measures of Child Poverty* (Cm 8483, London: DWP, 2012).

[85] Welfare Reform and Work Act 2016 c 7 ss 5–7.

[86] Ibid, s 4.

[87] Life Chances Act 2010 c 9 ss A1A–A1C.

[88] A Deacon and R Patrick, 'A new welfare settlement? The coalition government and welfare-to-work' in H Bochel (ed), *The Conservative Party and Social Policy* (Bristol: Policy Press, 2011).

[89] I Duncan Smith, 'Foreword – Secretary of State for Work and Pensions' in HM Government, above n 84 at 3.

[90] Ellison, above n 12.

level of benefits ensures that, for most, employment is the only way of accessing enough income, but paid work is also constructed as what a responsible and socially included citizen does. For those who fail to live up to this ideal, the Poor Law principle of 'less eligibility' has been reasserted.[91]

Reciprocity in the Active Welfare State

That 'conditionality has been a feature of benefit entitlement in the UK since the formation of the welfare state'[92] is a truism oft repeated in academic and political discourses on social security.[93] It is true that receipt of any benefit is subject to conditions of status (nationality, residence or age) and often of need (low income or exposure to a specified social risk). Conditions of conduct, such as contribution requirements, jobseeking or employment-related activities or other demonstrations of 'good' citizenship, are also a longstanding feature of social protection. While this aligns with Beveridge's view that recipients of low-income benefits should be required 'to fit themselves or to keep themselves fit for service',[94] the twenty-first century has seen work-related conditions become increasingly onerous and applicable to an increasingly wide range of claimant groups than was the case in the previous century.

To some, this trend is difficult to reconcile with the Marshallian citizenship paradigm. Marshall argued that 'the relief of the poor, the care of those who are unable to care for themselves, is among the unqualified objects of public duty'[95] and that 'the claim of the individual to welfare is sacred and irrefutable'.[96] Given such quotations, it is understandable that Marshall's has been interpreted as a 'theory of entitlement' with no regard for conduct, reciprocity or deservingness.[97] Yet other passages are clear that rights *are* coupled with duties. Marshall's ideal citizen should exhibit 'a lively sense of responsibility towards' the 'welfare of the whole community, which is something more complex than the sum total of the welfare of all its individual members'.[98] The very conception of citizenship as including a social element means citizens have positive obligations towards one another, in contrast with some earlier liberal visions.[99]

[91] PM Larkin, 'Delineating the gulf between human rights jurisprudence and legislative austerity: the judicial entrenchment of "less-eligibility"' (2016) 23(1) *Journal of Social Security Law* 42.

[92] Work and Pensions Committee, *Benefit Sanctions: Government Response to the Committee's Nineteenth Report of Session 2017–2019* (HC1949, London: House of Commons, 2019).

[93] See DR Fletcher, 'Workfare – a blast from the past? Contemporary workfare conditionality for the unemployed in historical perspective' (2015) 14(3) *Social Policy and Society* 329.

[94] Beveridge, above n 70 at [23].

[95] Marshall, above n 71 at 84.

[96] TH Marshall, 'Social selection in the welfare state', *Class, Citizenship and Social Development* (New York: Doubleday, 1964) 236.

[97] BS Turner and C Rojek, *Society and Culture: Principles of Scarcity and Solidarity* (London: Sage, 2001) 202.

[98] Marshall, above n 96 at 237; Marshall, above n 69 at 45.

[99] D Heater, *What is Citizenship?* (Cambridge: Polity Press, 1999).

Plant's view that 'individuals do not and cannot have a right to the resources of society unless they contribute to the development of that society through work or other socially valued activities, if they are in a position to do so' has broadly been reflected in the UK's social citizenship bargain.[100] However, the range of 'other socially valued activities' accepted as a contribution to society varies over time and in the twenty-first century has largely centred on the individual's duty to contribute through paid employment, and to seek (better) paid employment if in receipt of low-income benefits. This development is potentially compatible with the view, expressed in one of Marshall's later writings, that 'the obligation of the community to relieve destitution must somehow be matched by a duty of the individual not to become destitute, if he can help it'.[101] It is no great leap from such sentiments to the view of a former Secretary of State that, where a claimant is capable of paid work, the state has 'the right to insist that when work is available you take that work and work hard to keep that job', and that to support those who do not make sufficient effort to support themselves would be to 'waste' taxpayers' money.[102] That is not to say that Marshall would have approved of the particularly disciplinary approach to claimant activation that has emerged in the UK. While condemning laziness on the part of the unemployed,[103] Marshall assumed this would be so rare that 'the problem is not one of real importance'[104] and was explicitly tolerant of what Dunn terms 'choosiness' by jobseekers.[105] In contrast, the spectre of the early-rising shift worker taunted by the 'closed blinds' of a work-shy neighbour 'sleeping off a life on benefits' became a foundational myth of the Cameron Governments' reform project.[106]

If Marshall provides only a partial endorsement of the UK's conditionality regime, the question arises of whether developments in the twenty-first century better fit a different social citizenship paradigm. Watts and Fitzpatrick outline six ethical frameworks against which they suggest 'welfare conditionality' can be assessed:[107]

- Rights – social citizenship rights should be universal and essentially unconditional.
- Utilitarianism – policy should aim to maximise overall welfare.
- Contractualism – claimants have a duty to seek to limit/end their dependence on taxpayers.

[100] R Plant, 'Supply side citizenship?' (1999) 6(3) *Journal of Social Security Law* 124, 125.

[101] Marshall, above n 71 at 90.

[102] I Duncan Smith, Speech to the Conservative Party conference (Birmingham, 5 October 2010).

[103] TH Marshall, 'Work and wealth', *Class, Citizenship and Social Development* (New York: Doubleday, 1964).

[104] Marshall, above n 71 at 90.

[105] Marshall, above n 103; A Dunn, 'Activation workers' perceptions of their long-term unemployed clients' attitudes towards employment' (2013) 42(4) *Journal of Social Policy* 799.

[106] G Osborne, Speech to Conservative Party conference (Birmingham, 8 October 2012).

[107] B Watts and S Fitzpatrick, *Welfare Conditionality* (Abingdon: Routledge, 2018).

- Communitarianism – citizenship is primarily characterised by a duty to contribute to society.
- Paternalism – coercion may be necessary to ensure people act in their own interests.
- Social justice – distribution of resources must ensure people's basic needs are met before deservingness is considered.

Of these frameworks, paternalism and contractualism seem to best reflect UK elites' justifications for conditionality, although contractarian and communitarian arguments can be linked. Ensuring individuals work to move from 'dependence' on the state towards self-sufficiency is portrayed as being at once beneficial to the claimant, even if he or she does not realise it, integral to the claimant's contract with society and the taxpayer and a contribution to society.

The paternalist justification is summed up by a New Labour-era command paper. This argues that, while activating sick and disabled people, lone parents and older people would benefit the economy and taxpayers, 'the gains for individuals will be the greatest: respect, dignity, security, and achievement'.[108] The conditionality regime, from this perspective, represents a form of 'hard paternalism', using coercive means 'to induce people to act in ways that are argued to be in their own interests'.[109] A successful activation policy could help those who might otherwise have remained on benefits to enjoy greater economic welfare as well as the non-economic benefits of employment, with the opportunities for social inclusion that this brings.[110] Whether, as Mead argues,[111] hard paternalism is needed to ensure people act in their own best interests may be more questionable. Dunn finds that 'choosiness' and reluctance to work can represent a genuine barrier to employment, but only among a minority of the long-term unemployed, who, in turn, are a minority of unemployed people.[112] The paternalist justification for conditionality is also contingent on the regime's success in steering claimants towards behaviours that increase their chances of securing employment and social inclusion. A growing body of research calls into question whether the disciplinary approach succeeds on this front – particularly if the goal is *sustained* employment.[113]

[108] Department for Work and Pensions, *A New Deal for Welfare: Empowering People to Work* (Cm 6730, London: Department for Work and Pensions, 2006) 12.

[109] Watts and Fitzpatrick, above n 107 at 111.

[110] See G Waddell and AK Burton, *Is Work Good for your Health and Well-being?* (London: TSO, 2006).

[111] LM Mead, 'The new politics of the new poverty' (1991) 103 *Public Interest* 3; LM Mead, 'Citizenship and social policy: TH Marshall and poverty' (1997) 14(2) *Social Philosophy and Policy* 197.

[112] A Dunn, 'The "dole or drudgery" dilemma: education, the work ethic and unemployment' (2010) 44(1) *Social Policy and Administration* 1; Dunn, above n 105.

[113] J Griggs and M Evans, *Sanctions within Conditional Benefit Systems: A Review of Evidence* (York: Joseph Rowntree Foundation, 2010); R Patrick, *For Whose Benefit: The Everyday Realities of Welfare Reform* (Bristol: Policy Press, 2017); Welfare Conditionality, *Final Findings Report: Welfare Conditionality Project 2013–2018* (York: Welfare Conditionality, 2018); Fitzpatrick and others, above n 54; R Gerards and R Welters, 'Does eliminating benefit eligibility requirements improve unemployed

The contractarian justification for conditionality sets the claimant's right to support against 'the rights of taxpayers to see their taxes well spent and the obligations of out-of-work claimants … to demonstrate their deservingness'.[114] For some, to speak of a contractarian model of social citizenship is a contradiction in terms. Handler argues: 'the term "social citizenship" has no meaning in the United States' precisely because citizenship is construed as a contractual relationship.[115] From Handler's perspective, citizenship is fundamentally a status conferring rights – this status is undermined if entitlements only accrue in exchange for the fulfilment of responsibilities in a contractarian manner. It is far from certain that Marshall would have recognised this portrayal of his conception of social citizenship as conferring unconditional rights – although there is a subtle difference between duties owed to 'the community' or 'society' and those owed to 'the taxpayer'. A more convincing rebuttal of the contractarian justification is that it, to the extent that the claimant's obligations can be described as a contract, it is extremely one-sided. Handler highlights the chasm in the US between the bargaining power of the claimant and the state. For him, developments in recent decades are better understood as an attempt to exclude the 'undeserving' poor from support.[116] More recent authors, with a focus on European welfare states, similarly emphasise the power imbalance in the activation relationship that may mean 'people – in the name of empowerment – are being softly coerced into positions of powerlessness, bereft of autonomy, choice and dignity'.[117] Helping claimants into employment is a legitimate objective and need not operate in this manner, but if it does, and social entitlements are treated not as rights, but as a tools to undermine the civil rights to autonomy and freedom of contract, then the three-legged stool of citizenship is in danger of collapse.

Disability and Social Citizenship

Disability and disabled people barely feature in Marshall's writing. Yet how to ensure equal enjoyment of the social rights of citizenship despite impairments and societal barriers is an important question for the welfare state. Marshall's sole concession is that a minority of citizens are clearly unable to fulfil the duty to work and should not be penalised for failure to do so,[118] but there is little to

job search and labour market outcomes?' (2021) *Applied Economics* Letter, latest articles. Available at: https://doi.org/10.1080/13504851.2021.1927960.

[114] Patrick, above n 113 at 26.

[115] JF Handler, *Social Citizenship and Workfare in the United States and Western Europe: The Paradox of Inclusion* (Cambridge: Cambridge University Press, 2004) 76.

[116] Ibid.

[117] A Eleveld, T Kampen and J Arts, 'Welfare to work, social justice and domination: an introduction to an interdisciplinary normative perspective on welfare policies' in A Eleveld, T Kampen and J Arts (eds), *Welfare to Work in Contemporary European Welfare States: Legal, Sociological and Philosophical Perspectives on Justice and Domination* (Bristol: Policy Press, 2020) 8; and see other contributions.

[118] Marshall, above n 71 at 90.

indicate acknowledgement that disability can create a need for additional financial or practical assistance to enable social inclusion.[119] Only in *Social policy* is there explicit reference to the role of social security as a contribution towards additional disability-related costs, but the tone is descriptive of the development of benefits such as attendance allowance rather than advocative.[120] Sépulchre suggests that the progressive inclusion of 'previously excluded individuals', including disabled people, as full citizens is nonetheless implicit in Marshallian theory,[121] but it is hardly controversial to opine that such a state of affairs has yet to be fully achieved.[122]

The UK social security system does recognise that disabled people require an income if they lack capacity for paid employment (met by employment and support allowance or universal credit) and may need additional resources to meet the costs of disability (to which personal independence payment contributes). Both categories of benefit have undergone considerable reform in the twenty-first century. The evolution of incapacity-related benefits has been driven by the same forces as that of other low-income benefits, notably the construction of paid work as the route to social inclusion and, post-2010, the drive to reduce expenditure. However, the impact on experiences of social citizenship has varied. Claimants deemed capable of 'work-related activity', but not currently of 'work', have been targeted for both increased conditionality and reduced entitlement as part of an ongoing programme of 'coercion into "positive" citizenship'.[123] Those without capability for work-related activities have been relatively shielded from both austerity and conditionality. The picture is more complicated when it comes to disability benefits. At its introduction, personal independence payment was widely regarded as another austerity measure that would create 'absolutely no winners … just losers' in terms of entitlement.[124] In practice, some people have lost entitlement, due to more stringent rules.[125] However, the Office for Budget Responsibility estimates that, by 2018, annual expenditure on PIP was around 15 per cent higher than projected expenditure on its predecessor disability living allowance, had it been retained. The case load was four to eight per cent greater and the average

[119] M MacGregor, 'Citizenship in name only: constructing meaningful citizenship through a recalibration of the values attached to waged labour' (2012) 32(3) *Disability Studies Quarterly*. Available at: http://dx.doi.org/10.18061/dsq.v32i3.

[120] Marshall, above n 70.

[121] M Sépulchre, 'This is not citizenship: analysing the claims of disability activists in Sweden' (PhD thesis, Uppsala University, 2019) abstract.

[122] A Waldschmidt and M Sépulchre, 'Citizenship: reflections on a relevant but ambivalent concept for persons with disabilities' (2019) 34(3) *Disability and Society* 421.

[123] PM Larkin, 'Incapacity, the labour market and social security: coercion into "positive" citizenship' (2011) 74(3) *Modern Law Review* 385.

[124] R Sainsbury, cited by N Harris, 'Welfare reform and the shifting threshold of support for disabled people' (2014) 77(6) *Modern Law Review* 888, 892.

[125] For example, access to the enhanced rate mobility component of PIP depends on being able to walk no more than 20 metres, compared to 50 metres for the higher rate mobility component of disability living allowance – see P Alldridge, 'On being able to walk twenty metres: the introduction of personal independence payments' (2019) 46(3) *Journal of Law and Society* 448.

award 16 per cent higher.[126] Where disability benefits are concerned, the challenge for social citizenship appears to centre around access to entitlements rather than reduction of entitlement. PIP did not necessarily create, but has nonetheless been blighted by, problems around the complexity of the application form, claimants' perceptions of the assessment process as intrusive and undignified, and quality of decision making,[127] some of which have also been a challenge for incapacity benefits.[128]

Social Citizenship in a Pandemic

The coronavirus pandemic, which hit the UK in March 2020, has been both a public health and an economic crisis. Accordingly, it has required a range of interventions to support incomes. The UK's flagship response has been the coronavirus jobs retention scheme (CJRS), commonly referred to as the 'furlough' scheme. Delivered through HM Revenue and Customs (HMRC) and not, strictly speaking, a social security measure, the CJRS was designed to sustain the incomes and labour market attachment of people who might otherwise have faced redundancy due to the downturn in economic activity and the effective closure of certain sectors. The scheme was developed within the scope of an extremely broad provision in the Coronavirus Act 2020, under which '[HMRC is] to have such functions as the Treasury may direct in relation to coronavirus or coronavirus disease'.[129] As such, it could go through multiple incarnations in a short period; it is not necessary to spell out the detail of its evolution here. In essence, employees required by their employer to cease remunerative work, or in later versions of the scheme to work reduced hours, as a result of the pandemic continued to receive 80 per cent of their salary or of their average earnings in the previous financial year, up to a maximum of £2,500. Initially, employers could reclaim furlough payments from HMRC in full; later, employers were required to pay for any hours actually worked by the employee, plus a percentage of the gap between these and the individual's usual earnings.[130]

The most significant changes to social security benefits were the £20 per week uplift to the universal credit standard allowance and the restoration of the

[126] Office for Budget Responsibility, *Welfare Trends Report* (CP02, London: HM Treasury, 2019).

[127] Harris, above n 124; P Gray, *The Second Independent Review of the Personal Independence Payment Assessment* (London: DWP, 2019); Scottish Government, *Social Security Experience Panels: Personal Independence Payment Health Assessments – Part Two* (Edinburgh: Scottish Government, 2020); M Cavanagh, *Personal Independence Payment: A Second Independent Review of the Assessment Process* (Belfast: DfC, 2020); Northern Ireland Public Services Ombudsman, *PIP and the Value of Further Evidence* (Belfast: NIPSO, 2021).

[128] G McKeever (2014) 'Improving decision making in employment and support allowance' (2013) 21(1) *Journal of Social Security Law* 13.

[129] Coronavirus Act 2020 c 7 s 76.

[130] Coronavirus Act 2020 Functions of Her Majesty's Revenue and Customs (Coronavirus Job Retention Scheme) Direction, made on 15 April 2020, modified on 22 May 2020 and 25 June 2020, and extended by subsequent Directions.

maximum housing benefit for private tenants to the thirtieth percentile of rents in their area.[131] These interventions represented a significant increase to headline entitlements – at £408.89, the monthly standard allowance for a single claimant aged 25 or older in 2020–2021 was 30 per cent higher than in the previous financial year. Initially covering just the financial year 2020–2121 (whereas the LHA uplift was not time-limited), the standard allowance increase was subsequently extended for a further six months.[132] The significance of this increased generosity was not only in higher benefit payments at a time when many low-income households experienced a sharp rise in living costs,[133] but in the break with a decade of real-terms cuts to income replacement benefits.

It would, though, be too simplistic to baldly state that the coronavirus pandemic was met with more generous social protection. By maintaining incomes at 80 per cent of usual earnings, up to a maximum of £2,500 per employee, the CJRS had the potential to support the income of households with ongoing labour market attachment at a far higher level than social security benefits – depending on the number of earners and level of earnings. The extent to which the notional increase in generosity has been experienced depends on the interaction of family size, housing costs, disability and relationship with the labour market, mainly due to the household benefit cap of £23,000 per year in greater London and £20,000 elsewhere. Any claimant whose benefit entitlement was capped prior to the LHA and standard allowance increases – that is, anyone with two children and weekly housing costs of £146.18 or greater, not falling within an exempt group – will not have received any additional benefit.[134] Other households missed out on the full benefit of the two uplifts as their notional entitlement rose beyond the level of the cap. There were fewer than 80,000 capped households in Great Britain in December 2019, but 170,000 by August 2020.[135]

To a large extent, the cap targets higher benefits at those who are recognised as 'deserving' based on current or recent paid employment, disability or incapacity, as they are temporarily or permanently exempt from it.[136] Childless universal credit claimants are likely to benefit regardless of the exemptions because of lower overall entitlements. However, the uplift to the universal credit standard allowance was not mirrored in the out-of-work benefits it replaces – jobseeker's allowance,

[131] Social Security Benefits Up-rating Order 2020 SI No 234 arts 24, 33; Social Security (Coronavirus) (Further Measures) Regulations 2020 SI No 371 regs 3, 4.

[132] Universal Credit (Extension of Coronavirus Measures) Regulations 2021 SI No 313 reg 2; Trussell Trust, *Dignity or Destitution? The Case for Keeping the Universal Credit Lifeline* (Salisbury: Trussell Trust, 2021).

[133] R Patrick and M Brewer, *Pandemic Pressures: Why Families on a Low Income are Spending More During COVID-19* (London: Resolution Foundation, 2021).

[134] N Harris, C Fitzpatrick, J Meers and M Simpson, 'Coronavirus and Social Security Entitlement in the UK' (2020) 27(2) *Journal of Social Security Law* 55.

[135] Department for Work and Pensions, 'Benefit cap: number of households capped to August 2020' (London: DWP, 2020).

[136] Comptroller and Auditor General, *Rolling out Universal Credit* (HC1123, London: National Audit Office, 2018).

employment and support allowance or income support (the LHA increase applies to both universal credit and housing benefit). Remaining claimants of the legacy benefits have been out of work (or working very limited hours) for some time, as they no longer accept new applications. Claimants of contribution-based JSA and ESA, who have more recent paid employment, are entitled to universal credit in addition to these if overall household income is low, so do have potential to gain from the higher standard allowance.

The impact of coronavirus on social security has not been limited to benefit rates. The early stages of the pandemic saw a rapid increase in the number of universal credit claimants. At one point in March 2020 the daily number of applications in Great Britain was double the *weekly* average for 2019. The number of people receiving universal credit rose from about 2.8 million in January 2020 to almost 6 million a year later, with 2.2 million claimants added between 12 March and 14 May.[137] In Northern Ireland, the claimant count rose from 60,000 in January 2020 to 140,000 in November 2020.[138] In both Great Britain and Northern Ireland, large numbers of staff were moved from other roles to process the increased volume of applications. The online application process – part of a trend towards digitisation of welfare states that has received sharp criticism[139] – was essential to the departments' ability to handle the surge, although concerns remain about the digital literacy of some potential applicants.[140]

Hurried redeployment of staff, along with high levels of vulnerability to coronavirus among Department for Communities staff in Northern Ireland, appears to explain the suspension of behavioural conditionality for claimants.[141] However, the undertaking to review claimant commitments as part of its reintroduction from July 2020 in Great Britain must be a tacit acknowledgement that obligations imposed prior to the pandemic might be harder to meet in the context of ongoing infection control measures. Longer term, there is nothing to suggest that claimant activation will become less central to working age social security. A further enforced change was the suspension of face-to-face assessments for disability- and incapacity-related benefits, with greater reliance placed on medical evidence provided by the applicant. Given Scotland's stated intention to end 'assessments' and minimise the use of 'consultations' in its new devolved disability benefits,[142] this unscheduled experiment will have been watched with interest.

[137] Work and Pensions Committee, *DWP's Response to the Coronavirus Outbreak* (HC178, London: House of Commons, 2020); Department for Work and Pensions, 'Universal credit statistics, 29 April 2013 to 14 January 2021' (London: DWP, 2021).

[138] Department for Communities, 'Universal credit: Northern Ireland – data to November 2020' (Belfast: DfC, 2021).

[139] P Alston, *Digital Technology, Social Protection and Human Rights* (A/74/493, New York: United Nations, 2019).

[140] Department for Work and Pensions, above n 137.

[141] Social Security (Coronavirus) (Further Measures) Regulations 2020 SI No 371 regs 6–7; Social Security (Coronavirus) (Further Measures) Regulations (Northern Ireland) 2020 SI No 53 regs 6–7; A Mackley, *Coronavirus: Universal Credit During the Crisis* (BP8999, London: House of Commons, 2021).

[142] Scottish Government, *Consultation on Adult Disability Payment* (Edinburgh: Scottish Government, 2021).

Conclusion

This chapter has set out key developments for social citizenship at UK level in the twenty-first century, notably the increase, then decrease, in the generosity of low-income benefits for working-age people and the more consistent escalation of behavioural conditionality for claimants of these benefits. Access to the means required to live the life of a civilised being has become more remote to those reliant on benefits, while even the 'guarantee' of a modicum of economic welfare has become increasingly conditional. The coronavirus pandemic has disrupted these trends, but whether this represents a temporary pause or a permanent shift remains to be seen. While the ambiguities inherent in Marshallian theory mean it is difficult to definitively state whether the evolution of social protection is consistent with it or not, the findings presented in this book show that aspects of the UK approach are at odds with devolved elites' vision for social citizenship. Chapter 5 gives an overview of the areas in which social security in Scotland and Northern Ireland has diverged from England and Wales, paving the way for a discussion of the relationship between these legal and policy developments and the nature of emerging devolved social citizenships.

5

Constructing Devolved Social Citizenships: Divergence from the UK Model of Social Security

Introduction

Chapter 4 outlined key UK-level developments in social security (and some other aspects of income maintenance). In previous eras, this would have told the story of how social protection has evolved regardless of location in the UK. Post-2010, this is no longer the case – different countries within the UK are beginning to diverge. Scotland and Northern Ireland have sought to mitigate the effect of certain UK-level reforms, affecting both the level of awards and how benefits are paid. Scotland has enshrined a distinctive vision for social security in statute and begun to replace parts of the UK system with new devolved benefits. Perhaps less visible, but no less important, is the way in which social security policy and systems are developed, how social security is delivered in practice and, critically, how it is experienced by claimants. The importance of social security to the citizen's guarantee of a minimum level of economic welfare means the possibility and extent of divergence here is central to the question of whether it is plausible to speak of devolved social citizenships within the UK. This chapter examines the approaches taken by Scotland and Northern Ireland in each of these fields, using findings from interviews with politicians and officials in 2014–2015 and 2020 to guide the analysis. The next section contrasts Scotland's vision-led approach with Northern Ireland's more pragmatic responses to specific (perceived) problems flowing from UK-level reforms. Subsequent sections examine the implications for social security policy and system development, for legislation and policy around three broad areas of social security – low-income benefits, disability, carer and incapacity benefits and discretionary assistance – and for the operational delivery of benefits.

A Devolved-level Vision for Social Citizenship?

It is mainly in Scotland that the exercise of devolved social security competences is guided by a distinctive ideology of social citizenship. While it is possible to debate how well defined and widely shared this vision is, the Scottish Government has articulated a particular vision for social security and the Scottish Parliament has unanimously endorsed its exposition in the Social Security (Scotland) Act 2018. This is the first primary social security Act following the devolution of responsibility for parts of the system in the Scotland Act 2016. As a piece of framework legislation, it creates only one new payment (the carer's allowance supplement) but empowers the Scottish Government to establish various forms of social security assistance by Regulation. It also establishes guiding principles for the devolved system and scrutiny and accountability mechanisms to encourage their realisation. The vision is further distilled down into the strapline of 'Dignity, fairness, respect' adopted by Social Security Scotland, the agency responsible for delivery of devolved social security assistance.

The language of dignity and respect was not a feature of the social security discourse before or during the 2014 referendum campaign, or in the 2015 wave of fieldwork.[1] The terms surfaced as 'strong themes in terms of how people are treated by public services and, in particular, the social security system' in the Fairer Scotland action plan published in 2016.[2] The word 'fairness' is used in relation to social security elsewhere in the same document. This plan emerged from

[1] R Patrick and M Simpson, 'Conceptualising dignity in the context of social security: bottom-up and top-down perspectives' (2020) 54(3) *Social Policy and Administration* 475.

[2] Scottish Government, *It Takes All of Us to Build a Fairer Scotland: Fairer Scotland Action Plan* (Edinburgh: Scottish Government, 2016) 10.

a large-scale public engagement exercise designed to build on the conversation about social justice that was a prominent feature of the referendum campaign.[3] That applicants should be 'treated with respect' and have 'their dignity … preserved' became tenets of the Scottish welfare fund, the new system of discretionary assistance.[4] A commitment to dignity and respect, or respect for dignity, has remained at the heart of the narrative on devolved social security since. It is now enshrined in the 2018 Act as one of the Scottish social security principles. The principles are:

- social security is an investment in the people of Scotland
- social security is itself a human right and essential to the realisation of other human rights
- the delivery of social security is a public service
- respect for the dignity of individuals is to be at the heart of the Scottish social security system
- the Scottish social security system is to contribute to reducing poverty in Scotland,
- the Scottish social security system is to be designed with the people of Scotland on the basis of evidence
- opportunities are to be sought to continuously improve the Scottish social security system in ways which
  - put the needs of those who require assistance first, and
  - advance equality and non-discrimination
- the Scottish social security system is to be efficient and deliver value for money.[5]

These principles inhabit a space between the legal and the political. They represent a statement of intent about the nature and purpose of social security, how the devolved system should be designed and how it should be experienced. They play a role in accountability as the Scottish Commission on Social Security, an independent expert body established for the scrutiny of draft social security Regulations, must have regard to them when undertaking this task. The principles may be taken into account by a court or tribunal where relevant, although breach of a principle is not in itself justiciable[6] and how they might be deployed in legal argument remains to be seen.

Although there is no statutory hierarchy of principles, dignity and respect (with or without fairness) feature most prominently in Scottish Government literature and statements on social security. These are ambiguous terms. Interviewees were

[3] G Mooney and G Scott, 'The 2014 Scottish independence debate: questions of social welfare and social justice' (2015) 23(1) *Journal of Poverty and Social Justice* 5.
[4] Welfare Funds (Scotland) Act 2015 asp 5 s 5.
[5] Social Security (Scotland) Act 2018 asp 9 s 1.
[6] Social Security (Scotland) Act 2018 asp 9 ss 2, 97.

alive to this; some acknowledged challenges in determining what the various principles mean in terms of shaping a new system. One official acknowledged: 'We've never been able to put a value on them … it's really difficult to … think about what is it that the DWP aren't doing with dignity and respect and what is it we're doing differently' (W2I11, Scotland official). Others argued that in the context of codesigned policy and systems, it matters little that competing interpretations exist:

> We have never at any point attempted … to define what treatment with dignity means because we have always understood that to be an impossible task … There may be 200,000 different ideas … But that to an extent is the point, it is not about setting a definition as to what this treatment entails, it's about seeking in every single instance to meet the individual's expectations (W2I16, Scotland official).

This statement sits within a broader narrative that suggests a guarantee of dignity and respect is about the relational aspects of a social security system. Ultimately, the task may be to design processes where the experience is not one of *in*dignity or *dis*respect – and that incorporate the flexibility to ensure this is the case for every user. Other principles may speak more clearly to other aspects of the system, including its distributional function. However, by reserving income-replacement benefits to Westminster, the devolution settlement limits the scope for devolved-level action to address the distributional (adequacy) aspects of dignity.[7]

This kind of vision for social security has not been evident in Northern Ireland. In the absence of a shared ideological vision for social citizenship, a devolved approach to social security has been reactively shaped by the goal of mitigation. A genuine break with the UK model of social security has not received serious consideration, for reasons of cost, the difficulty of securing consensus on fundamental reform in the devolved political context and, to some extent, constitutional considerations. Instead, financial losses to claimants resulting from selected reforms have been temporarily deferred or made good on an ongoing basis by the provision of supplementary payments. These sit alongside administrative divergence, notably in universal credit payment arrangements and the operation of claimant activation. The one truly distinctive form of support provided for in the Northern Ireland legislation (but never actually introduced), the cost of working allowance,[8] would have reinforced a key objective of the 2012 reforms, removing financial disincentives to transition from out-of-work benefits to low-paid employment by providing a small subsidy towards 'the expenses those in employment incur'.[9]

[7] M Simpson, G McKeever and AM Gray, 'From principles to practice: social security in the Scottish laboratory of democracy' (2019) 26(1) *Journal of Social Security Law* 13.

[8] Welfare Reform (Northern Ireland) Order 2015 No 2006 (NI 1) art 137B – the necessary Regulations were never made, in part due to absence of a Minister or functioning Assembly from 2017 to 2020.

[9] Welfare Reform Mitigations Working Group, *Welfare Reform Mitigations Working Group report* (Belfast: OFMDFM, 2016) 14.

Developing Social Security Policy and Systems

Devolved social security in Scotland is portrayed as different to the UK system from the earliest stages of policy development, being 'designed with the people of Scotland'.[10] The move towards coproduction of policy and systems – which will extend to evaluation – has been a major undertaking. Northern Ireland has yet to embrace this approach in practice, but Ministerial statements and interview data show interest in the Scottish example. Expert scrutiny plays a role in the development and evaluation of policy, legislation and processes in both countries, but in different ways.

The existence of a 'Scottish approach' to policy development has been observed since the inception of devolution, but what this consists of has evolved. In 2016, the Scottish approach was understood to imply close cooperation on service design and delivery between the Scottish Government, local government, health authorities, voluntary sector, private sector, professional bodies and trade unions.[11] This may have emerged by necessity, due to limited policy development capacity within the Scottish Government in 1999.[12] The smaller scale and consequent strength of relationships within and between government and the wider policy community in Scotland also means the opportunity for this kind of approach is greater than at UK level.[13] The Scottish approach as originally understood continues to inform social security policy, with key stakeholders' role institutionalised through advisory bodies like the Disability and Carer Benefits Expert Advisory Group, and the Poverty and Inequality Commission, but a still more inclusive approach is emerging.

Today, the Scottish approach to service design officially aims to 'design service journeys around people' by 'seeking citizen participation in our projects from day one', using 'inclusive and accessible research and design methods so citizens can participate fully and meaningfully'.[14] Interviewees identified social security as a pioneering field in this respect – perhaps because 'the values of dignity, fairness and respect' inevitably lead to codesign (W2I14, Scotland politician, nationalist). However, this new Scottish approach was felt to have grown fairly organically from the original version:

> It's a paradigm shift … We always had this preference for a stakeholder engagement … What we've done in the social security sphere is extend that to continuing engagement with service users … the largest ongoing longitudinal piece of stakeholder engagement I've ever heard of the Scottish Government doing. (W2I16, Scotland official)

[10] Social Security (Scotland) Act 2018 asp 9 s 1(f).

[11] P Cairney, S Russell and E St Denny, 'The 'Scottish approach' to policy and policymaking: what issues are territorial and what are universal?' (2016) 44(3) *Policy and Politics* 333.

[12] P Cairney, 'Has devolution changed the "British policy style?"' (2008) 3(3) *British Politics* 350.

[13] Cairney et al., above n 11.

[14] Scottish Government, *The Scottish Approach to Service Design* (Edinburgh: Scottish Government, 2019) 12.

Codesign of social security policy and processes has centred on 'experience panels' composed of 2,400 people with experience of the areas of social security coming under devolved control. A lengthy list of reports documents the panels' work discussing shortcomings in the DWP system, aspirations for the various new forms of Scottish social security assistance and multiple facets of how claimants should interact with the system.[15] A key task was to agree the content of the social security Charter, which 'takes [the social security] principles and explains what they will mean in practice and what [claimants] are entitled to expect'.[16] Consultation on the Charter's content with people with experience of specified social security benefits was required by statute.[17] This process had a profound impact on participants, encapsulated by the Cabinet Secretary for Social Security and Older People's quotation of a member:

> People came out crying, because it was the first time for many of us that we'd been believed, and that people in authority were horrified at our experiences … Session after session, we'd see our words, fears and hopes take form … I will never be able to describe how important it is to us to be listened to, and to be respected and believed.[18]

It is clearly in the Cabinet Secretary's political interest to highlight positive experiences and the experience panels came in for some criticism in the fieldwork: that they operate in a 'dark world … out of public sight, out of parliamentary sight', leaving their membership open to manipulation to ensure support for the Scottish Government's agenda (W2I06, Scotland politician, unionist), or 'ignore the positive voices' about the UK system (W2I12, Scotland politician, unionist). Notably, though, a successful amendment to a Parliamentary motion calling for the development of the Charter to be treated as 'an exemplar that informs future Scottish public service design' was proposed by an opposition MSP.[19] This was more representative of research participants' view of the 'fiercely independent' panel members (W2I07, Scotland politician, nationalist) as crucial actors in ensuring the devolved system 'was going to be different' (W2I05, Scotland politician, nationalist). The voice of the claimant will continue to play a role in policy and service evaluation and in the five-yearly review of the Charter.[20]

Northern Ireland's approach to social security has not historically lent itself to this kind of approach. If the overriding objective is parity with the system in Great Britain, in-depth engagement with stakeholders may serve limited purpose. The post-2012 erosion of parity has been accompanied by a more active role for organisations outside government – conducting impact assessments and advocating the

[15] More than 100 experience panel reports are available at www.gov.scot/collections/social-security-experience-panels-publications/.

[16] Social Security Scotland, *Our Charter* (Dundee: Social Security Scotland, 2019) 5.

[17] Social Security (Scotland) Act 2018 asp 9 s 16.

[18] Social Security Committee, 31 January 2019, col 3.

[19] SP deb 2 October 2018, col 29.

[20] Social Security (Scotland) Act 2018 asp 9 s 18.

introduction and retention of measures to mitigate the impact of certain reforms.[21] The mitigations package itself was shaped by a working group mainly drawn from voluntary sector organisations.[22]

Wave two of the fieldwork brought expressions of enthusiasm for a more participatory approach in Northern Ireland. This followed a Ministerial commitment to 'look at co-design with the community and voluntary sector and the advice sector and also … people on the ground who receive those social security protections'.[23] At the time of writing, there was little obvious progress on this front. While the coronavirus pandemic was undoubtedly a major obstacle to launching an engagement exercise comparable to that in Scotland, one interviewee claimed devolved government has been institutionally 'inadequate on civic input to decision making' (W2I04, Northern Ireland politician, nationalist). Another felt politicians' own reluctance to 'give up the power' might be the problem (W2I19, Northern Ireland politician, nationalist). However, there were occasional suggestions that Ministers, legislators and officials in Northern Ireland are, in any case, less removed from the experiences and needs of social security claimants than many of their counterparts in England, and that this affects policy preferences and service delivery.

> It's not the millionaire cabinet that you kind of think of in England so I think there's less ignorance … amongst Northern Ireland politicians as to the level of poverty and deprivation in Northern Ireland. It's a small place, politicians are of their community, there isn't the same level of detachment. (W2I02, Northern Ireland politician, neutral)

If greater space is opening up, in Scotland at least, for experts by experience to shape devolved social security, more traditional forms of expertise remain important. Since 1980, the Social Security Advisory Committee (SSAC) has provided advice and scrutiny to the UK Government. In part, the SSAC serves to fill the scrutiny gap that might otherwise exist due to heavy reliance on secondary legislation to set out how benefits work. The legislature generally has an opportunity to veto or revoke Regulations, but cannot amend them, so pre-legislative scrutiny by the SSAC may be the only opportunity for refinement.[24] Reliance on secondary legislation is even heavier in the devolved Scottish system, with a single primary Act delegating very broad powers to the government to create new forms of social security assistance.

[21] C Beatty and S Fothergill, *The Impact of Welfare Reform on Northern Ireland* (Sheffield: Centre for Economic Empowerment, 2013); H Reed and J Portes, *Cumulative Impact Assessment of Tax and Social Security Reforms in Northern Ireland* (Belfast: Northern Ireland Human Rights Commission, 2019); Northern Ireland Welfare Reform Group, *Social Development Committee: Welfare Reform Bill (Northern Ireland) 2012* (Belfast: Law Centre NI, 2012); Advice NI, Housing Rights and Law Centre NI, *Welfare Reform: Mitigations on a Cliff Edge* (Belfast: Advice NI, Housing Rights and Law Centre NI, 2018).

[22] Welfare Reform Mitigations Working Group, above n 9.

[23] D Hargey, response to AQO 29/17–22, NIA deb 3 February 2020, vol 125 no 5 p 42.

[24] See G McKeever, 'Legislative scrutiny, co-ordination and the Social Security Advisory Committee: from system coherence to Scottish devolution' (2016) 23(3) *Journal of Social Security Law* 126.

With almost every aspect of the operation of devolved benefits left to Regulations, the potential for a scrutiny gap is arguably even greater than at Westminster, but the devolution legislation excludes the devolved Scottish system from the SSAC's remit.[25] The creation of a new expert scrutiny body, the Scottish Commission on Social Security, can be viewed as motivated by the necessity of filling this gap, but the Scottish Parliament has taken the opportunity to tailor the SCoSS's work to the Scottish context. For example, whereas the SSAC has a general duty to scrutinise social security Regulations and make 'such recommendations … as the Committee thinks appropriate',[26] the SCoSS is required to 'have regard' to the Scottish social security principles and human rights instruments ratified by the UK in its pre-legislative scrutiny.[27] The Secretary of State has discretion to lay Regulations before Parliament without scrutiny if they are deemed urgent or follow less than six months behind the primary legislation.[28] Regulations relating to areas of social security covered by the 2018 Act *must* be referred to the SCoSS and time allowed for scrutiny before they can be laid, a novel legislative process referred to as the 'super-affirmative' procedure.[29] The SCoSS has the further function of reporting on whether the Scottish Government and Social Security Scotland are fulfilling the commitments of the social security Charter, which in principle opens up virtually any area of social security legislation or delivery to scrutiny.[30]

Scottish interviewees occasionally voiced discontent that reliance on secondary legislation – defended by some because of the relative ease of future amendment compared to a primary Act – had been deepened following devolution:

> Regulations are a very blunt tool to pass legislation. As opposition MSPs, even if we are united … we can only say yes or no, you can't amend the Regulations … When you're talking about benefits which people rely on day by day to survive on, for us to push that nuclear button, it's going to have to be something very radical … So it gives a lot more power to the executive. (W2I06, Scotland politician, unionist)

There is no dedicated scrutiny body for social security in Northern Ireland. Instead, the SSAC's remit includes advising the Department for Communities.[31] While there is some controversy around how effectively this role has been discharged,[32] McKeever argues that the Committee *has* striven to take account of the likely impact on Northern Ireland of DWP's legislative proposals and to monitor the effects thereafter.[33] Arguably, for as long as parity with Great Britain remained

[25] Scotland Act 2016 c 11 s 33.
[26] Social Security Administration Act 1992 c 5 s 174.
[27] Social Security (Scotland) Act 2018 asp 9 s 97(6).
[28] Social Security Administration Act 1992 c 5 s 173.
[29] Social Security (Scotland) Act 2018 asp 9 s 97.
[30] Ibid, s 22.
[31] Social Security Administration Act 1992 c 5 s 17.
[32] D Birrell and D Heenan, 'Devolution and social security: the anomaly of Northern Ireland' (2010) 18(3) *Journal of Poverty and Social Justice* 281.
[33] McKeever, above n 24.

the guiding principle for social security in Northern Ireland, this was sufficient. If the two systems now begin to diverge (which remains uncertain), the question of whether a UK-wide body with a single Northern Ireland member can provide adequate pre- and post-legislative scrutiny in both may arise.

Divergence in Devolved Social Security Benefits

There are different drivers for the development of devolved social security systems in different locations. Northern Ireland has sought to mitigate the impact of specific reforms deemed particularly ill-suited to the country or to have an unacceptable impact on the 'most vulnerable' – a phrase that has become ubiquitous in the social security discourse there.[34] Scotland has promised a new system based on wholly different principles to the UK model. Despite these different starting points, there is some overlap between the types of divergence that have occurred between the devolved and UK systems.

Low-income Benefits

Devolved-level changes to low-income benefits include measures intended to assist with budgeting, without providing any additional income, and top-ups to claimant incomes. Budgeting measures focus on the payment arrangements for universal credit. In England and Wales, claimants receive their whole award (including the housing costs element) as a monthly payment by default. This reflects a policy of 'encouraging personal responsibility' by requiring claimants to manage their own budgets over a period that aligns with most employees' payment pattern.[35]

In Northern Ireland, the Committee for Social Development expressed concern that these arrangements would create budgeting difficulties, particularly for claimants 'used to receiving benefits on a more regular basis'.[36] It also heard evidence from social landlords that payment of housing costs to claimants would lead to increased arrears. Consequently, the default arrangement is twice-monthly payments and direct payment of housing costs to landlords.[37] In Scotland, monthly payment in full to the claimant remains the default, but the claimant has a right to twice-monthly payments and direct payment to

[34] See Welfare Reform Mitigations Working Group, above n 9 at 4.

[35] Department for Work and Pensions, *Universal Credit: Welfare that Works* (Cm 7957, London: Department for Work and Pensions) 34.

[36] Committee for Social Development, *Report on the Welfare Reform Bill (NIA Bill 12/11–15)* (NIA 74/11–15, Belfast: NI Assembly, 2013) 9.

[37] Universal Credit, Personal Independence Payment, Jobseeker's Allowance and Employment and Support Allowance (Claims and Payments) Regulations (Northern Ireland) 2016 NISR No 220, reg 42.

the landlord on request.[38] These different approaches have brought different outcomes in terms of payment arrangements. In Northern Ireland, 54 per cent of private and 96 per cent of social tenants avail of direct payment to their landlords, while only 36 per cent of those offered the choice in Scotland avail of direct payments. Thirty-nine per cent of Scottish claimants receive twice-monthly payments; no equivalent statistics are published for Northern Ireland, but as the Executive's official information website does not even mention that there is any alternative to twice-monthly payments it seems safe to assume that few claimants receive a monthly payment.[39]

Various income supplements have been introduced at devolved level, through passported awards rather than by increasing the rate of the main income-replacement benefits. In Scotland this is out of necessity, as those benefits are outside devolved competence. Northern Ireland has favoured supplementary payments due to the difficulty of changing award amounts in IT systems supplied by DWP. Both Scotland and Northern Ireland compensate social tenants whose award is reduced due to under-occupancy. Claimants in Northern Ireland receive a supplementary payment equivalent to the under-occupancy penalty, which is forfeited if the individual moves to a different social home without downsizing.[40] Those in Scotland receive a discretionary housing payment equivalent to the under-occupancy penalty. In an example of the 'Scottish approach' to service delivery, these payments are not statutory, rather the Scottish Government provides additional funding for DHPs to local government on the understanding it will be used for this purpose.[41] A further supplementary payment makes good any loss of income due to the household benefit cap for claimants in Northern Ireland who have been in continuous receipt of one of the capped benefits since 2016 and have dependent children.[42] Since the cap almost exclusively affects larger households in Northern Ireland – 88 per cent of capped households there had three or more children in February 2021[43] – this is a means of protecting children in larger families from disadvantage. Legislation creating these payments only covered the legacy benefits – Regulations to cover universal credit were never made due to the lengthy period during which the Assembly did not meet – and only until March 2020. Universal credit claimants

[38] Universal Credit (Claims and Payments) (Scotland) Regulations 2017 SSI No 227.

[39] Department for Communities, 'Universal credit: Northern Ireland data to November 2020' (Belfast: DfC, 2021); L Robertson, S Wright and ABR Stewart, *How Well is Universal Credit Supporting People in Glasgow?* (York: JRF, 2020); NI Direct, 'How much universal credit you will get' (Belfast: NI Direct, nd). Available at: www.nidirect.gov.uk/articles/how-much-universal-credit-you-will-get.

[40] Welfare Reform (Northern Ireland) Order 2015 SI No 2006 (NI 1) art 137A.

[41] Scottish Government, *Welfare Reform (Further Provision) (Scotland) Act 2012: Annual Report 2016* (Edinburgh: Scottish Government, 2016).

[42] Welfare Supplementary Payments Regulations (Northern Ireland) 2016 NISR No 178, Part 2.

[43] Department for Communities, 'Benefit cap: Northern Ireland data to February 2021' (Belfast: DfC, 2021).

up to 2020 and all claimants thereafter have received equivalent support in the form of administrative payments.

Scotland has also targeted additional funds at children, in keeping with its statutory commitment to the near-elimination of child poverty by 2030–2031.[44] The Scottish child payment is a top-up of £10 per week in respect of each child under six years old in a household in receipt of universal credit, one of the benefits it is replacing (excluding housing benefit) or pension credit.[45] The intention is to extend the payment to cover all under-16s in households that receive one of the qualifying benefits.[46] The Best Start grant is a more generous replacement for the Sure Start maternity grant, with a higher initial pregnancy and baby payment followed by new payments at two years old (the early learning grant) and the start of primary school (the school age grant).[47] Entitlement to the Best Start grant depends on receipt of the same qualifying benefits as the Scottish child payment, with the addition of housing benefit. Several other low-income benefits, not targeted at children, have also come under devolved control. The winter fuel and cold weather payments will be replaced by winter heating and cold weather assistance, but there are no plans to change eligibility criteria or rates of payment.[48] The funeral expenses payment has been replaced by a new funeral support payment.[49] This mirrors the UK benefit in its purpose as a contribution towards specific funeral-related costs, contingent on receipt of a qualifying means-tested benefit, and in the level of awards. However, the Scottish Government estimates that up to 40 per cent more people will be eligible, largely due to changes to the 'nearest relative' test used to determine who can claim in respect of the deceased person. Essentially, if there are two equally close relatives, one can claim support even if the other is financially better off.[50]

In legislative terms, devolution has brought little change to the behavioural conditionality regime for claimants of low-income benefits. Northern Ireland initially set the maximum sanction for repeated 'high level' failures, such as refusal to apply for a suitable position, at 18 months' suspension of benefit – half the maximum duration in Great Britain.[51] Parity would subsequently be restored

[44] Child Poverty (Scotland) Act 2017 asp 6.

[45] Scottish Child Payment Regulations 2020 SSI No 351.

[46] Scottish Government, 'Scottish child payment: position paper' (Edinburgh: Scottish Government, 2019).

[47] Early Years Assistance (Best Start Grants) (Scotland) Regulations 2018 SSI No 370.

[48] Scottish Government, *Cold Spell and Winter Heating Assistance: Policy Position Paper* (Edinburgh: Scottish Government, 2019).

[49] Funeral Expense Assistance (Scotland) Regulations 2019 SSI No 292.

[50] Scottish Government, *Consultation on Funeral Expense Assistance Regulations* (Edinburgh: Scottish Government, 2018); Scottish Government, *Funeral Expense Assistance: Fairer Scotland Duty Assessment* (Edinburgh: Scottish Government, 2019).

[51] Welfare Reform (Northern Ireland) Order 2015 SI No 2006 (NI 1) art 31(6).

as the maximum duration fell to six months across the UK.[52] Devolution has arguably had a greater impact on the application of conditionality. It is generally accepted that Northern Ireland has had a stronger 'culture of supporting people' into employment, with a sanction 'viewed as a failure' of the system as much as the claimant.[53] Under jobseeker's allowance, this was reflected in dramatically lower sanctioning rates compared to Great Britain where, in 2014, claimants were more than six times as likely to receive a higher-level sanction.[54] Rates have since converged. From mid-2018 to the eve of the coronavirus pandemic (which saw work-related conditionality suspended) the proportion of claimants in Great Britain serving a sanction was consistently just above 2 per cent.[55] In Northern Ireland, the proportion fluctuated between 1.5 and 3.5 per cent over the same period.[56] Scotland lacks competence to adjust the conditionality regime, but has attempted to 'design out' sanctions by stipulating that participation in devolved employment support programmes – which only cover disabled people and those at risk of long-term unemployment[57] – should be voluntary.

Disability, Carer and Incapacity Benefits

At face value, there are greater differences between the approaches to disability, carer and incapacity benefits taken by Northern Ireland and Scotland. In Northern Ireland, as with low-income benefits, supplementary payments have been used to mitigate some losses resulting from reforms introduced in 2015 (2012 in Great Britain), although on a time-limited basis. Most have essentially run their course. Scotland has temporarily continued with the top-up approach in respect of carer benefits but is launching a new suite of disability and carer's assistance to replace the UK benefits. Ultimately, the extent of divergence within the UK is limited to date.

The supplementary payments applied to disability, carer and incapacity benefits in Northern Ireland had the common purpose of allowing claimants longer to prepare for a fall in income, rather than deferring the drop indefinitely as with those applied to low-income benefits. One had the additional function of supporting the right of appeal.

[52] Jobseeker's Allowance and Universal Credit (Higher-Level Sanctions) (Amendment) Regulations 2019 SI No 1357; Jobseeker's Allowance and Universal Credit (Higher-Level Sanctions) (Amendment) Regulations (Northern Ireland) 2019 NISR No 201.

[53] Social Security Advisory Committee, *Young people living independently* (OP20, London: SSAC, 2018) 54.

[54] M Simpson, 'Renegotiating social citizenship in an age of devolution' (2017) 44(4) *Journal of Law and Society* 646.

[55] Department for Work and Pensions, 'Benefit sanctions statistics to January 2020' (London: DWP, 2020).

[56] Department for Communities, 'Universal credit: Northern Ireland data to February 2020' (Belfast: DfC, 2020).

[57] Scotland Act 2018 c 46 sch 5, part II, s H3.

Table 5.1 Supplementary payments to claimants of disability, carer and incapacity benefits in Northern Ireland[58]

Benefit claimed	Loss results from	Proportion of loss made up	Duration of payment
Contributory employment and support allowance	Time-limiting of entitlement to one year	100% (if in receipt of CESA when time limit introduced)	One year
Disability living allowance	PIP refused following transitional assessment	100%	Until conclusion of appeal
Disability living allowance	PIP award is at least £10 per week less than previous DLA award, or refusal of PIP upheld on appeal	75%	One year
Disability living allowance, as a result of a conflict-related injury or trauma	PIP refused, but claimant awarded at least four points in assessment for either daily living or mobility component	Payment is equal to the PIP daily living *or* mobility component at the standard rate	One year
Any benefit or tax credit with a disability-related premium	PIP refused or awarded at a lower rate than previous DLA award	100%	One year
Carer's allowance	Cared-for person, previously in receipt of DLA, refused PIP daily living component	100% (discounting any increase to other benefits due to loss of carer's allowance)	One year
Any benefit with a carer's premium	Cared-for person, previously in receipt of DLA, refused PIP daily living component	100%	One year
Income support (entitlement contingent on being a carer)	Cared-for person, previously in receipt of DLA, refused PIP daily living component	Equivalent to carer's allowance (about 83% of the IS personal allowance)	One year

[58] Welfare Supplementary Payments Regulations (Northern Ireland) 2016 NISR No 178 part 3; Welfare Supplementary Payment (Loss of Disability Living Allowance) Regulations (Northern Ireland) 2016 NISR No 250; Welfare Supplementary Payment (Loss of Disability-Related Premiums) Regulations (Northern Ireland) 2016 NISR No 254; Welfare Supplementary Payment (Loss of Carer Payments) Regulations (Northern Ireland) 2016 NISR No 253.

Disability benefits are the most significant area of social security to come under devolved control in Scotland. In 2014–2015, the parts of the system for which competence would later be devolved had a combined expenditure of £2.7 billion. Disability living allowance, personal independence payment and attendance allowance accounted for £2.1 billion, or 78 per cent of the total.[59] Work to replace these with three forms of disability assistance – child disability payment, adult disability payment and pension age disability payment – remains in progress at the time of publication. Initially, the new devolved benefits will mirror their predecessors in purpose (as a contribution to the additional costs of disability), claimant groups (with separate benefits for children and young people, working age people and older people), eligibility criteria and rates of payment. Parity in eligibility criteria is crucial to the commitment to a 'safe and secure transition' of claimants from DWP to Social Security Scotland,[60] as cases can transfer without reassessment of entitlement. Longer term, it helps ensure receipt of a disability benefit continues to act as a passport to other reserved payments.[61] A few differences will exist:

- Awards will have no end date, but will be made on an ongoing basis, subject to review at intervals to be determined based on the claimant's condition.[62]
- Claimants awarded child disability payment before their sixteenth birthday can continue to receive CDP until their eighteenth birthday,[63] whereas DLA claimants transfer to PIP at sixteen.
- Children in receipt of the highest rate care component of child disability payment (or disability living allowance) will automatically receive child winter heating assistance, a new payment of £202 per year.[64]
- A fast-track application process and automatic entitlement to the higher or enhanced rate of disability assistance is available to anyone with a terminal illness. In the UK system this only applies if death is expected within six months.[65]

[59] Scottish Government, *A New Future for Social Security: Consultation on Social Security in Scotland* (Edinburgh: Scottish Government, 2016).

[60] Ibid, at 34.

[61] Scottish Government, *Consultation on Adult Disability Payment* (Edinburgh: Scottish Government, 2020).

[62] Disability Assistance for Children and Young People (Scotland) Regulations 2021 SSI No 174 regs 26, 30; Disability Assistance for Working Age People (Scotland) Regulations (draft for consultation) regs 37, 39.

[63] Disability Assistance for Children and Young People (Scotland) Regulations 2021 SSI No 174, reg 4.

[64] Winter Heating Assistance for Children and Young People (Scotland) Regulations 2020 SSI No 352.

[65] Disability Assistance for Children and Young People (Scotland) Regulations 2021 SSI No 174, reg 15; Disability Assistance for Working Age People (Scotland) Regulations (draft for consultation) reg 26.

- As with all devolved social security assistance, a claimant whose award is terminated or reduced is entitled to short-term assistance at the same rate as the previously received benefit until the conclusion of any redetermination and appeal.[66]

Although competence for carer benefits has been devolved, at the time of writing proposals for the new Scottish carer's assistance are at an early stage of development. However, adult carers in Scotland who are eligible for carer's allowance are financially better off than their counterparts elsewhere in the UK thanks to the carer's allowance supplement. The supplement initially topped up a carer's allowance award to the same level as jobseeker's allowance – the combined total is now slightly higher as the supplement has been uprated in years when jobseeker's allowance was not.[67] Early indications are that a safe and secure transition, protecting passported entitlements to other DWP benefits, will be prioritised at the introduction of carer's assistance, as with disability assistance. Innovation is likely to focus on increasing take-up and smoothing or removing cliff-edges in entitlement resulting from changes to the carer's circumstances. A separate form of carer's assistance – the young carer grant – is already in payment. This is an annual payment of £300 to a young person aged 16, 17 or 18 who provides care to someone in receipt of a disability benefit for 208 hours across at least 10 of the 13 weeks prior to application.[68] The grant does not require the same intensity of caregiving as carer's allowance and does not act as an income replacement benefit, but provides some additional resources intended to help young carers 'look after their own health and wellbeing, improve their quality of life and … participate fully in society'.[69]

Discretionary Assistance

Since the devolution of responsibility for the provision of discretionary assistance to local government in England, schemes providing help in a crisis have become inconsistent, often unreliable and in some areas absent.[70] Scotland and Northern Ireland have sought to ensure greater consistency. The Scottish welfare fund is also delivered by local government but, unlike the English schemes, is a statutory function with a set of national standards and ring-fenced funding.[71] Unlike the

[66] Social Security (Scotland) Act 2018 asp 9 sch 10.
[67] Ibid, s 81.
[68] Carer's Assistance (Young Carer Grants) (Scotland) Regulations 2019 SSI No 324.
[69] Scottish Government, *Scottish Government Response to Consultation on the Draft Regulations of the Young Carer Grant* (Edinburgh: Scottish Government, 2019).
[70] I Porter, *Nowhere to Turn: Strengthening the Safety Net for Children and Families Facing Crisis* (London: Children's Society, 2019); C Fitzpatrick, G McKeever and M Simpson, 'Conditionality, discretion and TH Marshall's "right to welfare"' (2019) 41(4) *Journal of Social Welfare and Family Law* 445.
[71] Welfare Funds (Scotland) Act 2015 asp 5.

former social fund, but in common with many local authority schemes in England, support can be provided even in cases of hardship due exclusively to a benefit sanction and all awards are non-repayable.[72]

Northern Ireland's discretionary support scheme continues to mirror the social fund in that it can offer a grant or loan depending on the applicant's circumstances and the urgent need being met. Grants are only available where required to enable an applicant to live independently, to meet living expenses when the applicant cannot receive a loan due to pre-existing debt or inability to repay, or when the applicant is self-isolating due to the coronavirus pandemic. Neither grants nor loans are intended to cover living expenses on an ongoing basis and there are limits to the number of awards that can be made in a year.[73] The scheme is also the vehicle for the universal credit contingency fund. Effectively, new universal credit applicants who experience severe financial hardship while awaiting their first payment can receive a discretionary support grant to cover essential living expenses.[74]

Administration, Service Delivery and Culture

The administration of social security matters, most obviously because it is necessary to put policy into practice by identifying who is entitled to benefit and making payment. How social security is delivered can also profoundly affect how users experience the system.[75] The first piece of research with Scotland's social security experience panels focused on claimants' experiences of the UK system. Findings centre on administrative delivery – staff attitudes, simplicity and flexibility in the application process and multiple aspects of the assessment process for disability and incapacity benefits. All the priority areas for improvement concern administration – advice and support, the application, reconsideration and appeal process and communication.[76] Independent reviews of the personal independence payment assessment process in Northern Ireland further emphasise how

[72] Scottish Government, *Scottish Welfare Fund Statutory Guidance Update* (Edinburgh: Scottish Government, 2021); R Spence, 'Local welfare: tips and tactics' (2015) *Welfare Rights Bulletin* 248. Available at: https://cpag.org.uk/welfare-rights/resources/article/local-welfare-tips-and-tactics; Porter, above n 70.

[73] Discretionary Support Regulations (Northern Ireland) 2016 NISR No 270, part 3.

[74] Comptroller and Auditor General, *Welfare Reforms in Northern Ireland* (Belfast: NIAO, 2019); Department for Communities, 'Section 75 policy screening form: Universal Credit Contingency Fund (UCCF) (change to eligibility criteria effective from January 2020)' (Belfast: DfC, 2019). Available at: www.communities-ni.gov.uk/sites/default/files/publications/communities/dfc-uccf-change-to-eligibility-criteria-effective-jan20-screening.pdf.

[75] See EZ Brodkin and G Marston (eds), *Work and the Welfare State: Street Level Organisations and Workfare Policies* (Washington DC: Georgetown University Press, 2013); JL Mashaw, *Bureaucratic Justice: Managing Social Security Disability Claims* (Newhaven: Yale University Press, 2009).

[76] Scottish Government, *Social Security Experience Panels: About your Benefits and You* (Edinburgh: Scottish Government, 2018).

claimant-system interaction can shape experiences of benefit receipt,[77] while an ombudsman's report illustrates how a misfiring assessment and decision-making process can result in wrongful denial of entitlement.[78]

There is an obvious contrast between Northern Ireland, which has delivered its own social protection since pre-Beveridgean times and Scotland, which has had to establish social security infrastructure from scratch post-2016. Scottish officials were clear about the challenge this has presented and the necessity of having the administrative infrastructure in place to enable the delivery of a devolved policy agenda:

> I wouldn't say it was scaring us witless or anything, because nothing scares us, but it was a significant task … The transition towards recruiting DWP staff, copying DWP systems … and specifying new ones, getting a Scottish welfare department set up. These were major preoccupations and actually it's what we … spent more of our time on than thinking what our policy would be once we had the levers in our hands … If you can't administer the benefits system reasonably efficiently and accurately, you're not in the races. Policies don't matter, because you can't implement them (W1I27, Scotland official).

Parity has allowed Northern Ireland to take a shortcut to addressing some of these issues. By delivering the same set of benefits as in Great Britain, the Department for Communities and its predecessors have been able to buy systems developed for the UK department off the shelf, taking advantage of the greater economies of scale involved in designing a system for a population of (by 2019) almost 67 million, as opposed to less than 2 million in Northern Ireland. The trade-off is that dependence on those systems itself becomes a powerful force for parity. If Northern Ireland wishes to diverge in certain areas, it must negotiate with the DWP to ensure system design can accommodate this (as with the different payment patterns for universal credit) or make supplementary payments separate to the main benefit (as with most other mitigations). Officials, along with some politicians, argued that this is largely a price worth paying:

> There's no way Northern Ireland could actually pay for a welfare system as currently constructed … It's financially impossible in terms of the direct payments that are made to various members of the public and secondly it's financially impossible in terms of the mechanics of having to construct a welfare system, whether it's IT systems or whatever, it's just incredibly expensive business to get into. (W1I19, Northern Ireland official)

Scotland is developing its own devolved benefits and, accordingly, must build its own systems for delivery. This comes at a cost but allows more flexibility to diverge in policy and delivery – in principle. In practice, the need to ensure a safe and secure transition of existing caseload from DWP disability and carer benefits to their devolved replacements is a strong driver of parity in eligibility criteria in the

[77] M Cavanagh, *Personal Independence Payment: A Second Independent Review of the Assessment Process* (Belfast: DfC, 2020).

[78] Northern Ireland Public Services Ombudsman, *PIP and the Value of Further Evidence* (Belfast: NIPSO, 2021).

short term. The political risk that would be associated with putting passported entitlements under UK Government control in doubt will undoubtedly ensure the Scottish Government treads carefully when contemplating greater divergence in the longer term, without definitively ruling it out. Widening access to a disability benefit might result in the withdrawal of passported entitlements; it might equally be possible for the UK Government to calculate how many additional claimants gained entitlement and pass on the cost to the Scottish Government.[79] However, careful negotiation would be required in advance of any changes.

Given the constraints on policy divergence that exist, it is perhaps unsurprising that hopes for the development of a different approach to social security have largely been pinned on service delivery. This has been most explicit in Scotland. If Scottish participants in wave one often focused on the challenge of putting social security infrastructure in place, by wave two the narrative had shifted to how processes, culture and interactions with the system might contribute to the realisation of the social security principles. The strategy has two strands. The first is about making it as easy as possible for people to access their entitlements, building on a statutory duty to promote take up.[80] This means making automatic awards where possible, allowing application via multiple channels (online, telephone, on paper or in person) where this is required, providing pre-application advice, following up on applications that provide insufficient information, rather than rejecting them, and allowing prospective applications where the applicant does not yet fulfil the eligibility criteria, but soon will.[81] A Social Security Committee inquiry broadly commended Social Security Scotland's early work on take-up, but warned of inherent risks in basing entitlement on receipt of a reserved benefit, given the absence of a clear take-up duty and strategy in the UK system.[82] The second strand is about ensuring claimants are treated with dignity and respect. This takes in measures to address aspects of the UK system that the experience panels associated with *in*dignity – minimising the use of assessments for disability benefits, relying instead on evidence from a health or social care practitioner where possible, and excluding private providers from the assessment process.[83] Largely, though, it concerns

[79] HM Government and Scottish Government, *The Agreement between the Scottish Government and the United Kingdom Government on the Scottish Government's Fiscal Framework* (Edinburgh: Scottish Government, 2016).

[80] Social Security (Scotland) Act 2018 asp 9 s 3.

[81] See, for example, Winter Heating Assistance for Children and Young People (Scotland) Regulations 2020 SSI No 352, reg 5; Disability Assistance for Children and Young People (Scotland) Regulations 2021 SSI No 174, reg 24; Scottish Government, *Social Security Policy Position Paper – Disability Benefit Applications: Making Applications* (Edinburgh: Scottish Government, 2020); Scottish Government, *Social Security Policy Position Paper – Disability Benefit Applications: How Decisions are Made* (Edinburgh: Scottish Government, 2020); Scottish Government, *Social Security Policy Position Paper – Disability Benefit Applications: Extra Support Options* (Edinburgh: Scottish Government, 2020).

[82] Social Security Committee, *Benefit Take-up* (SP696, Edinburgh: Scottish Parliament, 2020).

[83] Social Security (Scotland) Act 2018 asp 9 ss 12, 14; Scottish Government, *Social Security Experience Panels: Personal Independence Payment Health Assessments* (Edinburgh: Scottish Government, 2019); Scottish Government, *Social Security Policy Position Paper – Disability Benefit Applications: How Decisions are Made* (Edinburgh: Scottish Government, 2020).

organisational culture within Social Security Scotland. Interviewees acknowledged that getting this right is harder than putting 'warm words' in a social security charter, but felt it is achievable if organisational and political leaders are clear about 'what the expectations are … what the rules of engagement are and the level of respect that has to be shown' (W2I07, Scotland politician, nationalist). An official explained how this is put into practice:

> The induction, even our offer before they join us, I think, is attracting people who come to an extent with those kind of values … People are coming to us because they believe that what we offer is a more values-based employment that will allow them to work in an environment that is, for want of a better word, nicer to people. (W2I16, Scotland official)

Several officials who took part in the study placed themselves among those who had been inspired by the chance to work for an organisation with 'those kind of values'. In particular, those who had left jobs at the Department for Work and Pensions for the new social security policy and delivery teams expressed pleasure at leaving an organisation whose practice 'just doesn't sit comfortably with me' for one that 'wanted to do things differently' (W2I09b, Scotland official).

Some participants in Northern Ireland argued that, with less fanfare, the devolved social security system there has long sought to achieve many of the things Scotland is now promising. Officials spoke of their desire to run 'a compassionate and empathetic service' (W2I26, Northern Ireland official) in which 'the interactions that our people have with our customers [are] really rich and honest and genuine' (W2I27, Northern Ireland official). One highlighted that 'we have run benefit uptake schemes much more openly throughout the time when, for example, England didn't do that so much' (W2I29, Northern Ireland official).[84] Several politicians suggested developments like the move to digital processes and algorithmic decision-making, leaving less space to take account of individual circumstances, might be undermining this culture, reflecting wider concerns about digital welfare states:[85]

> In Northern Ireland I think the system had been up till now a lot more interactive. And this online movement is distancing people … Everything's done remotely and it's far away from you and things happen to you and you want to talk to a human about it and they aren't there. And if you do try and talk to a human, it's all process driven as opposed to common sense and just sitting down and having a chat with people. (W2I19, Northern Ireland politician, neutral)

However, this was not universal. Another politician highlighted that telephone contact remains an option – and that 'the human touch' is still evident, at least

[84] See Department for Communities, 'Make the Call supports over 9000 people claim £43.2million in additional benefits and supports' (News Release, 18 November 2019). Available at: www.communities-ni.gov.uk/news/make-call-supports-over-9000-people-claim-ps432million-additional-benefits-and-supports.

[85] P Alston, *Digital Technology, Social Protection and Human Rights* (A/74/493, New York: United Nations, 2019).

in that aspect of the service (W2I31, Northern Ireland politician, nationalist). Officials stressed that the move to digital processes had allowed the Department for Communities and DWP to respond to the surge in universal credit applications in the early stages of the coronavirus pandemic:[86]

> I worked in income support for years. There's no way that 10,000 people in a week would have filled in application forms, posted them into the office, the post would have delivered them and we would have had the people to take those away, assess them, work them through, put them onto systems, work them out. That just wouldn't have happened. You'd have been lucky ... if half of those cases would have ever got a payment when they were due ... The [universal credit] system has been very, very robust and people have actually been able to access it and get their payments (W2I27, Northern Ireland official).

Conclusion

After a long period of almost complete parity in social security across the UK, some divergence is occurring. Some of the distinctive measures introduced in Scotland and Northern Ireland have the common aim of mitigating the impact on claimants of certain UK-level reforms, albeit those methods can differ. Research participants in both locations also expressed a common aspiration to run a social security system with a more human face than they felt the UK system offers. To date, only Scotland has moved beyond the language of mitigation to set out a distinctive vision for a devolved social security system and introduce new benefits. Divergence in discretionary assistance has become a more general feature of the social security landscape. However, in many areas no divergence has occurred; most of the system is not even devolved to Scotland. Even where new benefits have been introduced, they can be similar to those they replace in their purpose and how they operate. The nature of UK social security, then, continues to have much in common regardless of location. The following chapters consider what the changes that have occurred in Scotland and Northern Ireland, alongside the factors driving divergence, reveal about the nature of devolved social citizenships.

[86] See Work and Pensions Committee, *DWP's Response to the Coronavirus Outbreak* (HC178, London: House of Commons, 2020).

6

Rights and 'Fairness' in UK and Devolved Social Citizenships

Introduction

The year 1998 was a landmark year for the UK constitution, not only because of legislative devolution to Scotland and Northern Ireland, but also because of the incorporation of international human rights obligations into domestic law. Rights protection centres on the European Convention on Human Rights (ECHR), therefore on civil and political rights. This has not prevented attempts to use human rights as a legal and political tool to shape social security or resist certain reforms. The legal status of human rights differs at UK and devolved level and is moving in different directions in different devolved countries. There are also differences in how human rights are deployed politically. Successive UK governments have been critical of human rights in general and the Human Rights Act 1998, which incorporates the ECHR into UK law, in particular. Since 2010, human rights have been used in opposition to aspects of social security law, policy and practice rather than as an aspiration for the system. Other objectives, fairness among them, have been foregrounded in official explanations of policy decisions and legislative changes. Scotland's devolved social security system is explicitly human rights-oriented, with a commitment to protect dignity and an acknowledgement of rights beyond the ECHR. Fairness is also a stated objective, but the Scottish Government's understanding of the term differs from the UK Government's. In Northern Ireland, the restoration of devolution in 1998 was bound up with a political agreement that envisaged progression from a conflicted recent past to a peaceful, human rights-oriented future.[1] However, human rights language is not embedded in official accounts of the purpose of social security. This chapter examines the legal and political roles of human rights and fairness in shaping and contesting the social rights of citizenship, drawing on policy documents, case law and data from the two sets of interviews with devolved-level politicians and officials conducted for the project.

Human Rights and UK Social Security

The highest form of human rights protection at UK level is the Human Rights Act 1998. This brings most of the ECHR rights into domestic law,[2] but compliance is not an absolute requirement. The Act creates a presumption that Parliament does not intend to legislate contrary to the Convention rights. As such, courts must interpret legislation 'in a way which is compatible with the Convention rights' if possible, while public authorities must not 'act in a way which is incompatible with a Convention right' unless required to do so by primary legislation. If a provision of primary legislation cannot be read in such a way as to be compatible, the court can issue a declaration of incompatibility, but this does not affect the validity or operation of the provision. Incompatible secondary legislation also remains valid if primary legislation prevents its drafting in accordance with the Convention.[3] The UK has ratified other human rights agreements with a stronger focus on social rights, including the European Social Charter (1961 version) (ESC), International Covenant on Economic, Social and Cultural Rights (ICESCR), Convention on the Rights of the Child (UNCRC) and Convention on the Rights of Persons with Disabilities (CRPD). However, besides certain UNCRC provisions, in certain contexts,[4] none forms part of domestic law.[5]

[1] See C Harvey (ed), *Human Rights, Equality and Democratic Renewal in Northern Ireland* (Oxford: Hart, 2001).

[2] Protocols 4, 7 and 12 have not been ratified by the UK, therefore are not incorporated.

[3] Human Rights Act 1998 c 42 ss 3, 4, 6.

[4] Children (Northern Ireland) Order 1995 SI No 755 (NI 2) arts 3, 26(3); Children Act 2004 c 31 s 11; Borders, Citizenship and Immigration Act 2009 c 11 s 55; Rights of Children and Young Persons (Wales) Measure 2010 nawm 2 s 1.

[5] For an alternative approach – not one that has thus far been embraced by the judiciary – see *R (on the application of SG) v Secretary of State for Work and Pensions* [2015] UKSC 16 at [254–257] (Lord Kerr).

The only social right explicitly conferred by the ECHR is the right to education (Protocol 1, article 2). However, other provisions implicitly include social rights – albeit that these are typically minimal. The prohibition of inhuman or degrading treatment (article 3) requires states to refrain from the deliberate imposition of degrading living conditions, for example by excluding an individual lawfully present in the country from both the paid labour market and financial support from the state.[6] The right to respect for family life (article 8) may imply a right to financial support if necessary to protect children's welfare and the integrity of the family unit.[7] These rights engage in situations of extreme poverty carrying a risk of grave consequences for health and wellbeing.[8] Otherwise, the ECHR imposes no positive obligation to provide social protection where none exists. It can act as a shield for existing social security rights and against discrimination. A social security entitlement is a possession protected by protocol 1, article 1 (P1-1);[9] family or child-related benefits are a means of demonstrating respect for family life in accordance with article 8.[10] Consequently, any interference with (diminution of) the entitlement must be in accordance with the law, necessary in a democratic society and proportionate. If the scheme, or changes to it, results in differential treatment of persons in similar positions other than their membership of different protected groups, this must be in pursuit of a legitimate aim, with a 'reasonable relationship of proportionality between the means employed and the aim'.[11] Social security is an area of economic and social policy, in which the ECtHR allows states a wide margin of appreciation and the UK courts are similarly deferential to the executive and legislature. Consequently, a legal and necessary interference with a social security right or unequal treatment in pursuit of a legitimate aim will only be held disproportionate if it appears to the court to be 'manifestly without reasonable foundation'.[12]

Substantive violation of P1-1 will only found in cases where there has been a very substantial and apparently arbitrary reduction of an individual's benefit entitlement without any change in his or her circumstances.[13] Human rights-based

[6] *R (On the Application of Limbuela) v Secretary of State for the Home Department* [2005] UKHL 66.

[7] *Anufrijeva v Southwark LBC* [2003] EWCA Civ 1406; *R (JS) v Secretary of State for Work and Pensions* [2013] EWHC 3350 (QB).

[8] M Simpson, G McKeever and C Fitzpatrick, 'Legal protection against destitution in the UK: restoring a right to a subsistence minimum' (under review).

[9] *Stec v UK* (Admissibility) (65730/01) [2005] 41 EHRR SE18.

[10] *Petrovic v Austria* (20458/92) [2001] 33 EHRR 14; *R (on the application of DA) v Secretary of State for Work and Pensions* [2019] UKSC 21.

[11] *R (on the application of SG) v Secretary of State for Work and Pensions* [2015] UKSC 16 at [8] (Lord Reed).

[12] *Stec v UK* (Admissibility) (65730/01) [2005] 41 EHRR SE18; for a critical view of the 'manifestly without reasonable foundation' test as applied by the UK courts, see *R (on the application of DA) v Secretary of State for Work and Pensions* [2019] UKSC 19 at [147] (Lady Hale) and [163–177] (Lord Kerr); J Meers, 'Problems with the "manifestly without reasonable foundation" test' (2020) 27(1) *Journal of Social Security Law* 12.

[13] See *Lengyel v Hungary* (8217/15) [2019] 68 EHRR 4 at [28], in which the applicant's disability benefit was reduced by 54 per cent – the ECtHR, while stressing states' right to review the terms of social security entitlements, held this meant 'the impairment of the essence of her pension rights'.

social security cases in the UK typically feature a ritualistic, inevitably doomed, argument that there has been a substantive breach of P1-1 and/or article 8, but turn on whether a measure unlawfully discriminates against a class of claimants contrary to article 14. Claims of discrimination have largely come from women (as lone parents or domestic violence victims) or disabled people. In cases heard by the Supreme Court, litigants have successfully argued that they were unlawfully discriminated against by the suspension of a disability benefit following hospitalisation (in the case of a child) and by the reservation of certain bereavement benefits to married couples.[14] Claims that the household benefit cap and two-child limit on awards of child tax credits breached article 14 have failed.[15] The reduction of housing benefit to under-occupying social tenants produced a complex judgment. The under-occupancy penalty unlawfully discriminated against claimants in so far as the list of exemptions failed to recognise the need for an 'extra' bedroom for a disabled adult unable to share a room with her partner and a disabled child who regularly required an overnight carer. Failure to exempt multiple other applicants did not breach article 14. These included a father whose son stayed with him less than 50 per cent of the time, a 'hoarder' who compulsively collected papers and individuals who had more bedrooms than their family circumstances required but whose homes had been extensively adapted for reasons of disability or security.[16] In a rare example of a social security case in which discrimination played no part, the Supreme Court rejected a claim that mandatory work placements for jobseeker's allowance claimants violated the prohibition of forced labour in article 4 ECHR.[17]

Litigants using human rights to challenge diminution of social rights in the UK since 2010 have enjoyed very limited success. Van Bueren, writing before the arrival of this age of austerity, identifies the reason: 'the [Human Rights Act] is strangely silent over the rights of the poorer and more vulnerable sections of the community'.[18] Other international instruments explicitly confer a right to social security (article 12 ESC; article 9 ICESCR; article 26 UNCRC), social assistance (article 13 ESC) and/or an adequate standard of living (article 11 ICESCR; article 27 UNCRC; article 28 CRPD). Other rights are relevant to the conditions imposed on social security claimants, such as the right to a freely chosen occupation (article 1 ESC; article 6 ICESCR). Article 2(1) ICESCR implicitly prohibits 'deliberately retrogressive measures' unless these are 'fully justified' and the state

[14] *Mathieson v Secretary of State for Work and Pensions* [2015] UKSC 47; *Re McLaughlin's application for judicial review* [2018] UKSC 48 – *McLaughlin* was a Northern Ireland case, but concerned a benefit delivered under the same rules as its equivalent in Great Britain.

[15] *R (on the application of SG) v Secretary of State for Work and Pensions* [2015] UKSC 16; *R (on the application of DA) v Secretary of State for Work and Pensions* [2019] UKSC 21; *R (on the application of SC) v Secretary of State for Work and Pensions* [2021] UKSC 26.

[16] *R (on the application of Carmichael) v Secretary of State for Work and Pensions* [2016] UKSC 58.

[17] *R (on the application of Reilly) v Secretary of State for Work and Pensions* [2013] UKSC 68.

[18] G van Bueren, 'Including the excluded: the case for an economic, social and cultural Human Rights Act' (2001, aut) *Public Law* 456, 456.

continues to deploy its maximum available resources in pursuit of the realisation of the 'totality' of the rights conferred by the Covenant.[19] This appears particularly relevant to anyone resisting a trend towards less generous and more conditional social security, as the litigants in most of the cases above were seeking to do. However, the Committee on Economic, Social and Cultural Rights (CESCR) has long adopted a deferential attitude towards states where retrogression occurs and its resistance may have further softened since the 2008 economic crisis.[20]

There is little doubt that aspects of the UK social security system fail to live up to the minimum standards the state purports to embrace by ratifying some of these treaties. The European Committee on Social Rights has repeatedly found the level of income replacement benefits 'manifestly inadequate' for compliance with the right to social security and has sometimes found that provision for foreign nationals breached the right to social assistance.[21] CESCR does not make explicit findings of non-compliance, but its most recent concluding observations on the UK record its concern that austerity measures might be impeding the progressive realisation of the ICESCR rights and that social security cuts and conditionality might be in tension with articles 9 and 11.[22] The UNCRC is the only social rights treaty to be mentioned with any regularity, and other than as an aside, in the domestic courts.[23] The Supreme Court has held that the Secretary of State failed to treat the best interests of children as a primary consideration in establishing the household benefit cap, contrary to Article 3(1) UNRC[24] but reached the opposite conclusion in respect of the subsequent lowering of the cap.[25] It has also found that the suspension of a child's disability benefit while in hospital breached the same provision.[26]

Since these judgments, there has been a decided hardening of attitudes towards unincorporated international law on the part of the senior judiciary. While few have ever disputed the principle that such instruments 'are not contracts which

[19] Committee on Economic, Social and Cultural Rights, 'General comment no 3: the nature of states parties' obligations' (E/1991/23, annex III, New York: United Nations, 1991) para 9.

[20] M Craven, *The International Covenant on Economic, Social and Cultural Rights: A Perspective on Its Development* (Oxford: Oxford University Press, 1995); B Warwick, 'Socio-economic rights during economic crises: a changed approach to non-retrogression' (2016) 65(1) *International and Comparative Law Quarterly* 249.

[21] European Committee of Social Rights, *Conclusions XV-1–United Kingdom–Article 13-4* (Strasbourg: Council of Europe, 1997–98); European Committee of Social Rights, *Conclusions XVIII-1–United Kingdom–Article 12-1* (Strasbourg: Council of Europe, 2003–04); the author has argued that the Committee ought to have taken a more critical view of the right to social assistance in the UK in its most recent conclusions – M Simpson, 'Assessing the compliance of the United Kingdom's social security system with its obligations under the European Social Charter' (2018) 18(4) *Human Rights Law Review* 745.

[22] Committee on Economic, Social and Cultural Rights, 'Concluding observations on the sixth periodic report of the United Kingdom of Great Britain and Northern Ireland' (E/C.12/GBR/CO/6, Geneva: United Nations, 2016).

[23] Simpson, above n 21.

[24] *R (on the application of SG) v Secretary of State for Work and Pensions* [2015] UKSC 16.

[25] *R (on the application of DA) v Secretary of State for Work and Pensions* [2019] UKSC 21.

[26] *Mathieson v Secretary of State for Work and Pensions* [2015] UKSC 47.

domestic courts can enforce',[27] the last decade has at least seen Supreme Court majorities prepared to pronounce on questions of compliance. More recently, in a unanimous judgment that found the Secretary of State acted lawfully in limiting awards of child tax credits to two children in a household, the Court held that the UK courts 'cannot determine whether this country has violated its obligations under unincorporated international treaties' and 'cannot entertain' arguments concerning whether it has.[28] Lord Reed stated that he left the door open for the best interests of the child to be taken into account when considering compliance or discriminatory interference with the right to for respect family life. Lady Hale argued in 2015 that this was a well-established approach at Strasbourg and not unheard of in the UK legal system.[29] However, the courts' ability to do so must be seriously compromised if they cannot decide, or even hear arguments on, whether the best interests of affected children have been properly considered.[30]

Rights outside the ECHR have had some purchase in the political arena through the work of the Parliamentary Joint Committee on Human Rights (JCHR),[31] although not necessarily in plenary debates.[32] The JCHR's scrutiny report welcomed the Bill that would become the Welfare Reform Act 2012 as a 'potentially human rights enhancing measure' if successful in its headline purpose of 'support[ing] people to move into and progress in work, while still supporting those in greatest need', but made several procedural and substantive criticisms.[33] Members noted the absence of a detailed memorandum on the Bill's compliance with the ECHR and of 'any detailed analysis' of its compatibility with the UNCRC, ICESCR and CRPD.[34] They also expressed concern about the potential for the conditionality regime to result in inhuman or degrading treatment, for reforms including the introduction of the household benefit cap to have a discriminatory impact and retrogression in disabled people's rights associated with the introduction of personal independence payment. The report was cited on a handful of occasions during the Report Stage in the House of Lords,[35] but as this followed

[27] *R (on the application of SC) v Secretary of State for Work and Pensions* [2021] UKSC 26 at [76] (Lord Reed).

[28] Ibid, at [84] and [207] (Lord Reed).

[29] *R (on the application of SG) v Secretary of State for Work and Pensions* [2015] UKSC 16 at [211–224] (Lady Hale).

[30] The Child Poverty Action Group, which provided legal representation to the applicants in *SC*, has said it is considering bringing the case to the ECtHR – Child Poverty Action Group, 'Statement on Supreme Court decision on two-child limit' (News Release, 9 July 2021). Available at: https://cpag.org.uk/news-blogs/news-listings/statement-supreme-court-decision-two-child-limit.

[31] M Hunt, 'Enhancing Parliament's role in relation to economic and social rights' (2010) 3 *European Human Rights Law Review* 242.

[32] E Palmer, 'The Child Poverty Act 2010: holding government to account for promises in a recessionary climate?' (2010) 3 *European Human Rights Law Review* 305.

[33] Joint Committee on Human Rights, *Legislative scrutiny: Welfare Reform Bill* (HC233/HL1704, London: Houses of Parliament, 2011).

[34] Ibid.

[35] HL deb 12 Dec 2011, vol 733 col 1090; HL deb 14 Dec 2011, vol 733 col 1312; HL deb 11 Jan 2012, vol 734 col 123, 206; HL deb 23 Jan 2012, vol 734 col 820.

the completion of all stages in the Commons as well as the Second Reading and Committee Stage in the Lords, it is questionable how much scope there was for a meaningful impact. The Committee did not report on the subsequent Welfare Reform and Work Bill.

The future of rights protection at UK level seems more likely to involve a retreat from the ECHR than the embrace of additional human rights instruments. The Conservative party won a Parliamentary majority in 2015 with a manifesto commitment to 'scrap the Human Rights Act [1998] and curtail the role of the [ECtHR] in the UK legal system in favour of a British Bill of Rights'.[36] Repeal was put on hold due to the need to focus on withdrawal from the EU, but not definitively abandoned.[37] Although Fredman suggests that the prospect of moving from the 1998 Act to a Bill of Rights entails both 'the risk of jeopardising existing hard-won rights [and] the possibility of opening up new horizons',[38] from a social rights point of view it is not hard to imagine that the risks outweigh the possibilities. Announcing their intention to review human rights protection, the Conservatives endorsed 'the commitments made when we signed the [ECHR]',[39] but rejected subsequent judicial 'mission creep' in its application.[40] The inclusion of non-contributory benefits within the scope of the right to peaceful enjoyment of one's possessions was only confirmed in 2005[41] and could be an example of the sort of mission creep a Bill of Rights might be designed to reverse. Meanwhile, the Commission established to explore the possible content of a future Bill of Rights rejected the explicit inclusion of social rights.[42]

Human Rights in Devolved Social Security

Human rights protection at devolved level has also centred on the ECHR. The Northern Ireland Executive and Assembly, and the Scottish Government and Parliament, lack competence to act contrary to those provisions of the ECHR that

[36] Conservative Party, *Strong Leadership, A Clear Economic Plan, A Brighter, More Secure Future: The Conservative Party Manifesto 2015* (London: Conservative Party, 2015) 58.

[37] E Argar, letter to Lord Boswell, 4 January 2019. Available at: www.parliament.uk/globalassets/documents/lords-committees/eu-justice-subcommittee/CWM/EAtoLB-PolDeclationReferencetoECHR040119.pdf.

[38] S Fredman, 'New horizons: incorporating socio-economic rights in a British Bill of Rights' (2010, Apr) *Public Law* 297.

[39] Conservative Party, 'Protecting human rights in the UK: the Conservatives' proposals for changing Britain's human rights laws' (London: Conservative Party, 2014) 8.

[40] Ibid, at 3.

[41] *Stec v UK* (Admissibility) (65730/01) [2005] 41 EHRR SE18; for discussion, see N Harris, 'European Court of Human Rights confirms that both contributory and non-contributory benefits are covered by Article 1 of Protocol 1' (2006) 13(1) *Journal of Social Security Law* 3; I Leijten, 'From *Stec* to *Valkov*: possessions and margins in the social security case law of the European Court of Human Rights' (2013) 13 *European Human Rights Law Review* 309.

[42] Commission on a Bill of Rights, *A UK Bill of Rights? The Choice Before Us* (London: Commission on a Bill of Rights, 2012).

the UK has ratified.[43] This limit on legislative and Ministerial competence goes further than the Human Rights Act 1998: primary legislation can be held invalid by the courts, not merely declared incompatible.[44] Although the ECHR is not a particularly potent means of protecting social rights, there are examples of social security legislative provisions being held as incompatible, such as discrimination between bereavement benefit applicants based on marital status and between terminally ill disability benefit applicants based on life expectancy.[45] Such occurrences could force divergence, as the devolved legislatures could not imitate an incompatible provision passed at Westminster,[46] or promote convergence if a distinctive provision passed by one of the devolved legislatures were held invalid.

Other features of the devolution legislation place no hard-and-fast limits on legislative competence but could be used to nudge policy and legislation in a certain direction. The Secretary of State has discretionary powers to compel a devolved minister to take action, including tabling legislation, necessary to comply with international law, or to revoke devolved legislation that is incompatible with international law.[47] These powers could conceivably be used to force compliance with social rights treaties the UK has ratified but not incorporated. However, a UK minister is unlikely to require a devolved counterpart to comply with a social rights treaty when the UK Government's own compliance can be questioned. At present, when devolved social security offers stronger protection against poverty than the UK approach (to the limited extent that divergence has occurred), it is unlikely that there are any social rights with which the UK system complies, but a devolved system does not.

Looking beyond the devolution legislation, the Scottish Government and Parliament are taking active steps to enhance rights protection at devolved level. The Scottish Parliament unanimously passed a Bill incorporating the Convention on the Rights of the Child into Scottish law.[48] As the Human Rights Act 1998 does for the ECHR, this requires public authorities to act in accordance with the UNCRC, requires courts to interpret legislation so as to be compatible with the UNCRC where possible and provides for declarations of incompatibility where this is impossible. Going further than the 1998 Act, if enacted it would empower courts to strike down incompatible legislative provisions predating the enactment of the Bill. Prior to Royal Assent, the Supreme Court held that provisions of the

[43] Northern Ireland Act 1998 c 47 ss 6(2)(c), 24(1)(a); Scotland Act 1998 c 46 ss 29(2)(d), 57(2).

[44] *Salvesen v Riddell* [2013] UKSC 22.

[45] *Re McLaughlin's application for judicial review* [2018] UKSC 48; *Re Cox's application for judicial review* [2020] NIQB 53.

[46] Such an occurrence may be merely theoretical as thus far a declaration of incompatibility has always been followed 'eventually' by remedial action by the UK Parliament or Government, but remains a possibility – B Hale, 'The changing legal landscape' (2019) 19(4) *Legal Information Management* 217, 220.

[47] Scotland Act 1998 c 46 s 58; Northern Ireland Act 1998 c 47 s 26.

[48] United Nations Convention on the Rights of the Child (Incorporation) (Scotland) Bill – for discussion, see B Adamson and B White, 'Making it possible: realising children's rights in Scotland in a changing world' (2021) 2 *European Human Rights Law Review* 133.

Bill that related to reserved matters or had the effect of restricting the ability of the UK Parliament to make laws for Scotland within devolved policy areas (including those relating to the courts' interpretation of Acts of Parliament) were outside the Scottish Parliament's legislative competence.[49] At the time of writing the Scottish Government is considering its legislative response, but has stressed its continuing commitment 'to the incorporation of the UNCRC to the maximum extent' that the devolution settlement allows.[50] The Bill will clearly require amendment, but it and the planned incorporation of other instruments, including the ICESCR, retain potential to drive divergence in social security as the UNCRC offers stronger protection for social rights than the ECHR.[51] Even in advance of such developments, the primary legislation establishing the Scottish social security system states that 'social security is itself a human right and essential to the realisation of other human rights' and that 'respect for the dignity of individuals is to be at the heart of the … system'.[52] Earlier still, Scottish parliamentarians were scrutinising UK-level reforms through a human rights lens from at least 2014.[53]

Despite the Welfare Reform Committee's scrutiny work and a legislative commitment to protect the dignity of applicants to the Scottish Welfare Fund, which dates from 2015,[54] Scottish participants in wave one of the fieldwork seldom referred explicitly to human rights; dignity barely featured in the interview data.[55] Reading between the lines, it is possible to suggest that some participants alluded to the importance of a social security system based on respect for human rights, and implied that recent UK-level reforms came up short in this regard. Interviewees variously argued that the challenge for devolved legislators was to create a system in which 'everybody's dignity matters' (W1I21, Scotland politician, nationalist) and that the UK system denies claimants' 'individual worth' (W1I25, Scotland politician, unionist). The conditionality and sanctions regime was particularly singled out as 'dehumanising' (W1I24, Scotland politician, nationalist), based on arbitrary suspension of benefit for 'spurious' reasons without due process (W1I26, Scotland politician, unionist) and responsible for causing hunger.

The social security principles largely took shape in the year following wave one.[56] In wave two, most Scottish participants reflected on the commitment to

[49] *Reference by the Attorney General and Advocate General – UNCRC (Incorporation) (Scotland) Bill* [2021] UKSC 42.

[50] Scottish Government, 'Pledge on children's rights' (news release, 6 October 2021). Available at: www.gov.scot/news/pledge-on-childrens-rights/.

[51] Scottish Government, 'New Human Rights Bill' (news release, 20 March 2021). Available at: www.gov.scot/news/new-human-rights-bill/.

[52] Social Security (Scotland) Act 2018 asp 9 s 1.

[53] Welfare Reform Committee, *Interim Report on the 'Bedroom Tax'* (SP459, Edinburgh: Scottish Parliament, 2014).

[54] Welfare Funds (Scotland) Act 2015 asp 5 s 5.

[55] R Patrick and M Simpson, 'Conceptualising dignity in the context of social security: Bottom-up and top-down perspectives' (2020) 54(3) *Social Policy and Administration* 475.

[56] Scottish Government, *Creating A Fairer Scotland: Social Security – The Story So Far … and the Next Steps* (Edinburgh: Scottish Government, 2015); Scottish Government, *Creating a Fairer Scotland: A New Future for Social Security in Scotland* (Edinburgh: Scottish Government 2016).

develop a devolved social security system based on respect for dignity, widely assumed to be 'above all the principles … a core one' (W2I05, Scotland politician, nationalist). Again, though, there were few explicit references to human rights, with the dignity principle widely construed as being primarily about how people interact with Social Security Scotland, based on consideration of 'what would be the best for the client' (W2I16, Scotland official) rather than what international law demands. One politician thought a political commitment to human rights is not, in any case, about understanding the minutiae of treaty obligations. Rather, incorporation of the UNCRC would be a 'huge step forward' because it would ensure that 'everyone in [the Scottish] Parliament' was conscious of 'having a responsibility for ensuring that we are doing the very best for our young people and children' (W2I05, Scotland politician, nationalist). Even if the language used tends towards the political, or even that of customer service, rather than the legal, an official felt the Scottish Government's commitment to a holistic and maximalist view of human rights was genuine, a striking departure from its position a decade previously and not 'particularly controversial' within the Scottish Parliament. The change was depicted as a manifestation of the Scottish approach to policymaking, having been strongly advocated by the voluntary sector, as well as the 'personal and ideological commitment' of the First Minister, Nicola Sturgeon (W2I10, Scotland official).

Northern Ireland is perhaps more like the UK than Scotland in that future developments in rights protection are more likely to take the form of a Bill of Rights than explicit incorporation. The 1998 peace agreement envisages a Bill of Rights to supplement the ECHR with additional rights 'to reflect the particular circumstances of Northern Ireland, drawing as appropriate on international instruments and experience'. The Assembly would lack competence to legislate contrary to its provisions.[57] In common with the UK-level debate, and in contrast with Scotland's incorporation agenda, the inclusion of social rights in a future Bill of Rights is contentious. The Northern Ireland Human Rights Commission's advice to the UK Government on its content advocated the inclusion of social and economic rights.[58] For its advocates, this approach recognises that the 'particular circumstances of Northern Ireland' are to a large extent social and economic in nature (see Chapter 7) and that constitutional measures for rights protection invariably draw on the examples and experiences of other countries.[59] Opponents argue that simply transposing social and economic rights from international agreements is not tailoring a Bill of Rights to the needs of Northern Ireland in

[57] Northern Ireland Office, *Agreement reached in the multi-party negotiations* (Cm 3883, Belfast: NIO, 1998) chapter 6, para 4.

[58] Northern Ireland Human Rights Commission, *A Bill of Rights for Northern Ireland: Advice to the Secretary of State for Northern Ireland* (Belfast: NIHRC 2008).

[59] B Dickson, 'New human rights protections in Northern Ireland' (1999) 24(supp) *European Law Review* 3; A Smith, 'Internationalisation and constitutional borrowing in drafting Bills of Rights' (2011) 60(4) *International and Comparative Law Quarterly* 867.

the way the Agreement envisaged.[60] The UK Government is firmly in the latter camp[61] and there seems to be little prospect of securing the necessary agreement between unionist and nationalist political parties for the devolved institutions to take their own steps towards the protection of social rights,[62] as has been possible in Scotland.

Politically, it can be hard to identify a set of overarching principles for social security in Northern Ireland – human rights-based or otherwise. Parity with England and Wales remains the starting point (if no longer the presumption), with divergence from the UK Government's approach justified on more pragmatic social and economic grounds. Nonetheless, the progress of the Welfare Reform Bill through the Assembly during the 2011–2016 mandate shows a degree of concern about the equality and human rights implications of the proposed legislation.[63] In addition to the statutory committee stage, the Assembly referred the Bill to an ad hoc committee on conformity with equality requirements.[64] The ad hoc committee expanded its focus to include human rights obligations, consciously modelling its approach on that of the JCHR. However, the only international agreements referred to in the body of the report are the ECHR and UNCRC, with other instruments mentioned only in the appended minutes of evidence and written submissions. The committee concluded by majority vote that it could not 'identify any specific breaches of equality or human rights' law flowing from the Bill, but highlighted 'a number of areas of concern' requiring ongoing monitoring.[65] A complicating factor was the difficulty in determining whether specific provisions of the Bill were themselves in breach of human rights or equality requirements, or empowered the Department for Social Development to make secondary legislation that might (and that some members expected would) breach those requirements. Recommendations included steps to 'minimise the potential for … destitution' flowing from benefit sanctions, payment of universal credit by default to the main carer in the case of joint-claim couples with children, monitoring of the impact of the household benefit cap, measures to ensure human rights compliance in the assessment process for disability benefits and waiving the reduction of housing

[60] C Harvey and D Russell, 'A new beginning for human rights protection in Northern Ireland?' (2009) 6 *European Human Rights Law Review* 748; Northern Ireland Affairs Committee, 'A Bill of Rights for Northern Ireland: an interim statement' (HC236 incorporating HC360, London: House of Commons, 2010).

[61] Northern Ireland Office, *A Bill of Rights for Northern Ireland: Next Steps* (Belfast: NIO, 2009).

[62] M Simpson, 'The Agreement and devolved social security: a missed opportunity for socio-economic rights in Northern Ireland?' (2015) 66(2) *Northern Ireland Legal Quarterly* 105; A Smith, M McWilliams and P Yarnell, *Political Capacity Building: Advancing a Bill of Rights for Northern Ireland* (Newtownabbey: Transitional Justice Institute, 2014).

[63] As introduced, the Bill essentially replicated the reforms included in the Welfare Reform Act 2012 for Great Britain.

[64] NIA deb 20 November 2012, vol 79 no 6, p 2.

[65] Ad Hoc Committee, *Report on whether the provisions of the Welfare Reform Bill are in conformity with the requirements for equality and observance of human rights* (NIA92/11–15, Belfast: NI Assembly, 2013) 1.

benefit to under-occupying tenants 'where no reasonable alternative accommodation is available'.[66]

In wave one of the fieldwork, Northern Irish interviewees were more likely than those in Scotland to make explicit reference to human rights concerns as a factor informing their views on the UK Government's social security policy. However, this was not always accompanied by evidence of firm understanding of the issues raised. A politician who expressed the view that Northern Ireland's devolved institutions 'should be bound by international conventions' and specifically highlighted the impact of welfare reform on the right to family life as a potential issue of concern nonetheless seemed to base judgements in part on whether witnesses before Assembly committees were 'wishy-washy' or 'more assertive' in their evidence (W1I04, Northern Ireland politician, nationalist). An official stressed that Northern Ireland takes human rights obligations seriously, even those under non-justiciable agreements, as long as there is a 'rigorous reporting process' and does respond to criticism of its record (W1I10, Northern Ireland official). Yet the following year, the CESCR observed with regret that the Northern Ireland Executive had not taken part in the latest periodic review of the UK's implementation of the ICESCR. By wave two, the frequency of references to human rights had dwindled. A rare comment on the subject observed that 'there is always going to be political tension around equality and human rights and the primacy of those … Frankly, that's part of politics' (W2I31, Northern Ireland official). As in Scotland, although less often, there were more implicit allusions to the need for social security to adhere to what might be interpreted as human rights standards, or indeed as respect for claimants' dignity. For example, that social security should be based on 'humanitarian ideals' and avoid stigmatising claimants (W2I01, Northern Ireland politician, unionist), or that 'the worst thing in the world isn't somebody who gets money who was not entitled to [it]. The worst thing in the world is somebody who … will literally go hungry if they don't get it' (W2I02, Northern Ireland politician, neutral).

Fairness – To Whom?

The need for fairness in the social security system has been a central pillar of the UK Government's defence when facing judicial review of measures flowing from the Welfare Reform Act 2012 and the Welfare Reform and Work Act 2016. Indeed, the aspiration to a 'fairer' system has been a thread running through policy documents, parliamentary debates and litigation from the early days of the post-2010 coalition government – and in publications by the Centre for Social Justice predating the 2010 general election.[67] Adopting a different vision for and approach to

[66] Ibid, at 3.

[67] Economic Dependency Working Group, *Dynamic benefits: Towards Welfare that Works* (London: Centre for Social Justice, 2009) – the CSJ was established by Iain Duncan Smith, the future Secretary

social security has been equally central to the Scottish Government's stated aim of creating a 'fairer Scotland'.[68] Exploring the concept of fairness, then, can help illuminate both the judicial deference to the executive described above and the divergence between UK and Scottish approaches to social security with which the book as a whole is concerned. It is less relevant to the Northern Ireland context.

The coalition government's interpretation of 'fairness' is summed up by the Secretary of State's introduction to the second reading debate on the Welfare Reform Bill:

> The Bill says to the taxpayer, 'Your hard-earned money must be spent responsibly'... Taxpayers ... are constantly being asked to pay in taxes towards support for others. That is fair, but we have a responsibility to ensure that taxpayers too are properly supported.[69]

The Secretary of State went on to identify the capping of benefit incomes, so that no unemployed household can receive more than the average earnings for in-work households, and the introduction of 'tougher regimes' of job-seeking obligations as central to how 'fairness' would be achieved.[70] Policy documents additionally associate fairness with narrower targeting of disability benefits on 'people who face the greatest challenges to living independent lives',[71] ensuring that 'work always pays' and that social security does not pay 'excessive' rents on tenants' behalf.[72] Patrick views this emphasis on a direct link between 'the rights of taxpayers to see their taxes well spent and the obligations of out-of-work claimants ... to demonstrate their deservingness' as integral to the reframing of social citizenship as a contractual relationship between contributors and recipients, as opposed to one of mutual solidarity.[73]

The Supreme Court has accepted the pursuit of fairness in, and ensuring 'public confidence' in the fairness of, the social security system as a legitimate aim for policy and legislation.[74] A 'fair balance' between the interests of the individual and society is integral to the proportionality test for interference with an individual's enjoyment of his or her possessions.[75] Hence, fairness is capable of justifying the unequal impact of the household benefit cap, two-child limit on

of State for Work and Pensions. It is a measure of its influence that the phrase 'welfare that works' was adopted for the title of the white paper setting out proposals for universal credit.

[68] Scottish Government, *It Takes All of Us to Build a Fairer Scotland: Fairer Scotland Action Plan* (Edinburgh: Scottish Government, 2016).

[69] I Duncan Smith, HC deb 9 Mar 2011, vol 524 col 921.

[70] Ibid, cols 922, 925.

[71] Department for Work and Pensions, *Disability Living Allowance Reform* (Cm 7984, London: DWP, 2010) 1.

[72] Department for Work and Pensions, *Universal Credit: Welfare That Works* (Cm 7957, London: DWP, 2010) 1, 19.

[73] R Patrick, *For Whose Benefit: The Everyday Realities of Welfare Reform* (Bristol: Policy Press, 2017) 26.

[74] *R (on the application of DA) v Secretary of State for Work and Pensions* [2019] UKSC 21 at [152] (Lady Hale).

[75] Ibid, at [61] (Lord Wilson).

child tax credit awards and perhaps the reduction of housing benefit to under-occupying tenants[76] – as long as the measure and resulting inequality are not manifestly unreasonable means of attempting to ensure fairness. The senior judiciary has been unwilling to comment on what 'fairness' in social security might look like. As Lord Reed observes: 'the assessment of [what] would represent a fair balance between the interests of working and non-working households is a matter of political judgment'.[77] By and large, it has been almost as deferential in its acceptance of the Secretary of State's assertions that the policies adopted in the name of fairness have been the right ones.[78] Lady Hale provides a rare example of a more critical perspective, interrogating whether the Secretary of State's account of the characteristics of the benefit cap that are claimed to result in fairness – reducing costs to taxpayers, ensuring out-of-work benefit recipients are not financially better off than in-work households and incentivising employment – withstands scrutiny. She concludes:

> Families in work are already better off than those on benefits and so the cap is not necessary in order to achieve fairness between them; saving money cannot be achieved by unjustified discrimination; [and] the major aim, of incentivising work and changing the benefits culture, has little force in the context of lone parents.[79]

While Lady Hale found there could be no reasonable justification for the cap on this basis, the majority of the Court disagreed. Considering a challenge to the two-child limit on child tax credits, the Supreme Court went further. A unanimous judgment uncritically accepts the legitimacy of the Secretary of State's stated view that the automatic increase of an award in response to the birth of an additional child was 'unfair and unreasonable'[80] – despite the centrality of the principle that social security must respond in some fashion to households' actual living costs to Beveridge's proposals and to six decades of policy thereafter.[81]

Overall, it can be concluded that fairness in the post-2010 UK model of social citizenship is largely about controlling costs for the taxpayer, with more than a hint of the 'less eligibility' principle that underpinned the former Poor Law, namely that the support to an out-of-work household should be below the earnings of a

[76] *R (on the application of Carmichael) v Secretary of State for Work and Pensions* [2016] UKSC 58 – fairness is mentioned in the judgment as an objective of the 2012 reforms as a whole but is not discussed in detail as in the other cases cited in this paragraph.

[77] *R (on the application of SG) v Secretary of State for Work and Pensions* [2015] UKSC 16 at [69] (Lord Reed).

[78] C O'Brien, '"Done because we are too menny": the two-child rule promotes poverty, invokes a narrative of welfare decadence, and abandons children's rights' (2018) 26(4) *International Journal of Children's Rights* 700.

[79] *R (on the application of SG) v Secretary of State for Work and Pensions* [2015] UKSC 16 at [229] (Lady Hale); see also *R (on the application of DA) v Secretary of State for Work and Pensions* [2019] UKSC 21 at [153] (Lady Hale).

[80] *R (on the application of SC) v Secretary of State for Work and Pensions* [2021] UKSC 26 at [201] (Lord Reed).

[81] W Beveridge, *Social insurance and allied services* (Cmd 6404, London: HMSO, 1942).

low-paid worker. The fieldwork revealed a degree of sympathy for this perspective among some participants in both Northern Ireland and Scotland. In wave one, a significant number of Northern Ireland interviewees regarded the benefit cap at its then-level of £26,000 as ample for any reasonably prudent household to 'manage' on (W1I01, Northern Ireland politician, unionist), particularly in light of the country's relatively low earnings compared to other UK regions.[82] Job-seeking conditionality, backed by sanctions, also gained some support on the basis that, in or out of paid employment, 'if you can't be arsed to get out of your bed … you don't get paid' (W1I17, Northern Ireland politician, neutral). Other interviewees took a broader view of (un)fairness between in- and out-of-work households, questioning why low-income households should be prioritised in accessing services like preschool education and parenting support. Not everyone agreed with the UK Government's conception of fairness – one politician pointedly spoke of 'unfair reform' rather than 'welfare reform' (W1I07, Northern Ireland politician, nationalist) – and it was widely accepted that it would be unfair to financially penalise under-occupying social tenants in the absence of any realistic possibility of downsizing.

In common with UK-level reforms in the 2010s, fairness features prominently in the Scottish social security discourse, with the agency responsible for delivering assistance adopting the slogan 'Dignity, fairness, respect'. However, the Scottish Government has its own interpretation of fairness. Whereas the UK Government has presented reduced expenditure on income- and housing-related benefits and greater targeting of disability benefits as integral to the fairness of social security, the Scottish Government describes the mitigation or abolition of under-occupancy penalties and longer-term awards to some disabled people as examples of 'mak[ing] social security fairer'.[83] 'Decent pay' and 'flexible working', not conditional social security entitlements, are presented as the route to incentivising employment.[84] In the fieldwork, a handful of interviewees did argue that 'it offends most people's sense of fairness' to see low-earning taxpayers paid less than out-of-work households receive in benefits (W1I25, Scotland politician, unionist). Generally, though, understandings of fairness were closer to those of the Scottish Government. The social contract, it was widely argued, does not and should not set the interest of claimants and service users against those of the taxpayer, and certainly should not make 'moral judgements' about individuals' deservingness (W2I14, Scotland politician, nationalist). Rather:

> People have an entitlement to benefit support that comes from the contract that is there between the government and the citizen, that it is something that we collectively all contribute to, a bit like our NHS, in order that it is there for us, should we ever need it (W2I14, Scotland politician, nationalist).

[82] Average full-time earnings in Northern Ireland at April 2014 were £23,800 – Office for National Statistics, *Annual survey of Hours and Earnings, 2014 Provisional Results* (Newport: ONS, 2014).

[83] Scottish Government, above n 68 at 38.

[84] Ibid, at 66, 68.

Social security, according to this perspective, should not be designed to minimise costs to the taxpayer, but to ensure claimants 'have a minimum amount of money coming in every month allowing you to keep a roof over your head and have food on the table' (W2I11, Scotland official). For other interviewees, fairness was bound up with dignity in the sense that it is largely about interactions between claimants and the system – 'respecting the individual's preferences, needs, wishes and so on' (W2I16, Scotland official).

Conclusion

Social security, as the Scottish Parliament has observed, 'is itself a human right and essential to the realisation of other human rights'.[85] Consequently, as noted in Chapter 2, human rights may inform what the social rights of citizenship are, or ought to be. The UK has ratified numerous international agreements recognising social rights. However, the domestic human rights settlement privileges the ECHR, which underpins only a minimal set of social rights. Citizens enjoy a measure of protection against utter destitution, arbitrary withdrawal of social security entitlements and discriminatory treatment in their allocation. This protection only applies, though, to the extent that the state may not interfere with or discriminate in the enjoyment of those entitlements in a way that is deemed manifestly unreasonable by a judiciary that is instinctively, and at the highest level increasingly, deferential to the legislature and executive on questions of social policy. Nonetheless, the higher degree of protection for the ECHR rights in the devolution settlements compared to the Human Rights Act 1998 could conceivably act as a driver of divergence.

Rights beyond the ECHR have force mainly to the extent that they are taken seriously in the political arena. Although there are examples of human rights-focused scrutiny by UK Parliamentary and Northern Ireland Assembly committees, this can only really be said of Scotland – where, accordingly, moves are afoot to increase the domestic legal force of a range of treaties. Even there, the interview data often speak to an instinctive assumption that an appeal to human rights reinforces the project to build a devolved social security system based on dignity and fairness, rather than a deep understanding of what the treaties require and what incorporation would mean. In contrast, at UK level fairness appears to be understood as requiring that social security claimants should not enjoy too many rights, a view shared by a significant number of the Northern Ireland interviewees and several in Scotland. Contrasting views on rights, then, go some way towards explaining tentative divergence in social security within the UK – but are far from the whole story. Further factors are examined in Chapter 7.

[85] Social Security (Scotland) Act 2018 asp 9 s 1.

7

The Foundations of Devolved Social Citizenships

Introduction

Concern about aspects of the UK social security system, particularly following the reforms of 2012 and 2016, is not limited to Scotland and Northern Ireland. Nonetheless, the discourse around the coalition and Conservative governments' agenda has been framed in terms of specific, negative impacts on or incompatibility with the ideological preferences of those countries. Devolved elites discontented with the emerging UK model of social citizenship could seek to change the UK Government's position, or advocate (or proclaim) a distinct social citizenship at devolved level. This chapter draws on Béland and Lecours's analytical framework[1]

[1] D Béland and A Lecours, *Nationalism and Social Policy: The Politics of Territorial Solidarity* (Oxford: Oxford University Press, 2010).

to consider how socio-economic, ideological and institutional factors in Scotland and Northern Ireland might birth substate social citizenships. Some factors might lead substate leaders to conclude that their region wants or needs a welfare state that differs from that taking shape at UK level. Others could shape an alternative vision for devolved social citizenship. A final set affect the feasibility of changing social security law, policy and systems in a way that better reflects preferences in the devolved country.

Socio-economic Factors

Neither Scotland nor Northern Ireland fits with the conventional view that demand for the decentralisation of redistributive programmes is driven by 'material self-interest', as better-off regions seek to dismantle state-wide solidarity networks through which they subsidise poorer neighbours.[2] Northern Ireland has consistently been among the economically weaker UK regions. Consequently, it receives the largest 'subvention' through a combination of its block grant, the primary source of funds for devolved government, and direct UK expenditure.[3] Scotland's economic position relative to the rest of the UK is harder to gauge. According to some analyses, it would sometimes appear as a net contributor to the UK Exchequer if North Sea oil and gas revenues were territorially apportioned. Nonetheless, Scotland seems to have been a net recipient of funds in recent years.[4]

Northern Ireland's status as an economically weaker part of the UK means it feels the effect of social security reforms particularly keenly. Recent cuts have arguably weakened the direct economic advantages of the social union to the country. Beatty and Fothergill's early projection of the impact of reforms in the latter years of the New Labour period and under the coalition envisaged an annual economic loss to Northern Ireland of £650 per capita.[5] By way of comparison, the projected loss for Great Britain was £450 per capita, or £530 for the worst-affected areas (north-east and north-west England).[6] Scotland's projected annual economic loss was £480 per capita, limited to £440 by the Scottish Government's mitigation measures.[7] However, the local impact within Scotland varied. Glasgow showed

[2] Ibid, at 32.

[3] P Teague, 'Northern Ireland: the political economy of peace' (Belfast: Mitchell Institute for Global Peace, Security and Justice, 2016).

[4] M Keep, *Scotland: Public Spending and Revenue* (BP06625, London: House of Commons, 2020); E Ashcroft, 'Has Scotland already spent its oil fund?' (Scottish Economy Watch, 10 July 2013). Available at: www.scottisheconomywatch.com/beth-ashcrofts-scottish/2013/07/; Research and Library Services, 'A background paper on the Barnett Formula' (RP12/01, Belfast: Northern Ireland Assembly, 2001).

[5] C Beatty and S Fothergill, *The Impact of Welfare Reform on Northern Ireland* (Sheffield: Centre for Economic Empowerment, 2013).

[6] Alternative analyses by the same authors suggest a per-capita loss of £470 for Great Britain and £560 for north-east and north-west England – see C Beatty and S Fothergill, 'The local and regional impact of the UK's welfare reforms' (2014) 7(1) *Cambridge Journal of Regions, Economy and Society* 63.

[7] C Beatty and S Fothergill, *The Cumulative Impact of Welfare Reform on Households in Scotland* (SP paper 657, Edinburgh: Scottish Parliament, 2015).

the second-highest overall projected loss (after Birmingham) of any local government district in Great Britain and was one of eight districts in Scotland with a projected per-capita loss of £500 or more.[8] Portes and Reed's more recent analysis of the effect, on overall poverty rates and by income decile, in each UK country of tax and social security reforms and changes to the national minimum/living wage between May 2010 and January 2018 is outlined below.

Table 7.1 Projected relative poverty rates (after housing costs) in 2020–2021, following reforms and assuming no reforms[9]

Location	**Poverty rate following reforms**		**Poverty rate without reforms**		**Change due to reforms**	
	Households	Children	Households	Children	Households	Children
Great Britain	19.7%	41.3%	18.2%	30.9%	1.6pp	10.4pp
England	20.1%	42.1%	18.4%	31.4%	1.7pp	10.7pp
Wales	18.6%	37.4%	17.6%	29.6%	1.0pp	17.7pp
Scotland	16.8%	33.1%	15.9%	25.1%	0.8pp	8.0pp
Northern Ireland	22.4%	31.5%	19.8%	23.4%	2.6pp	8.1pp

Table 7.2 Percentage change in annual net household income by income decile due to tax and social security reforms, 2020–2021 (approximate)[10]

Income decile	**England**	**Wales**	**Scotland**	**Northern Ireland**
1 (poorest)	–0.2%	+4.1%	–0.8%	–1.9%
2	–4.0%	–3.7%	–3.2%	–4.1%
3	–2.9%	–3.4%	–3.4%	–3.6%
4	–2.1%	–1.3%	–2.1%	–1.1%
5	–1.0%	–1.6%	–1.3%	–1.0%
6	0	+1.0%	–0.3%	–0.2%
7	+0.7%	+1.4%	+0.1%	+1.2%
8	+0.9%	+1.2%	0	+1.8%
9	+0.7%	+0.9%	–0.7%	+0.2%
10	–0.1%	–0.1%	–2.3%	–0.1%
Average	–0.4%	–0.2%	–1.2%	–0.4%

[8] Ibid; Beatty and Fothergill, above n 6.

[9] J Portes and H Reed, *The Cumulative Impact of Tax and Welfare Reforms* (London: Equality and Human Rights Commission, 2018); H Reed and J Portes, *Cumulative Impact Assessment of Tax and Social Security Reforms in Northern Ireland* (Belfast: Northern Ireland Human Rights Commission, 2019).

[10] Reed and Portes, above n 9.

Already it can be seen that, even in its infancy, devolutionary divergence in social security (and taxation) complicates direct comparisons of the various UK countries. Nonetheless, it appears that the impact is greater in Northern Ireland than elsewhere, at least on incomes at the lower end of the distribution. The effect is more pronounced in Beatty and Fothergill's analysis, whose earlier model could not take account of some factors that inform Reed and Portes's subsequent work.[11] At face value Scotland is less affected than Northern Ireland, although this has not deterred critics from highlighting the negative impact of social security reforms and wider public spending cuts on Scotland.[12] The reasons for Northern Ireland's long-term economic underperformance relative to the rest of the UK are beyond the scope of this book. A link with the 30-year violent conflict from the late 1960s is likely, although the issue was already present in the 1920s.[13] In any case, consistently high levels of economic inactivity (although not unemployment), incapacity and disability mean reliance on low-income and disability benefits is higher than in other parts of the UK, therefore any increase or decrease in generosity, any tightening or loosening of eligibility criteria, has a disproportionate impact. Fifty-eight per cent of social housing tenants under-occupy their homes, compared to 19 per cent in England, and tenant mobility is restricted by ethno-religious segregation.[14] Consequently, reducing housing benefit in response to under-occupancy would mainly penalise those who could not downsize, even if they wanted to. Conversely, private rents are lower than anywhere else in the UK, except the cheapest areas of Wales, reducing the likelihood of notional benefit entitlement exceeding the household benefit cap. Finally, a relatively high fertility rate means households are more likely to exceed the cap because of large family size and to be affected by the two-child limit on universal credit and child tax credits.

[11] Namely the mitigation payments to claimants negatively affected by selected reforms in Northern Ireland, Scotland's higher income tax rates, the launch of the first devolved benefits in Scotland (best start grant and carer's allowance supplement) and the fact that, against expectations, expenditure on disability benefits increased due to the introduction of personal independence payment.

[12] SP deb 22 December 2011 session 4 col 4941; G Mooney, 'Scotland, the CSR and public sector cuts' in N Yeates, T Haux, R Jawad and M Kilkey (eds), *In Defence of Welfare: The Impacts of the Spending Review* (York: Social Policy Association, 2011).

[13] Teague, above n 3; M Simpson, 'Developing constitutional principles through firefighting: social security parity in Northern Ireland' (2015) 22(1) *Journal of Social Security Law* 31.

[14] K Gibb, *The 'bedroom tax' in Scotland* (SP paper 409, Edinburgh: Scottish Parliament, 2013) – while these figures are now dated, the time taken to plan, fund and deliver new social housing means there is unlikely to have been a significant increase in availability of smaller units; see also J Frey, *Social Housing in Northern Ireland: Challenges and Options* (Glasgow: UK Collaborative Centre for Housing Evidence, 2018).

Table 7.3 Selected socio-economic indicators in the UK and constituent countries[15]

	UK	England	Wales	Scotland	Northern Ireland
Unemployment (ILO definition, May–July 2020)[16]	4.1%	3.5–5.2% depending on region	3.1%	4.6%	2.9%
Economic inactivity (May–July 2020)	20.2%	17.4–22.0% depending on region	22.9%	22.0%	26.3%
PIP receipt by 16–64 population (2019)	5.8% (GB)	5.5%	8.9%	7.2%	12%
Incapacity benefit receipt by 16–64 population (2016)[17]	6.1% (GB)	6.1%	8.5%	7.8%	10.8%
Fertility rate (2019)	1.63	1.66	1.54	1.37	1.82
Local housing allowance, three-bedroom house (weekly, 2021–2022)	£90.90–£441.86	£103.56–£441.86	£90.90–£178.36	£115.03–£253.15	£95.33–£120.91

Both Northern Irish and Scottish interviewees argued that their countries' social and economic circumstances differed to (parts of) England's, but this was more

[15] B Watson, 'Labour market in the regions of the UK: September 2020' (Newport: Office for National Statistics, 2020); DWP caseload statistics at StatXplore. Available at: https://stat-xplore.dwp.gov.uk/; Department for Communities, 'Northern Ireland benefit statistics summary at November 2016' (Belfast: DfC, 2017); Department for Communities, 'Northern Ireland benefit statistics summary at November 2019' (Belfast: DfC, 2020); Scottish Government, 'Local Housing Allowance Rates: 2021–2022' (Edinburgh: Scottish Government, 2021); Welsh Government, 'Local housing allowance rates from April 2021 to March 2022' (Cardiff: Welsh Government, 2021); Valuation Office Agency, 'Local Housing Allowance (LHA) rates applicable from April 2021 to March 2022' (London: HM Government, 2021); Northern Ireland Housing Executive, 'Current LHA rent levels' (Belfast: NIHE, 2021); Scottish Government, *A Scotland for the Future: Opportunities and Challenges of Scotland's Changing Population* (Edinburgh: Scottish Government, 2021). Available at: www.gov.scot/publications/local-housing-allowance-rates-2021-2022/; https://gov.wales/local-housing-allowance-lha-rates-april-2021-march-2022; www.gov.uk/government/publications/local-housing-allowance-lha-rates-applicable-from-april-2021-to-march-2022; www.nihe.gov.uk/Housing-Help/Local-Housing-Allowance/Current-LHA-rent-levels.

[16] Unemployment and economic inactivity data are from a relatively early stage in the coronavirus pandemic. All parts of the UK saw a decrease in employment between the quarter ending February 2020 and the quarter ending February 2021 – the greatest decrease, 3.5%, occurred in Northern Ireland. See B Wilson, 'Labour market in the regions of the UK: April 2021' (Newport: Office for National Statistics, 2021).

[17] It is impossible to calculate equivalent figures for later years as published universal credit data do not distinguish between people who are not required to be available for employment due to incapacity or for other reasons, such as caring responsibilities.

pronounced in Northern Ireland. Most Northern Ireland-based interviewees in wave one had a relatively gloomy perspective on the region's economic performance and potential, which one official believed 'would take 25 years to turn … round' (W1I08, Northern Ireland official). Politicians blamed high energy costs, the legacy of conflict, a peripheral location in the UK and Europe and treatment as a 'backwater' (W1I15, Northern Ireland politician, nationalist) by successive UK governments. Views on both countries' economic prospects in wave two were distorted by uncertainty about the impact of the coronavirus pandemic, with the future withdrawal of the jobs retention (furlough) scheme a particular concern. This focus on the pandemic, though, was consistent with Scottish interviewees' tendency to highlight economic challenges common to the UK as a whole such as in-work poverty, precarious employment and housing costs. Aside from occasional references to its 'quite different migration needs' (W2I09a, Scotland official), it was felt that localised economic differences within Scotland were more significant than those between Scotland and the rest of the UK. In Northern Ireland, economic inactivity, low pay, poor childcare provision, high energy costs and rurality continued to be portrayed as challenges. Some interviewees argued that an excessive focus on unemployment rates had obscured the reality of high levels of worklessness and in-work poverty:

> We have been living in a bit of a cloud cuckoo land in Northern Ireland in the sense that … before we had Covid we were almost in full employment. We were down at three per cent unemployment and yet we still had the highest rates of economically inactive people … in the UK (W2I25, Northern Ireland official).

A rare, unprompted mention of the UK's withdrawal from the EU came in the context of the likely economic impact on Northern Ireland:

> How much are UK companies going to want to invest or sell into the Northern Ireland market if they've got to fill in lots of forms in Liverpool? … 30,000 people who cross the border regularly, not processed. How does that work out? … Undoubtedly there will be issues (W2I29, Northern Ireland official).

In both locations it was universally accepted in wave one that construction of sufficient one- and two-bedroom social housing units to facilitate downsizing in response to the social sector size criteria would be impossible in the medium term. Northern Irish interviewees in wave two remained concerned about the impact of any under-occupancy penalty while 'we don't actually have a housing market that enables people to downsize' (W2I19, Northern Ireland politician, neutral) and 'we are a very segregated society' (W2I20, Northern Ireland politician, nationalist). In Scotland, housing benefit reform was mentioned infrequently in wave two. It may be that interviewees considered that the issue had been resolved by action at devolved level.

Ultimately, while interviewees in both locations advocated some divergence from the UK Government's approach to social security – universally in wave two – it was mainly in Northern Ireland that this was framed as necessary due to social and economic circumstances. There were occasional warnings that imposing social security cuts on already-deprived areas could result in a new round of 'breakdowns in society ... unrest and that's the last thing we need here' (W1I10, Northern Ireland official), reflecting the contribution of poverty to past civil unrest.[18] Scottish interviewees were more likely to argue that key UK reforms were wrong regardless of location, the difference being that Scotland had the ideological and political drive to do things differently.

Ideological Factors

Béland and Lecours argue that the development of substate social citizenships is more likely 'when there are consistent differences with respect to the desired amount of social spending' between regional and national elites or electorates.[19] Since 2012, countries within the UK have differed in their desired amount of spending on social security and the benefits provided, albeit within a similar structure. The question is whether emerging differences are the manifestation of a fundamentally different vision for social citizenship. Jeffery suggests decentralised control of social policy allows substate tiers of government to 'reinstat[e] earlier social policy commitments, insur[e] against their future erosion [or develop] new ways of pursuing established policy aims'.[20] The first two scenarios envisage the emergence of 'new' ideas about social citizenship at the national level, with autonomous territories using devolved powers to resist retrenchment. The third is more ambiguous – a region might devise alternative ways of pursuing aims it shares with the central government or pursue its own distinctive agenda.

Scottish mobilisation in favour of devolution from the 1980s is presented by Béland and Lecours as the archetypal example of regional social democrats seeking greater autonomy so that 'their community [could] enjoy more generous social programmes' than a conservative national government was prepared to fund. Yet this push for autonomy may also be the latest manifestation of a centuries-old 'Scottish myth' or 'belief that Scottish society is fundamentally egalitarian'.[21] The extent to which modern Scottish society and/or elites are politically to the left of their UK or English counterparts, and the implications for welfare state and constitutional politics, is widely explored in the literature. Greer and Mätzke regard devolution as the product of 'an effort by Scottish and Welsh elites to quarantine themselves from English policies that change or erode social citizenship

[18] P Hillyard, B Rolston and M Tomlinson, *Poverty and Conflict in Ireland: An International Perspective* (Dublin: Institute of Public Administration/Combat Poverty Agency, 2005).

[19] Béland and Lecours, above n 1.

[20] C Jeffery, 'Devolution and social citizenship: which society, whose citizenship?', SL Greer (ed), *Territory, Democracy and Justice: Regionalism and Federalism in Western Democracies* (Basingstoke: Palgrave Macmillan, 2006) 90.

[21] Béland and Lecours, above n 1 at 33, 101; see also D McCrone, *Understanding Scotland: The Sociology of a Nation* (London: Routledge, 2001).

rights'. Two questions arise. First, whether the ambition is limited to resistance to 'Thatcher's "contract-breaking" policies'[22] or extends to the construction of a new, specifically Scottish, social citizenship. Second, whether this is essentially an elite project or reflects a wider societal view of how the social rights of citizenship should be defined.

It is undisputed that the political centre of gravity of the Scottish Parliament is to the left of the UK Parliament. Until the rise of the Conservatives to form the main opposition party since 2016, a social democratic government (Labour-led or SNP) faced a social democratic opposition. Alongside distinctive voting patterns sits an 'elite discourse [that] is much more prone to articulate strong communitarian, redistributive, pro-welfare values'.[23] In this account, 'Scotland is envisioned as a spontaneous collective, an imagined community, or even a sentient being whereby "Scotland" does and feels things'.[24] The interview data are peppered with suggestions that what Scotland 'feels' is a deeper commitment to 'egalitarianism' (W1I36, Scotland official) or a 'socialist' vision for society (W1I25, Scotland politician, unionist; W1I33, Scotland official) than the UK as a whole. One politician painted a vivid picture of an egalitarian mindset underpinned by historical and cultural factors:

> If you go right back to the 1700s and you look at some of the famous plays that were written in Scotland, this idea of the common weal and the good of the people and looking after people, it has been part of the Scottish psyche for so long. That was a church tradition as well … we've always had a left of centre outlook on life … Look at voting patterns and the rise of political parties, Scotland at the forefront of the development of the modern Labour party … Look at the poetry of Robert Burns, this aspect of caring for people that are in need runs through that whole literary history (W1I24, Scotland politician, nationalist).

Other interviewees' statements were more qualified. Some felt Scottish egalitarianism had been consistently 'overstate[d]' (W1I21, Scotland politician, nationalist) or 'exaggerated' (W1I22, Scotland politician, unionist) for political effect, others that the country is somewhat more left-leaning than the London-centric 'establishment' (W1I23, Scotland politician, nationalist) but not necessarily than the population of England or the UK as a whole. Even the chief exponent of the 'Scottish myth', quoted above, thought it possible that Scotland had retained a set of values that 'parts of the UK has lost' over time (W1I24, Scotland politician, nationalist).

[22] SL Greer and M Mätzke, 'Introduction: devolution and citizenship rights', SL Greer (ed), *Devolution and Social Citizenship in the UK* (Bristol: Policy Press, 2009) 11.

[23] Ibid, at 9; see also N McEwen, 'The territorial politics of social policy development in multilevel states' (2005) 15(4) *Regional and Federal Studies* 537.

[24] A Law and G Mooney, 'Devolution in a "stateless nation": nation-building and social policy in Scotland' (2012) 46(2) *Social Policy and Administration* 161, 162.

This more cautious portrayal of the Scottish take on social citizenship broadly reflects the findings of social attitudes research, which have not usually indicated 'particularly higher levels of social democratic feeling in Scotland and Wales relative to England'.[25] A decade ago, Curtice and Ormston fond some evidence that Scotland was 'more social democratic in outlook than England', but that the difference was 'modest at best'.[26] Although Curtice continues to argue that this modern 'Scottish myth' is 'partly true – but perhaps not as much as is sometimes suggested',[27] recent British Social Attitudes survey data do show a difference between Scotland and England. Scottish and English respondents show similar views on abstract questions, with 51 and 50 per cent respectively agreeing that most people should be 'in the middle' of the social hierarchy. However, there are significant differences in assessments of whether this sort of society exists in the UK (7 and 15 per cent respectively agreed) and in attitudes to income distribution, health or educational inequalities and income tax rates.[28] In contrast, surveys in 2012 and 2013 found Scottish respondents slightly *less* likely than average to favour redistributive measures.[29] If Scottish attitudes to the welfare state have diverged from England over the last decade, it is possible to suggest some reasons. A striking feature of the interview data was the extent of Scottish participants' belief in the power of political leadership to mould a society's view of itself and of citizenship. The campaigns prior to the 2014 independence referendum – both 'Yes Scotland' and 'Better Together' – form the backdrop to this discussion.

Two years before the referendum, it was observed that battle lines were being drawn around the welfare state.[30] Mooney and Scott argue that the debate – particularly on the pro-independence side – was 'dominated' by 'issues of social welfare, social justice and the creation of a more equal Scotland'.[31] While the

[25] Greer and Mätzke, above n 22 at 9; see also McEwen, above n 23.

[26] J Curtice and R Ormston, 'Is Scotland more left-wing than England?' (Edinburgh: ScotCen Social Research, 2011) 1.

[27] J Curtice, 'Is Scotland more egalitarian than England?' (ScotCen, 29 October 2020). Available at: www.scotcen.org.uk/blog/is-scotland-more-egalitarian-than-england.

[28] J Yarde and R Wishart, 'An unequal Union? Attitudes towards social inequality in England and Scotland' (London: NatCen Social Research, 2020).

[29] N Pearce and E Taylor, 'Government spending and welfare: changing attitudes towards the role of the state' in A Park, C Bryson, E Clery, J Curtice and M Phillips (eds), *British Social Attitudes 30* (London: NatCen Social Research, 2013); ScotCen Social Research, 'Do you agree or disagree that Government should redistribute income from better-off to less well off?' in *What Scotland Thinks: Non-partisan Information on Attitudes to How Scotland Should be Governed* (Edinburgh: ScotCen Social Research, 2013). Available at: http://whatscotlandthinks.org/questions/do-you-agree-or-disagree-that-government-should-redistribute-income-from-better#line; J Curtice, 'Is it really all just about economics? Issues of nationhood and welfare' (Edinburgh: ScotCen Social Research, 2013); YouGov, 'YouGov/Sunday Times survey results' (London: YouGov, 2013).

[30] Law and Mooney above n 24 at 162.

[31] G Mooney and G Scott, 'The 2014 Scottish independence debate: questions of social welfare and social justice' (2015) 23(1) *Journal of Poverty and Social Justice* 5, 5; see also N McEwen, 'Welfare: contesting communities of solidarity' in M Keating (ed), *Debating Scotland: Issues of Independence and Union in the 2014 Referendum* (Oxford: Oxford University Press, 2017).

referendum failed to secure independence, it succeeded in 'push[ing] an alternate vision of welfare to that which had come to dominate the UK-level discourse'.[32] The UK-wide referendum on EU membership allowed Scottish elites to reinforce the message that Scotland lives by different values – more internationalist, more respectful of human rights, more open and welcoming to immigrants – than the UK as a whole.[33] A former chair of the Scottish Human Rights Commission observes that through the two referenda 'Scotland has presented its credentials … what its outlook is and what kind of country it wants to become'.[34] This performance of the latest version of the 'Scottish myth' may have affected citizens' perception of what it is to be Scottish.

In both waves, research participants acknowledged the social justice debate as an important issue in the independence referendum. The expectation that 'Scotland could be a fairer country' (W1I23, Scotland politician, nationalist) was regarded as a significant driver of the 'yes' vote. Although one unionist claimed nationalists' pronouncements on the welfare state lacked substance – 'it wasn't an intellectually robust argument … the yes campaign never said what the Scottish welfare system would be … they just said they didn't like the UK system' (W1I20, Scotland politician, unionist) – for others this missed the point. While 'not many people would know the detail of the [2012] Act', the sense that the welfare state was under attack, and that this was not merely 'a Tory thing' but emblematic of 'where the UK's headed', could swing a certain type of voter in favour of independence (W1I25, Scotland politician, unionist). At the same time, Better Together was seen to have had some success with its own social rights-based message: 'Protect your pensions … the only way to do that is stay part of the UK' (W1I26, Scotland politician, unionist).

By 2020, interviewees could reflect on the impact of at least eight years' exposure to a pro-welfare discourse from the Scottish Government, Scottish Parliament, voluntary sector, both sides in the independence campaign and (in contrast to England)[35] much of the media. The existence of a distinctly Scottish narrative around social security, based on the principles in the Social Security (Scotland) Act 2018 and the slogan 'Dignity, fairness, respect' that appears on every Social Security Scotland publication, was undisputed. A minority of participants argued that this was government based on 'clichés' rather than a clear vision for how the new Scottish model should develop (W2I06, Scotland politician, unionist). Differences of opinion also remained as to how strongly Scottish society buys

[32] J Wiggan, 'Contesting the austerity and "welfare reform" narrative of the UK Government: forging a social democratic imaginary in Scotland' (2017) *International Journal of Sociology and Social Policy* 37(11–12) 639, 640.

[33] M Simpson, 'Brexit and devolved social security in Scotland: a tale of two referenda' 25(1) (2018) *Journal of Social Security Law* 56.

[34] R Johnston and A Miller, 'Interview with Professor Alan Miller' (2016) 75 *Scottish Human Rights Journal* 2, 3.

[35] See T Jensen and I Tyler, '"Benefits broods": the cultural and political crafting of anti-welfare commonsense' (2015) 35(4) *Critical Social Policy* 470.

into this narrative – one interviewee acknowledged that there might be 'a version of the Scotland that we would like to be versus actual reality' (W2I11, Scotland official). On balance, though, interviewees had become more confident in asserting that there is 'a societal difference' in what people want from a welfare state, including but not limited to social security (W2I14, Scotland politician, nationalist), a 'kind of a feeling out there in the streets and the press that it is genuinely a different approach' (W2I05, Scotland politician, nationalist), and that this is to be welcomed. Even the Scottish National Party's political opponents gave some credit for this to the government, epitomised by an interviewee who warned in wave one: 'you shouldn't be blind to the fact that people in Scotland … can have quite reactionary and negative attitudes to welfare' (W1I25, Scotland politician, unionist). Five years later, the same interviewee still remembered 'the Scotland I was brought up in [as] quite a narrow-minded, bigoted place' and cautioned that such attitudes are slow to change – but nonetheless felt change was afoot:

> We are on a journey and I actually think the more we say it, the more we become it, just like that American, fake it until you make it … We are dragging ourselves into the 21st century, but it is a difficult process … It has been great to have the SNP in particular portray … Scotland in the terms they do as a progressive, left-of-centre Scotland … Most nationalist forces around the world are … quite culturally reactionary. So, to have them very explicitly not is a huge boon to Scotland, and it has definitely helped (W2I15, Scotland politician, unionist).

Others had similar views about the power of political leadership, but spread the credit more widely:

> When all parties … even the Tories up here just don't seem to use the same language as the Tories down south about social security – you start to win that argument and then you start to convince people. We probably view it in a much more positive way than the rest of society. But I think it is up to us to keep making the case and society is and will continue to catch up with that view (W2I13, Scotland politician, unionist).

Conservative buy-in was highlighted by several interviewees as a sign of the social democratic (political) majority's success in articulating a particular vision for the welfare state.

The literature on devolved social citizenships in Northern Ireland is sparser, but unanimous that the country is unpromising ground for the emergence of a vision capable of uniting a fragmented polity and divided society. Greer observes:

> Northern Irish politics are not about public policy and it shows … In each of the [unionist and nationalist] big-party systems the politics are essentially about best, and most of the time most vociferously, representing the group against the other. In none is policy performance a major issue. Politicians might like making policy, and … some of them do, but that is not what elected them, because the logic of enemies routinely trumps policy preferences in Northern Irish elections.[36]

[36] SL Greer, 'The territorial bases of health policymaking in the UK after devolution' (2005) 15(4) *Regional and Federal Studies* 501, 510.

Research evidence on what the public thinks about or wants from the welfare state is limited. The Northern Ireland Life and Times Survey last included questions on 'welfare reform' in 2000. More recent data from the Department for Communities Omnibus survey show that in 2017, 51 per cent of respondents considered the social security system to be ineffective because benefits paid more than employment, 46 per cent because people were permitted to 'avoid work' and 43 per cent because there was a 'culture of not working'. Thirty-eight per cent of respondents said out-of-work benefits were too high, a significantly lower proportion than in either Great Britain in 2012 or Scotland in 2013. There was limited confidence in disability benefits, but for divergent reasons: 45 per cent of respondents agreed that 'too many people who don't need support are receiving it', while 40 per cent believed 'some people who need support don't get it'.[37] Compared to Scotland, the fieldwork saw limited discussion of what the Northern Ireland population might want from its welfare state, but some politicians argued that the small, close-knit nature of society acts as a bulwark against the sort of 'anti-welfare commonsense' that many interviewees felt had taken root in England, as people are less removed from the voices and experiences of those in poverty:[38]

> We're sociable beings and we're talkers … We're still small enough that some of our families have been impacted by long-term unemployment and poverty and struggling with mental health … it's almost like, "Well, but for the grace of god go I" … So you've got that sense of collegiality (W2I31, Northern Ireland politician, nationalist).

Where an elite vision is concerned, politicians acknowledged that 'we've a bad track record of agreement' (W1I01, Northern Ireland politician, unionist). Officials felt the issue was more fundamental than lack of agreement, rather that politicians had not given significant thought to social security and had not been required to pre-2012. In wave one there was some belief that the Welfare Reform Act 2012 had forced Northern Ireland's politicians to ask themselves 'what sort of a society do we actually want [and] how do we see social welfare actually supporting the type of society we want?' (W1I03, Northern Ireland official). By wave two – which followed three years with no Assembly sittings or Executive – such optimism was in short supply. While complimentary about certain individuals, officials were scathing about the level of interest in and knowledge about social security among the political class as a whole. This was the more remarkable as Northern Ireland officials had been relatively guarded in their comments in wave one, in comparison to their Scottish counterparts. One interviewee contrasted the reactive Northern Ireland discourse on social security, with a focus on 'just keeping the mitigations going [without] any discussion really around what social

[37] A Milligan and J Hughes, *Attitudes to Social Welfare and Reform* (Belfast: Department for Communities, 2018).

[38] See R Patrick, 'Unsettling the anti-welfare commonsense: the potential in participatory research with people living in poverty' (2020) 49(2) *Journal of Social Policy* 251.

security in Northern Ireland is really about and what they're trying to do with it', with Scotland's clarity of vision:

> Scottish Nats have got a very clear view about what they want and the idea of a 'Fairer Scotland' … a political party which has debated the idea around social welfare and which is creating forums for discussion around social welfare and what the role of social security in Scotland should be. There's none of that in Northern Ireland … even within the voluntary and community sector it's all about, 'No, no, it's about simply money. It's about giving people money in their pockets'. There's actually little discussion really about what is that we want and the Executive doesn't really have a set of values that it believes should be permeating through its policies (W2I25, Northern Ireland official).

None of this is to say that there are no politicians in Northern Ireland who think deeply about or take strong ideological positions on social security – some clearly do. Where it differs from Scotland is in the absence of a view of social citizenship capable of uniting the greater part of the polity, even in some cases a coherent vision within a single party. While nationalist parties are fairly consistently left of centre, unionist and neutral politicians (including interviewees from the same party) shared wildly divergent views on what the objectives of social security ought to be and on the deservingness of claimants. This has not prevented the Executive agreeing on the need to mitigate aspects of post-2010 UK governments' reform agenda on the basis of the socio-economic considerations above, but represents a serious barrier to taking the next step and thinking about what a Northern Irish social citizenship might look like.

Institutional Factors

Institutional factors play a more complex role in shaping devolved views of social citizenship. Some determine the ability of the devolved countries to make distinctive provision for citizens' welfare. Others have potential to push social security policy, or policy preferences, in a particular direction – or to constrain divergence. A related consideration concerns the extent to which, in so far as the devolved countries have particular needs and preferences, these carry weight in UK-level deliberations. For Béland and Lecours, the extent of regional autonomy, how clearly each tier of government's role is demarcated (factors grounded in the devolution settlement), how devolved legislative and executive institutions work and the degree of integration or separation between regional and national party systems (which form the political context) all play a role.[39] To this list may be added the role of guiding principles in either the constitutional or devolved legislation.

[39] Béland and Lecours, above n 1.

The Devolution Settlement

The most straightforward institutional factor in determining whether the legal status of social citizenship can take different form at devolved level is the devolution of welfare state competences. Lack of devolved competence does not, however, preclude the emergence of a distinctive normative vision. The constitutional settlement devolves responsibility for most arms of the welfare state to Scotland, Northern Ireland and Wales, but historically preserved central dominance in social security. Today, social security increasingly inhabits what one interviewee referred to as a 'shared space' (W2I07, Scotland politician, nationalist). In Scotland, receipt of a reserved benefit, particularly universal credit or one of its predecessor benefits, allows access to various devolved benefits. Conversely, Scottish disability assistance will give claimants access to various awards in the UK system. The need to preserve this passporting function limits the scope for divergence, at least initially.[40] Northern Ireland may, in principle, have autonomy in most areas of social security, but in practice this is constrained by the habit of parity, the associated funding model and reliance on DWP computer systems. Consequently, critical political rhetoric directed at the UK Government can obscure extensive cooperation behind the scenes and broad conformity with the UK approach.

This raises the question of the extent to which UK policymakers are aware and take account of the needs and preferences of the devolved countries in this 'shared space'. From one perspective, the primacy of the UK Government in social security means policy development is inherently unresponsive to the needs and preferences of countries outside England:

> I've made a series of recommendations … to the UK Government. You would be lucky to get a reply. You'd be even luckier to get to appear in front of the [Work and Pensions] Committee. It's unaccountable to the people that are responsible to the Scottish people through the Scottish Parliament (W2I07, Scotland politician, nationalist).

Not all Scottish interviewees felt Scotland's needs were sufficiently distinctive for this to matter, and it is worth considering whether the UK Government is inherently unaccountable to the Scottish electorate given that the last Labour Government held 41 of Scotland's 59 parliamentary constituencies. The current party of government at UK level holds only six Scottish seats, but this does not preclude the future reconvergence of Scottish and UK voters' preferences. Opinions in Northern Ireland differed as to whether UK Ministers acknowledged the different needs of the devolved countries. One interviewee suggested that the Executive had made some progress with its 'strategy … to convince [Minister for Welfare Reform David] Freud … that this place was so different … that you

[40] Scottish Government, *Disability Assistance in Scotland: Consultation* (Edinburgh: Scottish Government, 2019).

couldn't go in the direction that Freud and the rest of them were arguing'. However, this did not move the more 'dogmatic' Secretary of State, Iain Duncan Smith (W2I04, Northern Ireland politician, nationalist). Officials who had been involved in talks with the Department for Work and Pensions about divergence in the Northern Ireland legislation after 2012 painted a picture of greater willingness to accommodate. One recalled:

> They were very nervous about what we were doing here … and how they were going to present that in Parliament. So therefore there was a bit of management that needed to be done … but effectively it went OK. It didn't cause us any problems. It also then allowed us to get into the DWP machine and get in with the techies and get in with the policymakers in terms of understanding what they were doing and what we were doing and then being able to work that through (W2I25, Northern Ireland official).

The Political Context

The mainstream of Scottish politics is composed of the three main UK parties (Conservative and Unionist, Labour and Liberal Democrat), plus two Scotland-based parties – the currently dominant Scottish National Party and the Scottish Greens. These five parties hold all seats in the current Scottish Parliament; Alba, the nationalist party founded in 2021, holds two seats in the UK Parliament. Northern Ireland's party system is divorced from that in Great Britain, with the current Assembly composed of the Democratic Unionist Party, Sinn Féin, Social Democratic and Labour Party, Ulster Unionist Party, Alliance Party, Green Party, Traditional Unionist Voice and People Before Profit.[41] According to Béland and Lecours's thesis, the separateness of its party system should make Northern Ireland the more fertile ground for the emergence of a substate social citizenship. In practice, it is Scotland that shows a more developed ideology of social citizenship and may be diverging more extensively from the UK social security system.

Greer's claim about the irrelevance of policy to electoral politics in Northern Ireland aside, an explanation can be found in the country's fragmented party system, reinforced by how the devolved institutions function. Devolved legislatures use proportional electoral systems under which an absolute majority of seats is hard to obtain.[42] However, in Scotland a combination of electoral arithmetic and the way a Government is formed – Ministers must simply secure the confidence

[41] More or less formal links exist or have existed between the Conservatives and UUP, Labour and the SDLP, the Liberal Democrats and Alliance Party and between the Green Party in Northern Ireland and other European Green Parties.

[42] Elections to the Scottish Parliament use an additional member system based on single-member constituencies and multi-member regions elected on the basis of party lists. Those to the Northern Ireland Assembly use the single transferable vote system in five-member constituencies. Scotland Act 1998 c 46 ss 5–8; Northern Ireland Act 1998 c 47 ss 33–34.

of a majority of MSPs[43] – has always allowed the formation of an ideologically-coherent, one- or two-party, social democratic administration. A strong, relatively united executive can articulate a vision for social citizenship and put this into practice to the extent that devolved competences allow. Further, unanimous parliamentary support for key legislative measures like the Child Poverty (Scotland) Act 2017, Social Security (Scotland) Act 2018 and UNCRC (Incorporation) (Scotland) Bill indicates 'a pretty strong feeling of unity … across all parties' on social rights (W2I07, Scotland politician, nationalist).

Northern Ireland's institutional arrangements favour inertia over innovation. Ministerial positions are allocated on a proportional basis to as many parties as hold sufficient Assembly seats[44] – currently five, spanning unionist, nationalist and neutral constitutional positions and conservative, liberal and social democratic ideological outlooks. A politically disunited Executive struggles to reach a shared position on any matter. Often, the consensus necessary for innovation in social policy can only be built around a 'lowest common denominator' based on shared conservative social values and protection of the 'unambiguously deserving poor'.[45] Direct rule from Westminster (1974–1998) is claimed to have ingrained in the Northern Ireland Civil Service a habit of 'administer[ing] rather than chang[ing] the system' across policy areas,[46] with policy evolving in line with the UK Government or not at all. In social security, the practice of parity with Great Britain means this habit has been cultivated since 1926 rather than 1974. This tendency was reflected in the first wave of fieldwork, in which Northern Ireland officials were the strongest proponents of a shared UK approach to social security and some politicians criticised officials for 'trying to sell welfare reform' (W1I04, Northern Ireland politician, nationalist). Officials did not necessarily agree that they were too invested in replicating UK Government policy: 'The lack of imagination of civil servants? Political comment. But have civil servants ever been asked by their Ministerial masters to come up with something different?' (W1I02, Northern Ireland official). By wave two, officials had become keener to stress the ways in which social security *has* operated differently in Northern Ireland and the need to consider the desirability and feasibility of further divergence, while remaining cautious in comparison to their Scottish counterparts' enthusiasm for their project to develop an alternative approach.

> There's no sense having devolution if Ministers are basically just rubber stamping what comes across … We've all gradually grown in this together … There's a pragmatic issue around parity that people get, but we can tweak things and some of the mitigations are a really good example of that (W2I27, Northern Ireland official).

[43] Scotland Act 1998 c 46 ss 45, 47.

[44] The formula used is set out at Northern Ireland Act 1998 c 47 s 18; the positions of First Minister and Deputy First Minister are separately allocated to the nominee of the largest party representing each of the two largest community designations (of unionist, nationalist or 'other') – s 16A.

[45] AM Gray and D Birrell, 'Coalition government in Northern Ireland: social policy and the lowest common denominator thesis' (2012) 11(1) *Social Policy and Society* 15.

[46] Greer, above n 36 at 511.

> I have completely drank the Kool-Aid, I feel extremely invested in what … the Scottish Government is trying to do … It's a game changer … what potentially we're going to get out of the other side of that is just going to be wonderful (W2I22, Scotland official).

Assembly procedure presents a further institutional barrier to innovation in Northern Ireland. The petition of concern enables 30 members to secure a cross-community voting requirement on any motion, meaning that in practice it is unlikely to be adopted.[47] In the period 1998–2017 (after which the Assembly did not meet for three years), more petitions of concern were tabled in relation to social security than any other matter – 49 out of 159. The DUP used the procedure to block 45 amendments to the Welfare Reform Bill in 2015, which would have increased divergence from the Welfare Reform Act 2012. A subsequent petition signed by Sinn Féin, SDLP and Green MLAs prevented the Bill from passing its final stage.[48] The petition makes it relatively easy for a large party to block changes it opposes, but harder to introduce distinctive measures unless it is clear they will enjoy support across the chamber. The overall effect was not lost on Scottish interviewees: 'In dealing with colleagues in Northern Ireland you say, "What's your position?" "We don't have one and we're not going to have one because there's just no chance of anything being agreed"' (W2I10, Scotland official).

Guiding Principles

The final group of institutional factors consists of aspects of the wider legislative context that may help steer the development of devolved social security policy. The convention of parity in social security between Northern Ireland and Great Britain is an example (see Chapter 3). The human rights-related legislation to which the devolved legislatures and executives are subject is a second (see Chapter 6). Several others are briefly highlighted here.

The Northern Ireland Executive is subject to a unique duty to 'adopt a strategy setting out how it proposes to tackle poverty, social exclusion and patterns of deprivation based on objective need'.[49] Thus far the only concrete outworking of this provision has been a successful judicial review arguing that the Executive had failed to comply,[50] but a consultation on a proposed strategy was due to begin as this book was being completed. Whether the strategy has anything clear to say about social security remains to be seen, but the required focus on poverty, social exclusion and deprivation forms part of the social citizenship landscape in Northern Ireland. This is reinforced by being the only country still required by UK

[47] Northern Ireland Act 1998 c 47 s 42; Northern Ireland Assembly, *Standing orders* (Belfast: NI Assembly, 2020).

[48] Thanks to Leah Rea for this analysis.

[49] Northern Ireland Act 1998 c 47 s 28E.

[50] *The Committee on the Administration of Justice and Brian Gormally's application* [2015] NIQB 59.

legislation to publish a strategy 'for the purpose of ensuring as far as possible that children … do not experience socio-economic disadvantage'.[51]

The Scottish Parliament has approved various measures with potential to shape the future development of social security. The guiding principles and requirement for the creation of a social security charter in the Social Security (Scotland) Act 2018 are of particular importance. The Child Poverty (Scotland) Act 2017 reinstates statutory targets for the near-elimination of child poverty in Scotland following the repeal of UK-wide targets in 2016.[52] These have influenced some of the earliest forms of devolved social security assistance and may drive further interventions in the future.[53] This was followed by the introduction of the 'fairer Scotland duty', to which a range of public authorities are subject.[54] This duty, included in the Equality Act 2010 but never given effect in England,[55] requires authorities to 'have due regard to the desirability of exercising [strategic functions] in a way that is designed to reduce the inequalities of outcome which result from socio-economic disadvantage'.[56]

Besides imposing specific requirements on the Scottish Government that may influence future social security policy decisions, these pieces of legislation can be understood as an assertion of Scotland's ideological otherness from recent UK governments. The Parliament has unanimously affirmed that Scotland does not buy into the UK-level shift away from understanding poverty in terms of income, is more concerned with inequalities of outcome and is committed to strengthening protection of human rights, including social and economic rights, in contrast to a possible retreat at UK level.[57] Northern Ireland has been less proactive and slow to deliver even its constitutionally required strategy but possible drivers of a different approach exist nonetheless.

Conclusion

Socio-economic, ideological and institutional factors may each contribute to the development of a devolved vision for social citizenship and to decisions on how

[51] Life Chances Act 2010 c 9 s 12.

[52] Welfare Reform and Work Act 2016 c 7 ss 5–7.

[53] Scottish Government, *Every Child, Every Chance: The Tackling Child Poverty Delivery Plan 2018–2022* (Edinburgh: Scottish Government, 2018); C Birt and B Milne, 'Turning the tide on child poverty in Scotland' (York: JRF, 2021).

[54] Equality Act 2010 (Authorities Subject to the Socio-economic Inequality Duty) (Scotland) Regulations 2018 SSI No 101; Scottish Government, *The Fairer Scotland Duty: Interim Guidance for Public Bodies* (Edinburgh: Scottish Government, 2018).

[55] The duty was subsequently brought into force in Wales – see Equality Act 2010 (Authorities Subject to a Duty Regarding Socio-economic Inequalities) (Wales) Regulations 2021 SI No 295 (W72) – and an early day motion before Parliament calls for England to follow suit – EDM 591 Commencement and enforcement of the socio-economic duty.

[56] Equality Act 2010 c 15 s 1.

[57] Simpson, above n 33.

aspects of the devolved welfare state should work in practice. The three do not exist in isolation but interact to inform the thinking of devolved elites. In combination, the socio-economic, ideological and party-political factors can shape the emergence of a view of social citizenship and a set of social security preferences that differ to those of the UK elite. These and the legislative principles can bring about the emergence of distinctive approaches to social security, to the extent that the devolution settlement allows. If the devolution settlement (in law or political reality) limits the ability to diverge where divergence is desired, and there is seen to be insufficient opportunity to mould UK approaches in ways that meet the needs and preferences of the devolved country, then the constitutional settlement may come under pressure. Both Scotland and Northern Ireland have attempted to 'put the brakes on' UK-level 'austerity politics' since 2012 (W2I15, Scotland politician, unionist), but Scotland has shown greater desire to develop a distinctive normative vision for social citizenship and the welfare state.

8

Social Citizenship and the Constitutional Future of the UK: Welfare Unionism, Nationalism and Regionalism

Introduction

The drive for autonomy in social security since 2010 follows important developments in the electoral and constitutional politics of Scotland and Northern Ireland in 2007. The Scottish National Party established itself as the dominant party in

Scotland, at the expense of the unionist Labour party, while Sinn Féin emerged as the leading voice of Irish nationalism in Northern Ireland, at the expense of the more 'moderate' Social Democratic and Labour Party. The Scottish independence referendum of 2014 reflected the rise of political nationalism in Scotland and prompted the partial devolution of social security. Even before these developments, social policy divergence at devolved level could be interpreted as a manifestation of 'welfare nationalism', a desire for the region to take on the trappings of nationhood and to exploit real or perceived ideological differences to advocate more devolution or independence:

> Nationalist leaders always argue that the bonds between the members of their national community supersede the bonds between citizens of the central state. As such, they are likely to seek to make the community of social justice and redistribution congruent with their national community. This typically results in pressures to decentralize social policy.[1]

This chapter finds that it is too simplistic to associate pressure for Scotland and Northern Ireland to play a greater, and distinctive, role in ensuring citizens' economic welfare solely with the sort of welfare nationalism outlined by Béland and Lecours above. Two sections explore the question of what 'nation' the people of Scotland and Northern Ireland belong to and the contrasting ways in which national identities are constructed and performed. The third examines welfare unionist, nationalist and regionalist views of social citizenship, drawing on the views expressed by Scottish and Northern Irish elites in the fieldwork. The following section highlights that the proper role of devolved institutions in ensuring citizens' economic welfare is likely to remain contested.

Which Nation?

Béland and Lecours suggest:

> A nation is animated not only by a sense of togetherness but also by a belief in a common destiny supported by an overarching identity. Members of a nation are typically seen to exhibit a solidarity that overwhelms connections with outsiders and renders secondary internal cleavages of class and gender.[2]

In the UK, it is unclear which nation is bound by this 'sense of togetherness'. Scotland is widely acknowledged to have an overarching identity and (at least at

[1] D Béland and A Lecours, 'Does nationalism trigger welfare-state disintegration? Social policy and territorial mobilization in Belgium and Canada' (2010) 28(3) *Environment and Planning C: Government and Policy* 420, 430.

[2] D Béland and A Lecours, *Nationalism and Social Policy: The Politics of Territorial Solidarity* (Oxford: Oxford University Press, 2010) 15.

the level of its political leadership) some vision for a 'common destiny' based on a more social democratic politics (see Chapter 7 and below). Whether the sense of solidarity that Scots feel towards Scots trumps class politics is harder to say, since it is difficult to separate class from nationalism in the progressive rhetoric. For Béland and Lecours, the Scottish and British identities have been compatible for much of the period since the Act of Union 1707. McEwen argues that this is because Britishness has been a 'plurinational' identity; others point out that the UK or English elite was responsible for popularising or inventing various well-known symbols of Scottishness.[3] However, the compatibility of the two identities may have lessened since 2010.[4]

The position differs in Northern Ireland, where the competing national identities have historically been Irish and British. Adherence to a Northern Irish identity has grown in recent decades and is associated with stronger support for devolution than the alternatives (direct rule from Westminster or unification with the Republic of Ireland).[5] Unionism uses the symbols of Britishness and, for the most part, values the Union, but can sometimes appear to be a form of Ulster nationalism with a decidedly 'conditional loyalty' to the UK.[6] While no mainstream political movement has ever advocated independence for Northern Ireland,[7] it is fair to say that there is no consensus about whether the citizen's loyalty should lie with the UK, Ireland or Northern Ireland. In the 2011 Census, nine per cent of respondents ascribed to at least two of the British, Irish and Northern Irish identities.[8] In a divided, segregated and sometimes conflicted society, it would be ambitious to claim that Northern Ireland displays a nation's 'overarching identity', 'solidarity' and 'belief in a common destiny'. The dominance of identity politics is

[3] N McEwen 'Brexit and Scotland: between two Unions' (2018) 13(1) *British Politics* 65, 65; H Trevor-Roper, 'The invention of tradition: the Highland tradition of Scotland', E Hobsbawm and T Ranger, *The Invention of Tradition* (Cambridge: Cambridge University Press, 2012).

[4] A Scholes, 'The changing role of identity and values in Scotland's politics' (What Scotland Thinks, 28 April 2021). Available at: https://whatscotlandthinks.org/2021/04/the-changing-role-of-identity-and-values-in-scotlands-politics/.

[5] J Garry and K McNicholl, 'Understanding the "Northern Irish" identity' (Knowledge Exchange Seminar Series, NI Assembly, Belfast, 13 May 2015). Available at: www.niassembly.gov.uk/globalassets/documents/raise/knowledge_exchange/briefing_papers/series4/northern_ireland_identity_garry_mcnicholl_policy_document.pdf; J Tonge and R Gomez, 'Shared identity and the end of conflict? How far has a common sense of 'Northern Irishness' replaced British or Irish allegiances since the 1998 Good Friday Agreement?' (2015) 30(2) *Irish Political Studies* 276.

[6] A Aughey, 'Unionism and self-determination', PJ Roche and B Barton (eds), *The Northern Ireland Question: Myth and Reality* (Aldershot: Avebury, 1991) 23; J Todd, 'Two traditions in unionist political culture' (1987) 2(1) *Irish Political Studies* 1.

[7] K McNicholl, C Stevenson and J Garry, 'How the "Northern Irish" national identity is understood and used by young people and politicians' (2019) 40(3) *Political Psychology* 487; loyalist flirtation with secessionism is discussed in A Aughey and C McIlheney, 'The Ulster Defence Association: paramilitaries and politics' (1981) 2(2) *Journal of Conflict Studies* 32.

[8] R Russell, 'Census 2011: key statistics at Northern Ireland and LGD level' (NIAR005-13, Belfast: NI Assembly, 2013).

widely – although not universally – regarded as an obstacle to the development of class politics, particularly on the unionist side.[9]

National Identity as Ideological Identity

A welfare state can act as the glue that holds a state and a citizenry together and an important part of how a state (or its political elite) defines itself. The UK has no equivalent to Germany's constitutional 'social state' principle,[10] but the post-Second World War welfare settlement has been portrayed as equally fundamental to the national self-image.[11] However, if the post-war UK was by consensus a social state, by the 1980s it was far from clear that its political leaders viewed this as a positive. While stressing that the extent to which the Conservative era of 1979 to 1997 brought about a 'rolling back' of the welfare state is contested, McEwen argues that the New Right's 'impact upon political debate and on the prevailing conceptions of Britishness was nevertheless profound'. Notably, 'rather than drawing upon the achievements of the postwar welfare state in promoting Britishness, the post-war consensus and the "nanny state" it was accused of creating were regarded as symbols and causes of British decline'.[12] Perceived 'contract-breaking at the centre' represented an opportunity for those at the periphery to assert their continued adherence to the earlier, social democratic vision.[13] Scotland in particular had a ready-made national and political community that could mobilise behind devolution, and increasingly independence, in the name of defending the welfare state.[14] Despite the 'devolution paradox', which holds that citizens are more supportive of regional government in the abstract than of regional variation in public services, it was all but inevitable that a devolved legislature whose very existence reflected discontent at the central government's social policy agenda would oversee some divergence.[15]

Trevor-Roper states that 'when a society renounces politics, it can find other ways of expressing its identity'.[16] Hence, following Scotland's voluntary submission to union with England and Wales in 1707, the defining traits of 'Scottishness'

[9] See A Edwards, *A History of the Northern Ireland Labour Party: Democratic Socialism and Sectarianism* (Manchester: Manchester University Press, 2009).

[10] Grundgesetz für die Bundesrepublik Deutschland, art 20.

[11] N McEwen, 'State welfare nationalism: the territorial impact of welfare state development in Scotland' (2002) 12(1) *Regional and Federal Studies* 66; C Jeffery, 'Devolution and social citizenship: which society, whose citizenship?', SL Greer (ed), *Territory, Democracy and Justice: Regionalism and Federalism in Western Democracies* (Basingstoke: Palgrave Macmillan, 2006); MS Leith, 'The view from above: Scottish national identity as an elite concept' (2012) 14(1) *National Identities* 39.

[12] McEwen, above n 11 at 75.

[13] Jeffery, above n 11 at 83.

[14] Ibid, at 84.

[15] A Henderson, C Jeffery, D Wincott and R Wyn Jones, 'Reflections on the "devolution paradox": a comparative examination of multilevel citizenship' (2013) 47(3) *Regional and Federal Studies* 303.

[16] H Trevor-Roper, *The Invention of Scotland: Myth and History* (New Haven: Yale University Press, 2008).

were suddenly found in the hitherto marginalised Gaelic, Highland culture. On 12 May 1999, with the words 'the Scottish Parliament, which adjourned on 25 March 1707, is hereby reconvened',[17] Winnie Ewing MSP confirmed Scotland's re-engagement with politics. However, Scotland had begun to define itself in political terms again some time before legislative devolution.[18] Béland and Lecours are not alone in arguing that the metamorphosis of a long-established Scottish national identity into a genuine nationalist movement demanding devolution 'was partly animated by the desire to … enact social legislation distinct from England's then Thatcherite policies'.[19] As much as Thatcher argued that 'Tory values are in tune with everything that is finest in the Scottish character', it is widely accepted that 'the [Conservative] government's programme met with greater resistance in Scotland' than in England.[20] Opposition parties may have had a tactical interest in equating Scottishness with 'belief in social justice and egalitarianism', but this could only succeed if there were some truth to the claim that Scotland was politically to the left of England.[21]

In Scotland today, 'the nation is partly defined in terms of social policy preferences'.[22] The ideological positioning discussed in Chapter 7 is presented as an integral feature of Scottishness. As some authors argue that the construction of Scotland as a more social democratic polity reflects elite rather than popular views, Leith suggests that this version of the Scottish national identity is also an elite rather than a popular conception.[23] Greer seems to make a similar point when he hypothesises that the electoral decline of the Conservative party in the second half of the twentieth century had less to do with its place on the left-right political spectrum than its failure to clear the 'obligatory threshold of national identity'.[24] If social democracy *is* the essence of Scottish national identity, Greer is wrong to draw a distinction between the two. On the other hand, if the Conservatives' partial revival to the position of Scotland's second party since the referenda on independence (2014) and withdrawal from the EU (2016) has been based on a successful repositioning as the party representing the *British* identity and nation against calls for a re-run of either referendum, rather than any particular social policy agenda, Greer's thesis may be reinforced.[25]

[17] W Ewing, SP deb 12 May 1999, vol 1 no 1 col 5.

[18] McEwen argues that the formation of the Scottish Office in 1885 marks the true re-establishment of a 'distinctively Scottish political arena' – above n 11 at 71.

[19] Béland and Lecours, above n 2 at 9.

[20] McEwen, above n 11 at 76.

[21] Ibid, at 77.

[22] D Béland and A Lecours, 'The politics of territorial solidarity: nationalism and social policy reform in Canada, the United Kingdom and Belgium' (2005) 38(6) *Comparative Political Studies* 676, 677.

[23] Leith, above n 11.

[24] SL Greer, 'The territorial bases of health policymaking in the UK after devolution' (2005) 15(4) *Regional and Federal Studies* 501, 505; see also D Seawright, 'The Scottish Conservative and Unionist Party: "the lesser spotted Tory"?' in G Hassan and C Warhurst (eds), *Tomorrow's Scotland* (London: Lawrence and Wishart, 2002).

[25] J Curtice, 'The three characteristics of the Scottish Conservative revival' (What Scotland Thinks, 1 October 2017). Available at: https://whatscotlandthinks.org/2017/10/the-three-characteristics-of-

Greer's observation that 'Northern Irish politics are not about public policy' has been noted in Chapter 7.[26] In keeping with this analysis, the Northern Ireland political spectrum is conventionally drawn, not from left to right, but from republican/nationalist to unionist/loyalist. If Scottish national identity is constructed by some as an ideological identity then, in Northern Ireland, the dominant ideological positions are strongly based on national (and to some extent religious) identity. Nationalists and republicans tend to identify as Irish and as members of a 'Catholic' community, even if they do not practice the religion. Unionists and loyalists tend to identify as British, although some might subscribe to an Ulster identity, and as members of a 'Protestant' community, even if they do not practice the religion. The Northern Irish identity is chiefly associated with the middle of the political spectrum, which purports to be neutral on Northern Ireland's constitutional future.[27] Nonetheless, Northern Ireland's clash of nationalisms cannot be divorced from questions about social rights and social justice. The armed conflict that broke out in the late 1960s emerged in large measure from discontent about systemic discrimination against the minority Catholic/Irish community in their enjoyment of political rights (gerrymandering of electoral boundaries and extra votes for largely Protestant business owners) and social rights (discrimination in employment and the allocation of social housing).[28] The allocation of social goods continues to be contested at times,[29] but social citizenship is not at the heart of the national debate in the same way as in Scotland.

Béland and Lecours offer a possible explanation for the differences between Scottish and Northern Irish identity politics. Only when demands for cultural recognition have been met, they argue, can nationalisms afford to become more inclusive and focus on social policy, rather than cultural identity, as a tool for nation building.[30] There is no struggle over Scottish cultural identity, which is embraced by unionist and nationalist, left and right. Nor have 'modern Scottish nationalists … sought to deny the British component of Scotland's social make-up'.[31] Northern Ireland remains embroiled in the cultural struggle, as recent or ongoing disputes over parading, flag-flying and language rights attest.[32]

the-scottish-conservative-revival/; J Curtice, 'Scottish election 2021: how the SNP was denied a majority by tactical voting' (Scotsman, 10 May 2021). Available at: www.scotsman.com/news/opinion/columnists/scottish-election-2021-how-the-snp-was-denied-a-majority-by-tactical-voting-professor-john-curtice-3230002.

[26] Greer, above n 24 at 510.

[27] Garry and McNicholl, above n 5; Tonge and Gomez, above n 5; McNicholl and others, above n 7.

[28] J Whyte, 'How much discrimination was there under the unionist regime, 1921–68?' in T Gallagher and J O'Connell, *Contemporary Irish Studies* (Manchester: Manchester University Press, 1983); P Teague, 'Northern Ireland: the political economy of peace' (Belfast: Mitchell Institute for Global Peace, Security and Justice, 2016); see also Aughey, above n 6.

[29] L O'Dowd and M Komarova, 'Contesting territorial fixity? A case study of regeneration in Belfast' (2011) 48(10) *Urban Studies* 2013.

[30] Béland and Lecours, above n 2.

[31] M Keating and N McEwen, 'The Scottish independence debate', M Keating (ed), *Debating Scotland: Issues of Independence and Union in the 2014 Referendum* (Oxford: Oxford University Press, 2017) 18.

[32] K Hearty, 'The Great Awakening? The Belfast flag protests and Protestant/Unionist/Loyalist counter-memory in Northern Ireland' (2015) 30(2) *Irish Political Studies* 157; E DeYoung, 'Lest we

This has not stopped Northern Ireland debating, and at times taking a distinctive path on, questions of social policy. Nonetheless, the continued prominence of identity, constitutional and post-conflict politics impedes the prioritisation of other issues, hinders the development of a consensual view of social citizenship and undermines the stability of the devolved institutions, so that even if an agreed Northern Irish vision for social citizenship were achievable, the presence of a devolved legislature and executive to put it into practice could not be taken for granted.[33]

Welfare Unionism, Nationalism and Regionalism

The term 'welfare nationalism' is used in different ways in different contexts. It may attach to the nation state (or multinational state) or to a substate territory. Welfare unionism is a manifestation of nationalism, but for the avoidance of confusion in the UK context it is convenient to distinguish the two terms. In this book, welfare unionism represents 'a nationalist practice that reproduces the [multinational] state', roughly corresponding to 'social patriotism'.[34] Welfare nationalism is a nationalist practice whose ultimate aim may be to establish a substate territory as an independent state in its own right. Social patriotism and substate welfare nationalism may have similar objectives for the welfare state, but dispute whether these are best achieved by capturing the leadership of the state or through secession. Welfare regionalism represents a middle way, one that accepts (at least provisionally) the integrity of the state but argues that the needs or preferences of citizens in a specific territory demand a degree of welfare state autonomy. In 2010 Béland and Lecours would have regarded this as a nationalist position, arguing that the strength of 'mobilisation for political, institutional and/or constitutional change' by the 1980s meant virtually 'all Scottish politicians were nationalist'.[35] In the present context it is less convincing to depict support for devolution, but not independence, as 'nationalist'.

It is possible to make a connection between welfare unionism and Marshallian citizenship theory. Ruiz Jiménez and co-authors do not refer to Marshall, yet their conceptualisation of social patriotism seems based on the premise that reducing

forget: observations from Belfast's Twaddell Avenue' (2016) 25 *Streetnotes* 179; DA Dunleavy, 'Learning Irish amid controversy: how the Irish Language Act debate has impacted learners of Irish in Belfast' (2021) *Journal of Multilingual and Multicultural Development*. Latest articles available at: https://doi.org/10.1080/01434632.2020.1854272.

[33] C Coulter and P Shirlow, 'From the "long war" to the "long peace": introduction to the special edition' (2019) 43(1) *Capital and Class* 3.

[34] AM Ruiz Jiménez, D Romero Portillo and L Navarro Adoy, 'Social patriotism: populist glue for a multinational democracy' (2021) 23(2) *National Identities* 127, 130.

[35] Béland and Lecours, above n 2 at 95; McEwen, above n 3.

the 'skyscraper' of inequality to a 'bungalow' plays an important role in cementing the national community:[36]

> When the state guarantees social justice for the people living within its borders, this fosters a feeling of belonging to a single group of equals … By creating prosperous living conditions, the government creates attachment to the state.[37]

Ruiz Jiménez and others argue that, for a democratic state to be sustainable, its 'constituent groups' must agree on 'the need for and desirability of the collective'.[38] The welfare state binds citizens to that collective through the payment of taxes and the receipt of services and benefits, simultaneously lending legitimacy to the state by limiting inequality. As McEwen argues:

> In providing state welfare and employing the language of shared national identity and solidarity in so doing, the welfare state served a nation-building purpose, reinforcing identification with and attachment to the state as a nation. In multinational states … the development of the welfare state may have helped to promote solidarity across the state territory and integrate the citizens of sub-state nations within its boundaries.

Conversely, retrenchment may restrict 'the capacity of the state to promote a national unity built upon the solidarity of the welfare state', in turn 'diminish[ing] the continued appeal and security offered by national states vis-à-vis the uncertainty of enhanced sub-state autonomy'.[39]

The literature can portray 'welfare nationalism' as a rather instrumental, if not cynical, use of differing social conditions or preferences for the welfare state – real, exaggerated or fabricated – to push a constitutional agenda. As Ruiz Jiménez and others argue, substate leaders may strive to 'nurture dual (and compatible) political identities' or favour 'polarising identities as a first step to demanding political independence'.[40] This perspective downplays the fact that nationalisms adhering to established states can themselves be polarising forces, not least through their association with welfare chauvinism, the limitation of non-nationals' access to the welfare state.[41] This tendency can be observed in the 'welfare tourism' discourse that formed part of the backdrop to the UK's withdrawal from the European Union.[42]

[36] TH Marshall, 'Citizenship and social class' in TH Marshall and T Bottomore, *Citizenship and Social Class* (London: Pluto, 1992) 28.

[37] Ruiz Jiménez et al., above n 34 at 131.

[38] Ibid, at 128.

[39] McEwen, above n 11 at 66.

[40] Ruiz Jiménez et al., above n 34 at 128.

[41] S Keskinen, 'From welfare nationalism to welfare chauvinism: economic rhetoric, the welfare state and changing asylum policies in Finland' (2016) 36(3) *Critical Social Policy* 352; JH Jönsson and BH Kojan, 'Social justice beyond neoliberal welfare nationalism: challenges of increasing immigration to Sweden and Norway' (2017) 5(3) *Critical and Radical Social Work* 301; H Tange and J Kirsten, 'From Bologna to welfare nationalism: international higher education in Denmark, 2000–2020' (2021) 21(2) *Language and Intercultural Communication* 223.

[42] N Harris, 'Demagnetisation of social security and healthcare for migrants to the UK' (2016) 18(2) *European Journal of Social Security* 130; M Simpson, 'Brexit and devolved social security in Scotland: a tale of two referenda' (2018) 25(1) *Journal of Social Security Law* 56.

In Northern Ireland, the unionist elite in the first devolution era imported the emerging UK welfare state model wholesale, yet was implicated in compromising the economic and social (as well as political) rights of a large section of the native population who did not share its British identity and constitutional aspirations, as well as some of those who did.[43]

Elite welfare nationalism and unionism featured in the campaigns for and against Scottish independence prior to the 2014 referendum.[44] McEwen contends that a popular welfare nationalism – or 'welfare expectations' of the new Parliament – sat alongside cultural nationalism and a desire for self-determination as a key driver of the 'yes yes' vote in the preceding referendum on legislative devolution, despite the relative lack of emphasis on the welfare state in elite campaigning.[45] Devolution in Northern Ireland has not been driven by a public policy agenda in the same way, but in both 1921 and 1998 formed one plank of the UK's attempts to find a resolution to centuries of conflict on the island of Ireland. Restoring peace has been portrayed as a means of advancing economic and social rights by bringing prosperity,[46] but there is a less obvious link between a constitutional agenda and a social policy agenda.

In wave one of the fieldwork, unionist or nationalist political positions were strongly predictive of views on the desirability of a distinctive devolved approach to social security. A spectrum emerged, as shown in the table below, along which only a very small number of Scottish unionists and officials deviated from their group's overall positioning:

Table 8.1 Welfare unionism, regionalism and nationalism among welfare one participants (2014–2015)

Most supportive of parity	⟷				**Most supportive of divergence**
Northern Ireland officials; Northern Ireland politicians (neutral)	Scotland politicians (unionist)	Northern Ireland politicians (unionist)	Scotland officials	Northern Ireland politicians (nationalist)	Scotland politicians (nationalist)

[43] Teague, above n 28.

[44] G Mooney and G Scott, 'The 2014 Scottish independence debate: questions of social welfare and social justice' (2015) 21(3) *Journal of Poverty and Social Justice* 5.

[45] McEwen, above n 11 – the referendum on Scottish devolution consisted of two questions, the first concerning whether a Scottish Parliament should be established, the second whether it should have tax-varying powers. A majority voted 'yes' to each question.

[46] G Horgan, 'Devolution, direct rule and neo-liberal reconstruction in Northern Ireland' (2006) 26(3) *Critical Social Policy* 656.

Despite the close association between political unionism or nationalism and particular views on social security divergence, welfare unionism and nationalism were not badges any participant wished to wear, but criticisms to be pinned on one's opponents. This was particularly evident in Scotland. Here, nationalists portrayed unionist ideology as an obstacle to the creation of 'a fairer system' (W1I23, Scotland politician, nationalist), heedless of the fact that 'there's a whole host of areas where … social provision is not the same in different parts of the UK already' (W1I21, Scotland politician, nationalist). From the unionist point of view, 'although I'm sure [the SNP] do sympathise with better welfare benefits, they're always just an argument … to further independence' (W1I25, Scotland politician, unionist). In Northern Ireland, wave one saw a definite unionist–nationalist divide in terms of how radically participants thought the devolved social security system ought to depart from the tradition of parity with the UK system. Unionists might regard nationalist aspirations for divergence as 'naïve in the extreme' (W1I06, Northern Ireland politician, unionist). Nationalists could claim unionist caution reflected a 'cowering attitude' to confrontation with the UK Government (W1I15, Northern Ireland politician, nationalist). However, politicians tended to present themselves as committed devolutionists, neither 'ideologically wedded' to parity (W1I06, Northern Ireland politician, unionist) nor 'particularly bothered what flag was flying where' when questions of citizens' economic welfare were at stake (W1I04, Northern Ireland politician, nationalist) – and to accept the same of their opponents.

By wave two (2020), the positions of the various groups had converged to some extent. Scottish nationalists remained more likely than unionists to aspire to the devolution of further social security competences, but unionists accused the nationalist Government of an excessively cautious approach to divergence from the UK system in those areas already under devolved control. Scottish officials remained excited by the possibilities opened up by devolution and their Northern Ireland counterparts had become much more enthusiastic about (limited) departures from parity with the UK system. There was little change in the positions of Northern Ireland unionists or nationalists, but neutral politicians were less convinced of the arguments for parity than in wave one.[47] Perhaps due to the passage of time since the Scotland Act 2016 and the Welfare Reform (Northern Ireland) Order 2015, responses in wave two were also more nuanced and reflective.

There was widespread recognition that the question of whether the welfare state is likely to fare better in UK, Scottish, Northern Irish or Irish hands is an important one for the constitutional debate:

> This Government's position is that Scotland should be an independent country so, on one level everything this Government does … will demonstrate Scotland's capability to be an independent country … Doing social security right has the potential to be one

[47] Election results between the two waves meant two constitutionally neutral parties were represented in wave two, compared to one in wave one.

> of the strongest arguments for Scottish independence this Government has yet been able to manifest [and] a headline argument in future debates around the constitutional question, if we can demonstrate that we can do it (W2I16, Scotland official).

> I took [relative] to an A&E in [Ireland] and within an hour he'd had every test he could possibly think of … It cost a lot of money … but you know if he was here and he lay in a hospital bed for 24 hours before he's getting those tests, you sort of look at that and go what way's the best way? These are the sort of questions that I need … a conversation about, what's better for everybody here (W2I19, Northern Ireland politician, neutral).

In Scotland, some unionists continued to accuse nationalists of approaching this intersection from a position of cynicism: 'The SNP is against everything in Westminster' (W2I12, Scotland politician, unionist). However, with unionists also accusing the Scottish Government of being too slow or timid to forge a distinctively Scottish path in the devolved areas, this argument had become harder to sustain. More often, it was observed that the SNP Government was in a fortunate position where its welfare state and constitutional objectives were complementary. Scotland might have 'different needs … a different demographic … different political leanings' to the rest of the UK, demanding a distinctive policy response from any government, 'but it fits with the SNP's position for a constitutional change' (W2I11, Scotland official). A Scottish social security system would inevitably differ from the UK system in certain respects, reflecting the different social, economic, demographic and ideological context. Importantly, though, under a nationalist Government 'it should have a Scottish identify, it should be recognisably different to the United Kingdom' (W2I16, Scotland official). Some unionists were conscious of this possible double motive for constructing a distinctly Scottish social citizenship, while others felt that divergence was simply devolution in action, in a way that could serve a nationalist, unionist or no particular constitutional agenda:

> We have had a few very good signs, the £10 family allowance [Scottish child payment] that has just been introduced is really good … Is the driver for everything that is happening the desire to create a more generous system? I am not sure it is … That is not what gets them out of the bed in the morning (W2I15, Scotland politician, unionist).

> Those of us who believe staying part of the UK would argue that showing the strength of a devolved Scottish Parliament shows the UK system working and I suppose the arguments of those who see an independent Scotland would say showing how well run the Scottish social security system can be is just an example of how the whole state would be if it was independent. But I don't think they're primary motivators (W2I13, Scotland politician, unionist).

Nationalists, perhaps unsurprisingly, did not portray the SNP's approach to social security since 2016 as motivated by their constitutional agenda, but were happier to admit that the transfer of further social security powers to Holyrood was something that, as nationalists, they were bound to pursue.

In Northern Ireland, there was an acknowledgement that welfare state and constitutional politics could overlap, but reluctance to argue that positions on social security were dictated by a unionist or nationalist perspective. Whereas wave one took place with the question of how, and to what extent, social security in Northern Ireland should diverge from the UK system still unresolved, by wave two limited divergence had been a reality for almost four years. With the benefit of this experience, the pragmatic argument for limited departures from parity became one that all interviewees – unionist, nationalist, neutral or official – could embrace. From a unionist point of view, 'the desire isn't to be different. The desire is to have something which is appropriate … because we do have unique circumstances' (W2I01, Northern Ireland politician, unionist). Nationalists argued for devolution of 'the maximum number of powers … to local elected and accountable politicians' (W2I20, Northern Ireland politician, nationalist), but foregrounded policy-based justifications for divergence:

> Parity serves you well if you have … a compassionate, fair, socially just Government in place that looks out for the many and not for the few. So parity under … this Conservative administration over the past 10 years has not served us well (W2I20, Northern Ireland politician, nationalist).

Officials felt that unionist and nationalist politicians may hold different views of parity in principle, but ultimately arrive at a similar destination in terms of their view of what is best in practice for Northern Ireland:

> I worked for Ministers from all parties in my time and some will lean more heavily on parity than others. But … every one of them will do the right thing for people locally; if they see an opportunity to do it, they'll do it (W2I24, Northern Ireland official).

> The DUP and UUP would like to ensure that they stay broadly in line with the UK … in principle terms, but for individual ministers, whenever they are in the social security hot seat, they sometimes also want to have the freedom to do things themselves. Whereas with [Sinn Féin] at the other end of the spectrum, they want to do everything differently … but they want to make sure that they can get whatever money is available, maximise it from London (W2I25, Northern Ireland official).

Some politicians argued that the gap between parties' positions was rather greater than the officials quoted above acknowledged, but seldom attributed this to divergent constitutional objectives. One interviewee argued that – contrary to Greer's assertion of the irrelevance of public policy to Northern Ireland politics – reactions to UK-level reforms reflect a more conventional left-right fault line in the polity.

> The two unionist parties are clearly to the right … The two national[ist] parties are to the left of centre. That's where we sit on the sort of left-right spectrum … I'm not sure being a nationalist means you're more likely to be opposed to the welfare reform. I think being a nationalist means you're more likely to be a member of a left of centre party, which means you're more likely to be opposed to elements of welfare reform, but I don't think they're necessarily linked in the sense of a constitutional question (W2I17, Northern Ireland politician, unionist).

None of this is to say that politicians in Northern Ireland shied away from attributing relatively instrumental or cynical motives to their opponents, but these tended to stress the pursuit of electoral gain or avoidance of blame for unpopular policy choices rather than constitutional manoeuvring.

Virtually every participant in wave two could reasonably be described as a welfare regionalist. Some wanted divergence between the devolved and UK social security systems to go further and some in Scotland aspired to the devolution of further social security competences. Scottish participants acknowledged that arguments about the (un)accountability of UK policymakers to the Scottish electorate or the ability of devolved government to successfully deliver social security assistance were as relevant to the debate on independence as to ideas about social citizenship. In Northern Ireland, though, suggestions of a clear link between welfare state and constitutional aspirations were rare and no participant suggested that the social security system ought to be more closely aligned with that of the Republic of Ireland. Whatever their constitutional aspirations, participants seemed united in their desire to use the opportunity provided by devolution to act in the interests of citizens in their country.

An 'Enduring Settlement' Achieved?

Despite the Scottish electorate's decision to remain within the Union, the October 2014 referendum spurred the furthest-reaching revision of the devolution settlement since 1998. The Smith Commission – composed of delegates from the five political parties represented in the Scottish Parliament – was convened with a view to reaching a shared vision for the future of devolution.[48] The UK Government accepted the Smith proposals as the blueprint for 'an enduring settlement'.[49] It was almost immediately apparent that neither the Scottish Government nor the Scottish Parliament accepted that this drew a line under the constitutional debate.[50] Subsequent developments confirm that aspirations for independence have not been abandoned. Nationalist leaders had described the 2014 referendum as a 'once in a generation opportunity'[51] but argued that the UK's departure from the EU represented a 'a significant and material change in the circumstances that prevailed in 2014', justifying a further vote on independence.[52] A majority of MSPs

[48] Smith Commission, *Report of the Smith Commission for further devolution of powers to the Scottish Parliament* (Edinburgh: Smith Commission, 2014).

[49] HM Government, *Scotland in the United Kingdom: an enduring settlement* (Cm 8990, Edinburgh: Scotland Office, 2015).

[50] Devolution (Further Powers) Committee, *New powers for Scotland: an interim report on the Smith Commission and the UK government's proposals* (SP paper 720, Edinburgh: Scottish Parliament, 2015); Scottish Government, 'Further devolution beyond the Smith Commission' (Edinburgh: Scottish Government, 2015).

[51] A Salmond, interview on Andrew Marr show (BBC One, 14 September 2014).

[52] N Sturgeon, speech at Bute House, 13 March 2017. Available at: www.gov.scot/publications/first-ministers-speech-bute-house-march-2017/.

elected to the Scottish Parliament in 2021 stood on manifestos calling for a second referendum.[53]

Nationalist discontent with the post-Smith extent of Scotland's social security competences was evident in the fieldwork. In wave one, nationalists and some officials argued that for Scotland to better support citizens' economic welfare, it must have control of out-of-work benefits, the national minimum wage and further areas of taxation. Unionists were largely sympathetic to nationalists' objectives for social security but felt that where income-replacement benefits are concerned, 'pool[ing] your resources' (W1I25, Scotland politician, unionist) against social risk across the UK's economic base made more sense, with pooled decision making an inseparable element of this arrangement. By pursuing changes to social security and employment law at Westminster, Scottish MPs 'might actually benefit those who are subjected to the faults in the rest of the UK as well' (W1I26, Scotland politician, unionist). This unionist-nationalist split remained in wave two. Nationalists typically argued:

> You could make an argument that social security for those in retirement would be retained across the UK … you can see a logical argument for that. When you've got a Scottish Parliament that's in charge of employability, that's in charge of skills, and universal credit isn't just there to support folk that are not in employment, but also to support [people] who are in employment, I can't think of a reason why that would still sit with a UK Government (W2I07, Scotland politician, nationalist).

Unionists were less enthusiastic about further revisions to the settlement. One acknowledged a possible case for further devolution but felt the dominance of politics by the independence question rendered a reasoned debate on the subject impossible.

> I was reasonably comfortable with the decisions around what was devolved because I think it is a relatively stable portion of the benefits system, wouldn't disrupt Scotland's finances overly but would allow some creative thinking and creative developments … I also felt it would be good for both governments to have to work together … I don't think it should go any further for a long time now (W2I12, Scotland politician, unionist).
>
> If you were to try and devolve anything else right now it would become a fault line in the independence divide. If we were to say, 'Look, devolve drugs policy to Scotland', which I think there is an argument for, it's not something I'm shouting about right now because [other unionist parties] would paint me as going soft on independence (W2I08, Scotland politician, unionist).

[53] See A Paun and J Sargeant, 'Explainer: Scottish independence' (London, Institute for Government, 2021). Available at: www.instituteforgovernment.org.uk/explainers/scottish-independence. For a discussion of political and legal issues relevant to a second referendum, see A Tickell, 'The technical Jekyll and the political Hyde: the constitutional law and politics of Scotland's independence "neverendum"'and A McHarg, T Mullen, A Page and N Walker (eds), *The Scottish Independence Referendum: Constitutional and Political Implications* (Oxford: Oxford University Press, 2016).

The Smith settlement can claim to be a relative success in as much as its recommendations have largely been implemented – those of the Calman Commission had not fully taken effect by the time they were superseded. However, it seems reasonable to expect that, whether or not a further referendum on independence takes place, pressure for further change will come. Despite the stark unionist–nationalist split on the desirability of transferring further social security competences to Holyrood, whether and in what form this happens will be a pragmatic question as much as an ideological one. The Scottish and UK systems rub against each other in numerous places – notably through passported entitlement to Scottish child payment for universal credit claimants, and to various premia associated with reserved benefits for Scottish disability assistance claimants. This will demand a considerable degree of intergovernmental cooperation[54] – how smoothly this works in practice will be one factor that helps determine how long the current settlement in fact endures.

Northern Ireland's constitutional settlement has long been viewed in different terms, with a significant section of the polity and society regarding the country's place in the UK as provisional, if not illegitimate, since its foundation in 1921.[55] As in Scotland, the UK's withdrawal from the EU has galvanised advocates of a referendum on unification with the Republic of Ireland[56] – something that, in contrast to Scotland, is specifically envisaged in the constitutional legislation.[57] At the same time, recurring political instability means the possibility of devolution being replaced by a further period of direct rule from Westminster can never be wholly dismissed.[58] A development of this nature would be unthinkable in Scotland, where the 'permanence' of the devolved institutions is enshrined in the devolution Act[59] – albeit that this is a symbolic provision, as the UK Parliament is presumably unable to fetter its own future ability to make or unmake any law.[60]

Even from a social security-focused perspective, the constitutional question looks different in Northern Ireland. Advocates of divergence need not demand the devolution of further competences, as social security is already fully devolved. The one exception might be control of the national insurance fund, probably a precondition for any significant divergence from Great Britain on contributory benefits,

[54] N McEwen and B Petersohn, 'Between autonomy and interdependence: the challenges of shared rule after the Scottish referendum' (2015) 86(2) *Political Quarterly* 192.

[55] J Tonge, *Northern Ireland* (Cambridge: Polity Press, 2006).

[56] C Gormley-Heenan and A Aughey, 'Northern Ireland and Brexit: three effects on "the border in the mind"' (2017) 19(3) *British Journal of Politics and International Relations* 497.

[57] Northern Ireland Act 1998 c 47 s 1, sch 1.

[58] D Birrell and D Heenan, 'The continuing volatility of devolution in Northern Ireland: the shadow of direct rule' (2017) 88(3) *Political Quarterly* 473.

[59] Scotland Act 1998 c 46 s 63A.

[60] C Himsworth, 'Legislating for permanence and a statutory footing' (2016) 24(1) *Edinburgh Law Review* 361; for the contrary suggestion that the referendum and its aftermath have struck a significant blow for popular sovereignty in the UK, see L Gow, 'Permutations of popular sovereignty before, during and after the Scottish independence referendum' in H-J Heintze and P Thielbörger (eds), *From Cold War to Cyber War: The Evolution of the International Law of Peace and Armed Conflict over the Last 25 Years* (Cham: Springer, 2016).

but no research participant advocated this. Nor is there any strong reason why those who feel citizens in Northern Ireland should continue to be treated 'precisely on the same level as similar people are treated in [Great Britain]', in line with the first Prime Minister's wish,[61] should be driven to see the settlement amended so that social security becomes a reserved matter. The parity convention has shown itself capable of achieving this state of affairs as long as that is the wish of the devolved legislature.[62] The temporary transfer of competences to Westminster in November 2015 was more about managing internal political disputes and side-stepping Assembly legislative deadlines than the principle of where responsibility for citizens' social rights ought to reside,[63] the irony of which was not lost on some participants:

> We ended up in the bizarre situation, where having had a deal made in Northern Ireland, the regulations to enforce it were put through by the very Parliament that we said we need to change what they had originally agreed (W2I03, Northern Ireland politician, unionist).

One consequence of the events of 2015 has been the shedding of light on the sometimes-murky question of what the parity convention actually requires. Parity in social protection has been an enduring feature of Northern Ireland's devolution settlement, from the 1920s to the present, but it has not necessarily been clear whether accepting the associated subvention from the UK Exchequer requires or merely facilitates equivalence of provision on the two sides of the North Channel. While the constitutional legislation requires consultation between the two governments on the matter,[64] 'it's never been defined … what it means in terms of consultation' (W1I03, Northern Ireland official). In wave one, some interviewees felt parity was nothing more than 'kind of a gentleman's agreement' (W1I04, Northern Ireland politician, nationalist); others, that even if the legislation is 'quite vague', the Treasury has considerable power in practice to press, if not force, the Executive into toeing the Westminster line (W1I19, Northern Ireland official). By wave two, no one could dispute that, in social security, Northern Ireland 'can do whatever tweaks [it] desire[s] provided that (a) you can pay for them and (b) you can operationally deliver them' (W1I02, Northern Ireland official). What Northern Ireland can pay for and operationally deliver is, to some extent, a question about the constitutional settlement, which devolves fewer fiscal powers than those for Scotland. However, it is also an economic and political question – some interviewees suggested economic conditions mean Northern Ireland could not raise as much revenue as Scotland even if it had comparable fiscal autonomy, others that legislators who have worked to hold down or reduce the taxes under their control

[61] J Craig, HC deb 1 Mar 1929, vol 225 col 2361.

[62] M Simpson, 'Developing constitutional principles through firefighting: social security parity in Northern Ireland' (2015) 22(1) *Journal of Social Security Law* 31.

[63] NIA deb 18 Nov 2015, vol 109 no 7 p 14; Northern Ireland (Welfare Reform) Act 2015 c 34.

[64] Northern Ireland Act 1998 c 47 s 87.

since 2007 might be unwilling to do so. A report by the Northern Ireland Audit Office in 2021 found the budget process complied with only one of 10 OECD best practice principles and may cast further doubt on the country's readiness for further fiscal autonomy.[65]

Conclusion

The relationship between national identity and ideologies of social citizenship is complex. Even articles with an author in common appear to reach different conclusions about whether debates around social justice in Scotland are one of the processes through which Scottishness is produced, performed and harnessed,[66] or whether visions for social justice are separate to national identity.[67] Nonetheless, the notion that both British national identity in the twentieth century and Scottish national identity in the twenty-first are intimately linked with ideas about the welfare state and the mutual solidarity it embodies has some pedigree. That said, it would be mistaken to assume that unionists automatically prioritise the integrity of the social union while nationalist critiques of the UK welfare state largely serve as barely disguised attacks on the political union. By wave two, every participant in Northern Ireland – whatever their constitutional aspirations – was a confirmed welfare regionalist. The picture was somewhat different in Scotland, but welfare unionism tended to manifest in opposition to the devolution of further competences rather than advocacy of UK-wide uniformity in the areas of social security now under devolved control. The Scottish settlement clearly remains contested, but in Northern Ireland, too, the question of how far policy should or can depart from parity is unresolved. Chapter 9 takes stock of developments to date and considers what the next steps might be.

[65] Comptroller and Auditor General, *The Northern Ireland Budget Process* (Belfast: NI Audit Office, 2021).
[66] A Law and G Mooney, 'Devolution in a "stateless nation": nation-building and social policy in Scotland' (2012) 46(2) *Social Policy and Administration* 161.
[67] Mooney and Scott, above n 44.

9

Towards Devolved Social Citizenships: How Far Have We Come and Where Are We Going?

Introduction

A partial regionalisation of social citizenship in the UK predates 2012 but has been taken further by developments in social security since then. Just how far Scotland and Northern Ireland have gone towards establishing a genuinely different approach to social security at devolved level remains an open question. Rhetoric that says a fundamentally different model is being put in place may not be matched by reality. Equally, the important question may not be the current extent of divergence, but whether trajectories or ways of thinking are being established that may cause the various systems to drift further apart in the future. Drawing again on the views expressed by research participants, this chapter assesses the extent to which distinctively Scottish and Northern Irish models of social security have either emerged or are emerging. It also highlights some of the likely centrifugal and centripetal forces for the future and assesses the extent to which the two countries' approaches may have influenced each other.

Scotland: From Principles to Practice

From the campaigns prior to the independence referendum onward, social security in Scotland has been associated with rhetoric advocating or promising radical change from the UK system. The Expert Working Group on Welfare suggested independence could be an opportunity to break with the liberal welfare state model in favour of a more insurance-based or universal approach to social security.[1] Any such ambitions will have been curtailed by the vote for continued union in 2014 – even the enhanced post-2016 devolution settlement places considerable constraints on autonomy in this field. Radical rhetoric has nonetheless remained, but sits alongside a degree of (mainly unionist) scepticism as to whether significant divergence is likely, or even possible, in reality:

> The yes campaign worked very hard to give the impression that in some future independent Scotland welfare payments and benefits would be a lot higher … People voted yes in an expectation that these promises would be acted on … You can promise the earth, but there's a limited amount of resource[s] available (W1I22, Scotland politician, unionist).

Nationalists, too, sometimes recognised that aspects of the pre-referendum vision might not be deliverable:

> If we woke up in the cold light of day and realised that we'd just voted for independence there might have been … a rowing back to ideas that the right wing very often present as mere pragmatism … that the world is this mean and nasty [and] that there is no alternative, to quote the lady [Margaret Thatcher] (W1I21, Scotland politician, nationalist).

The Scottish social security principles are the legislative embodiment of the Scottish Government and Parliament's vision for the devolved system. Most Scotland-based research participants argued that putting dignity and rights at the heart of its vision compels the Scottish Government to do social security differently to the UK system:

> That recognition that social security is indeed a right and … essential to … the realisation of other rights … is a hugely important recognition … If that were applied in the UK social security context it would significantly change the approach to sanctioning claimants, for example. If the consequence of refusing social security to somebody is

[1] Expert Working Group on Welfare, *Re-thinking Welfare: Fair, Personal and Simple* (Edinburgh: Scottish Government, 2014).

> that they go hungry then clearly you're starting to violate other rights as well and the system should not … allow that to happen (W2I10, Scotland official).

This book emerges at a point when the process of replacing UK benefits with devolved social security assistance, in fields where competence has been transferred, is still in progress. Its assessment of whether the same level of ambition is reflected in law, policy and practice is therefore an early one. As Chapter 5 emphasised, in policy innovation terms, the Scottish Government has sought to 'make effective use of [its] new social security powers but proceed with caution'.[2] Where a new form of devolved social security assistance acts as a direct replacement for a UK benefit, there tends to be little divergence in eligibility criteria or rates of payment – although this does not preclude distinctive administrative practices. In the short-term, this approach is driven by the imperative of a 'safe and secure transition', a mantra for those with responsibility for social security.[3] Longer term, there may be other obstacles to radical departures from the UK model – examined later in the chapter. Where a new, distinctive payment is introduced, divergence is more evident.

This cautious approach has been a source of frustration for some, particularly unionist politicians:

> It is a big practical challenge … We are talking about vulnerable people who don't have any money or an income. So you can't get these things wrong and also, you don't want to lose your reputation for competence as a government. But at the same time, I think the lack of drive in this area is quite revealing … If you want to make something happen quickly, you can make it happen quickly (W2I15, Scotland politician, unionist).

Nationalists and officials defended the government's approach, warning that 'the unintended consequences of making sudden changes, even quite minor changes, can be quite significant from an individual perspective' (W2I21, Scotland official) and that 'it's always got to be about the safe and secure transition, about people getting money that they need when they need it' (W2I11, Scotland official).

The Scottish Government emphasises its approach to the administrative delivery of social security as the primary means of ensuring that claimants' experiences of the devolved system are more positive than has been the case with parts of the UK system (see Chapter 5). Most participants – even some of those who argued that the Scottish Government exaggerates the shortcomings of the DWP approach – agreed that progress has been made on this front:

> I think the majority of us actually are quite happy with how DWP have done it … One thing I have been impressed with is the funeral expenses. [Stakeholders] were saying that system has really worked very well, it had been streamlined administration wise. Form filling was somewhat easier et cetera, so they had really been quite positive about that (W2I06, Scotland politician, unionist).

[2] Scottish Government, *It Takes All of Us to Build a Fairer Scotland: Fairer Scotland Action Plan* (Edinburgh: Scottish Government, 2016) 92.

[3] See S-A Somerville, SP deb 6 March 2019, col 19.

One interviewee argued that good intentions to improve the user experience may not be realised since, ultimately, applicants are interested in outcomes and any set of processes will result in some people being refused assistance:

> A lot of people's experience is not bad already. So, for the vast proportion of people, you're changing absolutely nothing. For the other portion of people, their main gripe is the outcome, not just the process. However nice the process is, [if] the outcome still leaves somebody in the situation that they were complaining about, they're not going to really get any happier (W2I12, Scotland politician, unionist).

There is evidence that this is not necessarily the case, that procedural justice – the fairness of the process, clarity about the reasons for a decision and the opportunity to participate effectively – can be as important as substantive justice (the outcome) to users' perceptions of administrative justice systems like social security.[4] The Scottish Government has sought to improve how people experience these aspects of the system: providing a range of options for how people interact with it (from online to home visits); scrapping target durations for telephone calls; changes in the nature of disability assessments (rebranded as 'consultations'); and encouraging people to exercise their right to appeal following an adverse decision through the payment of short-term assistance. The success or otherwise of these changes will not really be apparent until the various forms of disability assistance have rolled out, as interactions and determinations will be more complex than with the earlier forms of social security assistance.

These new processes are bound up with the aspiration to build a social security agency with a fundamentally different organisational culture to the Department for Work and Pensions. Officials' buy-in to the Scottish Government vision has been documented in Chapter 5. It is important to note that those interviewed were in relatively senior roles, whose enthusiasm may or may not be reflected in frontline staff – although a client survey does show that more than 85 per cent of respondents felt staff made them feel comfortable, listened to them and were kind.[5] Politicians, too, were largely enthusiastic about the cultural dimension of the project, but there were some sceptical voices:

> [Devolution] was a real chance to make a fresh start … Despite the fact that the people working at the [DWP] were equally well-intentioned, most of them were having often to manage a difficult situation … So, starting from afresh without that baggage I think is good. The approach they have taken with treating people like humans with value in them, I think it does matter (W2I15, Scotland politician, unionist).

> A lot of the staff have … come from DWP. Particularly for the slightly better pay … They're saying it's going to be a different culture, you have to buy into that culture.

[4] A Bryson and R Berthoud, 'Social security appeals: what do the claimants want?' (1997) 4(1) *Journal of Social Security Law* 17; M Adler 'Understanding and analysing administrative justice', M Adler (ed) *Administrative Justice in Context* (Oxford: Oxford University Press, 2010); G McKeever, 'A ladder of legal participation for tribunal users' (2013) (Win) *Public Law* 575.

[5] Social Security Scotland, *Client survey: 2018–20* (Dundee: Social Security Scotland, 2021).

> If you've been embedded in DWP working practice … that rubs off on how you do your work (W2I06, Scotland politician, unionist).

Major questions for the future of devolved social security in Scotland concern the UK Government's response to pressure for the devolution of further competences and the evolution of disability assistance after migration of claimants from the UK to the Scottish system has been completed. The division of responsibilities in the devolution settlement matters because of the constraints it places on the development of a distinctive devolved system. Nationalist interviewees' stated desire for further devolved social security competences is outlined in Chapter 8. Given these participants' ultimate political goal of achieving independence, it is possible to question – and unionists in the study did – whether this aspiration is primarily motivated by welfare state preferences or constitutional priorities. However, officials also highlighted what they saw as points of incoherence in the post-Smith settlement and the desirability of further devolution if the vision for a 'fairer Scotland' is to be achieved:

> I don't know if there's a rationale for what benefits [were devolved] because it feels very fragmented to me … We've got people who are basically being served by UK Government and Scottish Government in terms of the benefit package. It just makes things very complicated in manning. I probably would go back to some of the submissions that came in [to the Smith Commission]. Most of them did make clear that it was almost better to have an all or nothing. I think you see that now (W2I09b, Scotland official).

> Only 15 per cent of the overall spend [was devolved]. It's not unimportant, but neither is it anywhere near the kind of control over the heart of the system that really allows you then to start making changes that work right across the policy environment … That's a huge problem when it comes to things like food security or the day-to-day impacts that people face as a consequence of universal credit and the way in which DWP works (W2I10, Scotland official).

Eagerness in some quarters to take on a larger share of social security sat alongside reservations about the operational implications of doing so, at least until the dust has settled on the initial wave of devolution. Several officials were fearful of any 'rapid political acceleration with further devolution that would mean us having to take further responsibility … Anything this side of 2025 has the potential to be catastrophic' (W2I16, Scotland official). Some also suggested the Scottish Government was a long way from the 'worked-out policy position' (W2I11, Scotland official) on what further social security competences it wanted and how it would use them that would be needed to even open a discussion on more devolution.

Given the similarities between Scottish disability assistance and the UK benefits it is replacing – disability living allowance, personal independence payment and attendance allowance – it is fair to describe it as the latest development in 'a system that has evolved rather than been designed'.[6] The Scottish Government's

[6] Scottish Campaign on Rights to Social Security, *Beyond a Safe and Secure Transition – A Long Term Vision for Disability Assistance in Scotland* (Glasgow: SCoRSS, 2020) 10.

case for focusing on a safe and secure transition to the new, devolved system has largely been accepted by stakeholders, some frustration about lack of divergence in the descriptors that are used to assess entitlement notwithstanding.[7] However, a coalition of third-sector organisations has made it clear that they see a need for a 'fundamental review of disability assistance' in the future. They argue that the review should take the social security principles and disabled people's right to independent living and participation in society (CRPD article 19) – not the system inherited from the UK – as its starting point. Among the specific challenges identified are ensuring adequacy, eliminating problems associated with having separate payments for different-aged people and increasing cohesion with other areas of devolved social security. However, there is no call to change the core functions of disability benefits, identified as compensation for additional disability-related costs and passporting to other forms of support.[8] A first-principles review of social security for disabled people might go some way to placating the Scottish Government's critics in the research, one of whom said the focus on a safe and secure transition would be easier to accept if accompanied by a 'broad debate' on future aspirations (W2I23, Scotland politician, unionist). Whether or not such a review materialises, at some point decisions will have to be taken on whether a broad parity with the reserved system remains desirable. A 2021 consultation indicated that the UK Government is itself prepared to consider significant change to the current disability benefits in pursuit of simplification, reduced expenditure, greater focus on employment and, potentially, more emphasis on non-cash support.[9] If the Scottish Government considered that future UK-level changes were likely to take the reserved system further from the aspirations of the social security principles, but felt other forces in favour of parity remained strong, it would face a difficult decision on whether to make comparable changes.

Difficult decisions may also flow from the social security principles themselves, which can appear to push in different directions. For example, the Scottish Government has observed that different carers have diverse needs, with the implication that these may need to be reflected to a greater extent in a system that puts the needs of those who require assistance first. At the same time, it recognises the need for clear eligibility criteria and administrative simplicity – which might contribute to the development of an efficient system. It has yet to indicate how it might reconcile these objectives.[10] Each potentially points towards a different conclusion about the extent to which Scottish carer's assistance ought to diverge from the carer's allowance eligibility criteria, which make it fairly easy to determine

[7] Scottish Government, *Adult Disability Payment: Consultation Analysis* (Edinburgh: Scottish Government, 2021).

[8] Scottish Campaign on Rights to Social Security, above n 6 at 3, 15.

[9] Department for Work and Pensions, *Shaping Future Support: The Health and Disability Green Paper* (CP470, London: DWP, 2021).

[10] Scottish Government, *Scottish Carer's Assistance – Discussion Paper* (Edinburgh: Scottish Government, 2021); Social Security (Scotland) Act 2018 asp 9 s 1(g) and (h).

who is entitled to support but exclude many people with significant caring responsibilities because they do not provide care for sufficient hours, care for more than one person or have too much household income.

Northern Ireland: Commitment to Parity Wanes, the Practice of Parity Remains

One of the most striking developments between the two waves of fieldwork was the change in Northern Ireland participants' language when discussing parity with Great Britain (or England and Wales) in social security. As Chapter 8 explained, officials and constitutionally neutral politicians in Northern Ireland had the greatest reservations about divergence in wave one. Unionist politicians broadly favoured parity in principle, while recognising that some aspects of law and policy emerging from Westminster might not be in Northern Ireland's best interests. By wave two, regionalisation since 2015 was universally recognised as a positive response to UK-level developments. At the same time, the language used to describe divergence – mitigation of specific reforms rather than the development of an explicitly Northern Irish model – continues to position the system for England and Wales as the norm, or at least the starting point.

In 2010, McKeever argued that 'parity cannot simply be justified by default'.[11] One research participant suggested that even at that point work was underway to stimulate 'more of a conversation', within devolved government and with the UK Government, about what might be possible at devolved level to 'mitigate some of [the] worst excesses' of UK-level reforms (W2I04, Northern Ireland politician, nationalist). The mitigations package outlined in Chapter 5 reflects this shift in thinking, with claimants compensated for loss of income as result of selected reforms for a fixed period (loss of disability benefits) or on an ongoing basis (benefit cap and social sector size criteria). This represented a clear, if limited, break with parity. However, while the various supplementary payments have clearly been significant to their beneficiaries, their existence does not in itself reveal how far the pendulum might have swung from acceptance of parity as the default. Notably, the underpinning legislation limits the period for which the payments are available – until March 2020 in all cases and to a maximum of one year in the case of those compensating for loss of disability benefit.[12] Mitigation of the benefit cap is further limited to households that have been in continuous receipt of a capped benefit

[11] G McKeever, 'Reforming social security appeal tribunals in Northern Ireland: parity whether we Leggatt or not' (2010) 17(2) *Journal of Social Security Law* 71, 77.

[12] Welfare Reform (Northern Ireland) Order 2015, SI No 2006 (NI 1) art 137A; Welfare Supplementary Payment (Loss of Disability-related Premiums) Regulations (Northern Ireland) 2016, NISR No 254 regs 8, 17, 30, 36; Welfare Supplementary Payments Regulations (Northern Ireland) 2016, NISR No 178, reg 4(6).

since 2016.[13] In practice, the legislative sunset clauses have been circumvented by the making of administrative supplementary payments with no statutory basis since 2020, based on the authority of a political agreement.[14] As this text was being finalised, the Executive agreed to support legislation extending the current mitigations for a further three years while widening protection against the benefit cap and social sector size criteria.[15] This divergence between legislation and practice reflects the absence of functioning devolved institutions from January 2017 to January 2020, but also speaks to a lack of certainty about the purpose of the mitigations – to smooth the transition between systems, or as the first steps along a different path for social security in Northern Ireland.

The extended quote below shows that at least some officials regarded selective mitigation of certain reforms as a means of smoothing the transition, rather than the launchpad for a new, Northern Ireland-specific approach. The official is reflecting on the Stormont House agreement in December 2014, intended to reconcile the positions of the various political parties on issues – including social security reform – that threatened the viability of the consociational Executive:

> Welfare was the poison, the boil that needed to be lanced and so we got it lanced … The deal was done, and after that things went reasonably smoothly, probably for about four months and then again broke down over … the issue around whether or not future claimants were covered by the agreement. It was quite clear in the agreement which [the parties] signed it was future claimants were not included. It was all existing claimants … I think Sinn Féin got very nervous about what they'd signed up to and at that point then they … walked away from the agreement on the basis that future claimants needed to be included (W2I25, Northern Ireland official).

Extending the 2012 and 2016 reforms to Northern Ireland by Order rather than by Acts of the Assembly, then appointing an independent working group to propose a mitigations package, offered 'a way out' to parties uncomfortable with the changes to the system, but did not (in this official's view) result in any substantive departure from what had been agreed in 2014. Some – although not all – unionists agreed that 'the logic around the mitigations package was to ease Northern Ireland into a new welfare reform regime' (W2I17, Northern Ireland politician, unionist); parity deferred rather than abandoned. Some interviewees with a less favourable view of parity agreed: 'mitigations really are a way of phasing in the welfare cuts more gently. My fear is that in 10 years' time our welfare system, England's welfare system will be mirror images, that we won't use devolution' (W2I02, Northern Ireland politician, neutral).

Despite these views, by the time of wave two there was little expectation that the restoration of parity was imminent. On one hand there was seen to be an

[13] Welfare Supplementary Payments Regulations (Northern Ireland) 2016 NISR No 178 reg 4.

[14] Northern Ireland Office, *New Decade, New Approach* (Belfast: NIO, 2020).

[15] Department for Communities, 'Communities Minister Hargey announces welfare protections extension' (DfC news release, 15 November 2021). Available at: www.communities-ni.gov.uk/news/communities-minister-hargey-announces-welfare-protections-extension.

indefeasible case for continued mitigation of the social sector size criteria, due to the nature of Northern Ireland's social housing stock:

> We understood the magnitude of the shortfall that people would face simply because there wasn't the level of two bedroom and single bedroom housing stock in Northern Ireland and it wasn't going to be built any time soon … You can't expect people, through no fault of their own, to have to head 30, 40, 50 miles to try and find accommodation that might not even exist. (W2I24, Northern Ireland official).

On the other hand, closer scrutiny of and reduced willingness to simply accept social security reforms emanating from Westminster was seen as an example of the 'maturing' of the devolved institutions and devolved politics: 'OK, we have these powers, what does that mean? … A sort of learning and testing of what were the limits' (W2I29, Northern Ireland official). This kind of thinking could lead some to overstate the extent of divergence. One official suggested: 'UC … was delayed in getting underway. When you set that to the side, really any of the reforms that led to a loss of money for anybody … was mitigated' (W2I23b, Northern Ireland official). Clearly, this has not been the case. Losses flowing from reform of the local housing allowance for private tenants, the two-child limit on universal credit and child tax credits and below-inflation uprating of social assistance have not been mitigated.

If the point of the mitigations was contested in 2016, arguably the imperative for the four-year period covered was to establish just what the guiding principle for social security in Northern Ireland ought to be in the future. One official made just this point: 'The mitigations … would have created a sufficient window … for proper policy discussion … on what they're trying to do in social welfare' (W2I25, Northern Ireland official). The absence of functioning devolved institutions for most of that period meant an opportunity to consider that question had been missed. By the time the Assembly resumed business and wave two took place, the urgency of decisions on the immediate future of mitigation meant the time that discussion would take was a luxury politicians could ill afford:

> I actually don't know whether all of the mitigations that we had put in place have been for the better. I don't know if we could have done it differently … That's what worries me about going forward with the mitigations, we're rushing through emergency … That's a major issue, that none of this has been reviewed by the Assembly since it was brought about and that's actually quite shameful (W2I18, Northern Ireland politician, unionist).

As this book was nearing completion, an independent review of the mitigations programme was getting underway.[16] Its recommendations – and the political reaction – will provide an early insight into what the future holds for social security in Northern Ireland. Certain mitigations may be declared redundant – the supplementary payments to disability, incapacity and carer benefit claimants were explicitly a transitional measure. Payments to mitigate losses due to the

[16] The author is a member of the review panel.

social sector size criteria and benefit cap will almost certainly be retained and the Minister for Communities has stated her intention to 'close "loopholes" in the Benefit Cap and Social Sector Size Criteria schemes that prevent some people from receiving mitigation payments'.[17] In the case of the benefit cap, this would transform a transitional measure into ongoing divergence. Ministerial statements show an aspiration to respond to the two-child limit on universal credit and child tax credits and the removal of the coronavirus uplift to the universal credit standard allowance, but the cost of mitigating either in full would dwarf that of any previous mitigation.[18] Besides the substantive decisions on what divergence exists in future, signs of Northern Ireland taking a distinctive path might include steps to put into practice expressions of interest in 'co-design' with claimants (W2I23c, Northern Ireland official) or a change in language from mitigation to the development of a Northern Irish system. However extensive divergence might be post-2022, the days when the Department for Communities' predecessors could regard themselves as 'primarily a parity department [that] took whatever came from England, changed a few titles on it and put it through the Assembly' (W1I03, Northern Ireland official) are gone.

At the same time, neither public statements nor the interview data show any appetite for a fundamentally different set of benefits for Northern Ireland or, as one Scottish interviewee advocated, 'to send away [experts] and say devise us a new social security system and give them two years to go away and think what's possible' (W2I06, Scotland politician, unionist). Nor is the author aware of any political calls for convergence with the Republic of Ireland, although there has been some academic examination of the possibility.[19] While a measure of ongoing divergence appears likely, it will almost certainly be limited to what can be achieved through top-up payments and administrative practice. If the Communities portfolio, held by Sinn Féin at the time of writing, reverts to a unionist minister following the 2022 Assembly election, the true extent of unionists' conversion to welfare regionalism will be tested.

Forces for Parity

Previous chapters have examined the forces in favour of divergence in social security between the devolved countries of Scotland and Northern Ireland and the reserved system serving England and Wales. Given the limited nature of

[17] Department for Communities, 'Communities Minister Hargey addresses Committee on Welfare Mitigations' (news release, 17 June 2021). Available at: www.communities-ni.gov.uk/news/communities-minister-hargey-addresses-committee-welfare-mitigations.

[18] D Hargey, response to AQO 1423/17-22, NIA deb 19 January 2021 vol 135 no 2 p 33; D Hargey, response to AQO 2410/17-22, NIA deb 20 September 2021, vol 142 no 4 p 21.

[19] C Fitzpatrick and C O'Sullivan, 'Comparing social security provision in the North and South of Ireland: past developments and future challenges' (2021) 32(2) *Irish Studies in International Affairs* 283.

divergence to date, it is equally necessary to consider the forces in favour of parity. Even if a straightforward welfare unionist desire for a largely uniform welfare state has declined, Chapter 8 has noted the continued association of political unionism with somewhat greater caution about divergence in Northern Ireland or the devolution of further competences to Scotland. However, this is not the only factor promoting conformity with the UK system.

The cost of divergence is arguably the key constraint on Northern Ireland's use of its devolved social security powers. Under the parity arrangement, the UK Exchequer meets the cost of non-contributory benefits in Northern Ireland as annually managed expenditure (that is, outside the block grant to the devolved Executive) to the extent that overall expenditure matches what would be spent if parity in rates and eligibility criteria were maintained. Any divergence agreed upon at devolved level that results in higher expenditure must be paid for from the devolved budget. The statement of funding policy explains:

> The UK Government is … committed to ensuring that the Northern Ireland Executive has sufficient funding available to maintain welfare payments to recipients in Northern Ireland to the same level as those funded by the equivalent UK Government departments … If the Northern Ireland Executive opts to depart from arrangements in place in Great Britain such that the AME costs borne centrally by the UK Government are greater than the equivalent costs borne by the relevant UK government departments, the Treasury will seek to recover additional costs from the Executive's … block grant.[20]

The statement further confirms that 'the Northern Ireland Executive retains the capacity to provide additional funding to recipients in line with its own priorities'.[21] In the immediate post-2012 period, this aspect of the arrangement was often misconstrued. Northern Ireland politicians regularly spoke of the 'fines' or 'penalties' that the UK Government would impose if reforms equivalent to those in the Welfare Reform Act 2012 were not implemented.[22] In reality, the Treasury simply recovered the relative overspend resulting from Northern Ireland's decision not to – or indecision over whether to – follow in Westminster's footsteps. While the language of 'fines' was also used by politicians in the first wave of fieldwork, officials saw things in a different light:

> The first of April [2015], Treasury will take £114 million out of the Northern Ireland block, which is what they call the savings foregone in welfare reform … It's not really a fine, it's the savings that would have accrued if Northern Ireland had implemented welfare reform at the same rate as in England … the money the Treasury has lost because we have lagged behind (W1I19, Northern Ireland official).

By 2020, with the mitigation programme well established, there was more or less universal acceptance that extra investment in social security was a political decision

[20] HM Treasury, *Statement of funding policy: Funding the Scottish Parliament, National Assembly for Wales and Northern Ireland Assembly* (London: HM Treasury, 2015) 70.

[21] Ibid, at 71.

[22] V Boland, 'Stakes high in Northern Ireland welfare reform crisis' (*Financial Times*, 27 May 2015). Available at: www.ft.com/cms/s/0/1172b9c8-0478-11e5-a5c3-00144feabdc0.html.

to be taken at devolved level rather than any kind of penalty imposed by the UK Government. Such decisions were not to be taken lightly – to the approval of those who felt Northern Ireland 'need[s] to be realistic and cut our cloth according to our means' (W2I17, Northern Ireland politician, unionist) and the frustration of others:

> There is an attitude that [if] it's AME then it comes straight from the UK Treasury and it doesn't come out of [devolved] budgets so take as much as you can get. If it comes out of block grant, then it's a huge decision, but my argument then as now is … to use your block grant for the most vulnerable in society (W2I02, Northern Ireland politician, neutral).

Finance, then, will remain a key consideration, and probably a brake on divergence, as Northern Ireland considers the future for devolved social security. Broad 'consensus over what's desirable' sits alongside greater 'divergence on what is affordable' (W2I20, Northern Ireland politician, nationalist). In part this is due to the direct cost of supplementing incomes. Some possible candidates for future mitigations would require far greater annual expenditure than their predecessors. Offsetting the two-child limit on universal credit and child tax credits has been estimated to require £56 million per year, retaining the £20 top-up to the universal credit standard allowance £110 million per year, compared to £22 million per year for continued offsetting of the social sector size criteria.[23] In other cases the cost of implementation appears to be the main obstacle to divergence. This applies when a possible change is not just about topping up incomes – which can be achieved through a supplementary payment additional to the main benefit – but about changing the fundamentals of how a benefit operates. To replace any benefit with a Northern Ireland-specific payment, or make changes to awards, waiting periods, assessment periods or tapers, would require changes to DWP software or the commissioning of a new package. Any significant change to the IT systems underpinning the major benefits was widely regarded as unaffordable. Several participants warned that failure to legislate for reform in 2015 and 2016, instead continuing to operate benefits that will eventually cease to receive IT support from DWP, could have had disastrous consequences: 'Nobody would have got benefits, we'd have been outside the system' (W2I19, Northern Ireland politician, neutral). In practice, the existence of different payment patterns for universal credit in Northern Ireland shows that limited changes to delivery are not out of the question. Given that direct payment to landlords and more frequent payments are available in England and Wales under specific circumstances, though, it might be that this was a relatively easy – and therefore cheap – tweak to make.

The main constraint on Scotland's ability to diverge from UK approaches to social security is its limited range of devolved competences. The current division

[23] H Reed and J Portes, *Cumulative Impact Assessment of Tax and Social Security Reforms in Northern Ireland* (Belfast: NIHRC, 2019); D Hargey, response to AQO 2410/17-22, NIA deb 20 September 2021, vol 142 no 4 p 21.

of responsibility for social security, though, is not just an obstacle to divergence in the sense that the Scottish Parliament cannot make changes to benefits that are reserved to the UK Parliament (although it can make top-up payments to claimants in Scotland). The interdependence of the two systems means Scotland must tread carefully when designing certain forms of social security assistance and can experience challenges with the delivery of others. Research participants were frustrated that the Department for Work and Pensions had been unable – or, as one official suggested to a Parliamentary inquiry, unwilling[24] – to provide Social Security Scotland with details of children aged six years or older living in households in receipt of social assistance benefits in Scotland. This meant that awards of Scottish child payment could only be made in respect of children under six, whereas the aspiration was to provide extra support to all under-16s. Whatever the reasons (DWP officials have stressed that there were practical reasons why the missing data could not be provided), this was a major setback to a policy that is 'critical to how [the Scottish Government] deal[s] with child poverty'.[25]

Passporting is also a potential constraint on divergence between UK and devolved disability benefits, although in this case the function works in the opposite direction. Claimants of disability benefits may receive passported entitlement to various cash and non-cash benefits provided by the UK Government. Examples include disability premia paid to claimants of some social assistance benefits, exemption from the household benefit cap and discount on vehicle excise duty or rail fares. There is a risk that the UK Government would no longer make these entitlements available to Scottish disability assistance claimants if the eligibility criteria diverged too much from DWP disability benefits. Consequently, the Scottish Government does not 'consider it safe to make any significant changes to the … eligibility criteria' at the point of transition.[26] While this does not definitively rule out the development of alternative criteria in the future, there is an ongoing possibility that divergence between the two sets of disability benefit could put passporting at risk and this may constrain Scottish ambition for some time to come.[27] At the very least, divergence that results in more people in Scotland receiving passported entitlements through disability assistance than would be the case through UK disability benefits would represent 'a policy decision that affects the … expenditure of the other [government]' for which 'the decision-making government [must] reimburse the other'.[28] If the systems diverged to the point that it became impossible to identify a clearly-defined group of Scottish claimants

[24] Scottish Affairs Committee, *Welfare Policy in Scotland* (HC55, London: House of Commons, 2021).

[25] Ibid, at 22.

[26] Scottish Government, *Consultation on adult disability payment* (Edinburgh: Scottish Government, 2020).

[27] Scottish Commission on Social Security, *Scrutiny Report on Draft Regulations: Disability Assistance for Working Age People (Scotland) Regulations* (Edinburgh: SCoSS, 2021).

[28] HM Government and Scottish Government, *The Agreement between the Scottish Government and United Kingdom Government on the Scottish Government's Fiscal Framework* (Edinburgh: Scottish Government, 2016) 7.

whose circumstances are analogous to a group in England and Wales who receive a particular passported entitlement, that entitlement would presumably cease to be available in Scotland.

Unlike Northern Ireland, Scotland has been content to meet the cost of bespoke systems for the delivery of devolved social security assistance, even in areas like disability benefits where parity is largely maintained. One reason might be that it keeps open the option of greater divergence in future, but some participants argued that Scotland should in any case avoid reliance on the 'antiquated' system used for delivery of UK benefits (W2I07, Scotland politician, nationalist).

Policy Learning between Northern Ireland and Scotland

Northern Ireland and Scotland have been on a journey towards more distinctive approaches to social security in the same period. There are also similarities in the points of divergence and the methods employed to deliver them. Each has supplemented the incomes of social assistance claimants by protecting under-occupying social tenants from loss of income (both), disapplying the benefit cap in most cases (Northern Ireland) and making additional child-related payments (Scotland). Each has done so by making separate, passported payments rather than increasing the rates of the main income replacement benefits. Each has introduced a payment to support the right of appeal and offer transitional support to claimants whose award is reduced or terminated, albeit more extensively in Scotland. Each retains a more comprehensive, more geographically uniform approach to discretionary assistance in a crisis than England's localised model. Each offers different payment arrangements for universal credit. Each has a stated focus on the human face of the system, although this has been more explicit in Scotland. While there are differences, the commonalities beg the question of whether, and to what extent, there has been conscious policy learning.

The author has previously suggested that Scottish interviewees in wave one of the fieldwork looked at Northern Ireland primarily as an example of 'how *not* to do things' when developing a devolved approach to social security.[29] With hindsight and the benefit of the wave two findings, this was, in some respects, a harsh conclusion. It is certainly the case that Scottish participants saw the financial and administrative constraints on Northern Ireland's use of devolved social security powers as a warning. Scotland, they argued, must not fall into a Treasury-constructed 'straitjacket' (W1I21, Scottish politician, nationalist) in which 'it appear[s] that you have power over these things, but if you don't do what you're told it ends up costing you a lot of money' (W1I27, Scotland official). There was also bemusement at how, politically, 'things [weren't] working too well'

[29] M Simpson, 'The social union after the coalition: devolution, divergence and convergence' (2017) 46(2) *Journal of Social Policy* 251, 257.

(W1I23, Scotland politician, nationalist) as the Welfare Reform Bill limped its way through the Assembly – and subsequently at the prolonged, absence of functioning devolved institutions between the two waves and its 'ridiculous' consequences for social policy (W2I15, Scotland politician, unionist). However, many Scottish officials and a smaller number of politicians were clear that they had and 'continue to have a wide range of things that we can learn from our Northern Irish colleagues' (W2I16, Scotland official) about the day-to-day business of running a social security system, even if they did not acknowledge much influence in policy terms:

> We've met officials from [Northern Ireland] on a fairly regular basis … to learn lessons, best practice … Northern Ireland had a really good benefits take-up way of making sure that participants knew about what they were eligible for … There was definitely lots that we learned from that (W2I09a, Scotland official).
>
> I went to Northern Ireland and met the folk running devolved social security and visited a couple of places … The main lesson actually was the local staff who helped people know everything they were entitled to, and that is kind of reflected in our system (W2I14, Scotland politician, nationalist).

A Northern Ireland official expressed the frustration some felt that, because of the political context, the Scottish Government had been able to claim greater credit than the Northern Ireland Executive for what, in many cases, are comparable measures:

> The Scots are doing, on the social security, all the things that … at administrative level, we were doing quite a lot in Northern Ireland for a long time. And of course then the Scots came and talked to us a lot about how we did this stuff … The frustration for us is … we are trying to do all the things they want to do but they had a much more positive political process to do it (W2I29, Northern Ireland official).

Interviewees in Northern Ireland kept a keen eye on Scotland in turn. Its example was seen as significant at a fundamental level. The fact that Scotland had been empowered – and was beginning – to diverge from the UK social security system served as an 'eye-opener' (W1I11, Northern Ireland politician, unionist) that parity need not be maintained at all costs, or at least that a 'different form of parity' was possible (W1I03, Northern Ireland official). Scotland was observed to have 'its own uniqueness' (W2I01, Northern Ireland politician, unionist), so that the two countries were unlikely to diverge from England and Wales in the same way. Nonetheless, several participants identified specific Scottish innovations – particularly around disability benefits for people with terminal illnesses – that might be followed. Others felt elected representatives could learn more from the Scottish Parliament Welfare Reform Committee's approach to 'interrogating' Westminster social security policy and identifying areas where devolution might make a difference (W2I04, Northern Ireland politician, nationalist). There were also some expressions of approval for Scotland's principle-based approach to building 'a social security system that values a human being rather than degrading them' (W2I20, Northern Ireland politician, nationalist) and its commitment to codesigning policy and systems – tempered with concerns that 'some parties [in Northern Ireland] actually are … fearful about hearing too much from the external world' (W2I04, Northern Ireland politician, nationalist). The independent review of Northern Ireland's welfare reform mitigations and the political decisions that follow may reveal much about the true extent of Scottish influence.

In addition to their influence on each other, research participants sometimes reflected on interest in social security developments in Scotland and Northern Ireland from England and Wales. Members of the National Assembly (now Senedd) Equality, Local Government and Communities Committee visited Edinburgh as part of the inquiry that led to recommendations for Welsh devolved institutions to take on some role in social security.[30] Some interviewees in both Scotland and Northern Ireland were conscious of increased attention from Wales in recent times. There were obvious aspirations for action by the UK Government to address areas of devolved-level concern, not least because this would avoid additional expenditure from devolved budgets. This has been reflected in recent appeals from Ministers and Children's Commissioners for a UK-level retreat from the two-child limit on universal credit and child tax credits and the October 2021 cut to the universal credit standard allowance.[31] However, the interview data reveal little expectation that the UK Government would heed such appeals or be interested in learning from social security initiatives in the devolved policy laboratories. One interviewee accused both the UK and Scottish Governments of being more concerned with 'slagging off the other system' than learning from it (W2I06, Scotland politician, unionist). Whether or not this is a fair assessment of the UK Government's position, UK legislators and the Social Security Advisory Committee have recommended that the DWP consider some changes to policy and practice grounded in Scottish objectives of poverty reduction, more flexible, claimant-friendly administrative practice, relaxation of behavioural conditionality and coproduction.[32]

Conclusion

Social security has unquestionably taken on a more regional or devolutionary character within the UK. However, the extent of divergence has been limited.

[30] Equality, Local Government and Communities Committee, *Benefits in Wales: Options for Better Delivery* (Cardiff: National Assembly, 2019).

[31] S Holland, B Adamson and K Yiasouma, letter to Thérèse Coffey MP, 21 May 2021. Available at: https://cypcs.org.uk/resources/childrens-commissioners-for-scotland-northern-ireland-and-wales-letter-to-secretary-of-state-for-work-and-pensions/; Department for Communities, 'Communities Minister Hargey and Scottish and Welsh Ministers call for reversal of UC £20 uplift decision' (news release, 27 August 2021). Available at: www.communities-ni.gov.uk/news/communities-minister-hargey-and-scottish-and-welsh-ministers-call-reversal-uc-ps20-uplift-decision.

[32] Scottish Affairs Committee, above n 24; Social Security Advisory Committee, *How DWP Involves Disabled People When Developing or Evaluating Programmes That Affect Them* (OP25, London: SSAC, 2021).

Regardless of location in the UK, the system continues to be mainly composed of the same type of benefits, responding to the same social risks, providing a very similar level of financial support, subject to a very similar set of eligibility criteria. This is the case even when, as with Scottish disability assistance, the benefits themselves have different names. Still, the significance of divergence (in the form of top-up payments, tweaks to eligibility criteria and differences in operational delivery) to claimants should not be underestimated. The question of whether devolved social citizenships are emerging, though, is not just about the extent of divergence to date. Once it has been established that divergence is permissible in principle and possible in practice, mindsets can change and it can take on its own momentum. Parity ceases to be the default, although it may – and for now does – remain the norm. Devolved social security is in the early stages of a journey, but the implications of that journey for social citizenship in the UK demand assessment. The final chapter draws some conclusions about the state of the social union in the early 2020s.

10

Conclusion: The State of the Social Union

Introduction

How the state protects people from poverty varies over time. The early twenty-first century has seen significant developments in the minimum standard of living the state supports through the social security system, the obligations it imposes on recipients of support and the tier of government that determines approaches to and operates systems for poverty relief. This concluding chapter assesses the state of the UK's social union in 2021, asking whether there can be said to be a single UK social citizenship, or whether there are now distinct, territorially bounded social citizenships in (some of) its constituent countries. This requires consideration of legislative trajectories, ideological visions and whether it is empirically credible – if it ever was – to speak of a single UK welfare state. The relationship between developments in the social union and political union is then considered and reflections given on what current welfare state and constitutional developments mean for the applicability, reinterpretation or otherwise of Marshall's theory of citizenship. The chapter concludes with some thoughts on future research priorities for devolved social citizenships.

Trajectories in Social Citizenship(s)

As Chapter 2 noted, it is possible to examine citizenship from an empirical or a normative perspective.[1] TH Marshall's writing blends both approaches and this book has sought to do the same. To the extent that social citizenship is a legal status whose nature can be empirically examined, its twenty-first century evolution is sketched out in the legislative developments outlined in Chapters 4 and 5. At UK level, a simplified version is: a decade-long trend towards somewhat greater generosity, followed by a decade of austerity, with future trajectories uncertain following the coronavirus pandemic; alongside this, a more continuous escalation of the citizen's responsibilities when financial support from the state is required. There have been other changes, notably the restructuring of incapacity-related benefits by the Welfare Reform Act 2007 and of social assistance in general as well as adult disability benefits by its 2012 successor, but retrenchment has been central post-2010. Innovations including the household benefit cap and two-child limit on universal credit and child tax credits have broken the Beveridgean link between need and benefit awards, reasserting the principle of less eligibility.

Social citizenship has provided no obstacle to this retrenchment. Nor has human rights law, save in a few cases concerning housing support to the most 'deserving' poor.[2] The reassertion of the less eligibility principle has won judicial acquiescence without so much as a passing mention of the ICESCR's general prohibition of retrogression in social rights in the UK Supreme Court. Perennial dissenters Lady Hale and Lord Kerr argued that certain reforms displayed a disregard for gendered impacts and the best interests of children that the ECHR (read with the UNCRC) could not tolerate.[3] Following their retirements, the new Court has moved swiftly to shut the door on such arguments.[4] It is too soon to

[1] M Lister, '"Marshall-ing" social and political citizenship: towards a unified conception of citizenship' (2005) 40(4) *Government and Opposition* 471.

[2] *R (on the application of Carmichael) v Secretary of State for Work and Pensions* [2016] UKSC 58.

[3] *R (on the application of SG) v Secretary of State for Work and Pensions* [2015] UKSC 16.

[4] *R (on the application of SC) v Secretary of State for Work and Pensions* [2021] UKSC 26.

definitively state that the era in which O'Cinneide could depict the Supreme Court as the engine for reading social rights into the ECHR has come to an end,[5] but the possibility must be considered. While the situation might differ in states with constitutionally entrenched social rights, the Court appears to confirm that in the UK 'social citizenship rights … can only be as strong as politics makes them'.[6]

The rather different story of devolved-level developments can similarly be glimpsed in statute. The principles set out in the Social Security (Scotland) Act 2018 hold the promise of a different sort of social security system at devolved level. At the same time, the Scotland Act 1998, as amended in 2016, makes clear that the 'Scottish' social security system accounts for a relatively small share of social security in Scotland. The Northern Ireland Act 1998 devolves a far greater role in social protection, but its provision requiring consultation on the desirability of shared, UK-wide systems foretells the confusion that has emerged as to how meaningful this devolved competence is in practice.[7] The very form of Northern Irish social security legislation post-2010 tells its own story. The fact that the Welfare Reform Act 2012 is mirrored in the Welfare Reform (Northern Ireland) Order 2015, made at Westminster, rather than an Act of the Assembly, speaks to the challenges recent UK-level reforms have presented a polity accustomed to parity but fearful of its implications in an age of austerity. Returning to Scotland, the Regulations establishing the various forms of disability assistance – still a work in progress as this book was nearing completion – themselves show something not far removed from parity with England and Wales and raise the question of how easy or otherwise it will be to develop a distinctively Scottish approach.

A Vision for Social Citizenship – Or Visions for Social Citizenships?

Concerns about the impact on the people affected by UK-level reforms since 2010 have not been confined to the devolved countries, but specific claims have been made about the inappropriateness of aspects of the UK system to Scotland and Northern Ireland. A key question for this book has been the extent to which these claims reflect the existence or emergence of distinct social citizenship ideologies in the different UK countries.

At UK level, Beveridge's proposals for a post-Second World War welfare state envisage a partnership between the state, individual and private sector.[8] In practice, the liberal welfare state model, to which the UK social security system largely

[5] C O'Cinneide, A modest proposal: destitution, state responsibility and the European Convention on Human Rights' (2008) 5 *European Human Rights Law Review* 583.

[6] SL Greer (ed), *Devolution and Social Citizenship in the UK* (Bristol: Policy Press, 2009) cover matter.

[7] Northern Ireland Act 1998 c 47 s 87.

[8] W Beveridge, *Social insurance and allied services* (Cmd 6404, London: HMSO, 1942).

adheres, places primary responsibility for poverty avoidance on the individual. The state's role is to protect against the most severe forms of poverty, with limited regard for egalitarianism or income maintenance, guiding principles of the social democratic and conservative models respectively. Within this paradigm, the generosity and conditionality of provision have evolved over time, reflecting – as Chapter 4 noted – changing conceptions of poverty. From 1997–2010, the individual's primary responsibility for his or her own economic welfare through paid employment sat alongside a resurgent belief (compared to the 1979–1997 period) in the necessity of redistributive measures to reduce relative poverty. Post-2010 austerity in social security has sometimes been couched in technocratic terms as a necessary response to a crisis in the public finances, sometimes in more ideological terms as removing obstacles to self-reliance and voluntary, community-led action to address social problems. It also reflects hints of renewed scepticism that relative poverty ought to be a concern of the state at all.

As Chapters 6 and 7 highlighted, it was clear that Scottish interviewees were accustomed to thinking about what they wanted from their welfare state and the sort of society it ought to underpin. This reflected the wider political and public conversation about social justice that predates the 2014 referendum and has continued thereafter. While the debate as to whether public opinion in Scotland differs significantly to that in England will likely continue,[9] findings in Chapter 7 showed a general desire among the elite participants for a more rights-based, kinder and (less unanimously) more redistributive approach to social security. There was a near-consensus that the UK system had lost its way in some respects, although disagreement as to the extent to which it had done so, how far Scotland ought to diverge and whether radical rhetoric from the Scottish Government would be matched with action. The devolution settlement places legal and practical constraints on Scotland's scope to diverge from England and Wales on social security, as described in Chapter 9. There were some hints in the interview data that, given independence or greatly enhanced autonomy, appetite for the universalist, social democratic approach periodically endorsed by the Scottish Government could take flight.[10]

In Northern Ireland, academic writing and officials who took part in the fieldwork suggest that questions of social citizenship do not command elected representatives' attention. The findings suggest this characterisation may not be altogether fair. Given the opportunity, politicians – admittedly recruited based on a likely interest in social security – could express strong views on the matter. Officials were typically reticent about discussing the 'proper' function of social protection in wave one, but less so in wave two. However, thinking tended to be more reactive than in Scotland, stressing the need to protect citizens from specific

[9] For some recent findings on the question, see C Deeming, 'Social inequality: is Scotland more Nordic than liberal?'in E Clery, J Curtice, J Frankenburg, H Morgan and S Reid (eds), *British Social Attitudes 38* (London: NatCen, 2021).

[10] Ibid.

problems flowing from UK-level reforms rather than expounding a vision for a Northern Irish social citizenship. Even participants who believed the trajectory of UK policy since 1980 has delivered 'nothing that has been of benefit to claimants' (W1I04, Northern Ireland politician, nationalist) offered only a solution based on somewhat higher benefits and the relaxation of conditionality. There was no evidence of appetite for a wholly new approach based on fundamentally different principles. To the extent that a Northern Irish vision for social security emerges from the research, it takes the UK model as its starting point but seeks to remove features deemed not to work in the social, economic and housing context of Northern Ireland, somewhat enhance protection against poverty and improve relational aspects of the system. Arguably, agreement even on these matters is an achievement in a fragmented polity and a five-party Executive.

Still a UK Social Security System?

A truly unitary, uniform UK welfare state has never existed. Divergence in multiple public services predates legislative devolution to Scotland and Wales (devolution in Northern Ireland predates the foundation of the modern welfare state), but has widened since 1998.[11] Social security is central to the question of whether it is appropriate to speak of a single UK social citizenship not only because of its importance to the guarantee of a minimum standard of living, but also because of the lack of divergence and (outside Northern Ireland) devolved competence prior to 2012. The period since 2012 has opened up space for a tentative, partial but real regionalisation of social security. In Northern Ireland, this has involved greater use of long-held devolved powers to diverge from the Westminster approach. In Scotland, the crucial change has been the devolution of social security competences in 2016, from which some divergence has followed. Whether a recognisable UK approach to social security still exists, or will continue to exist in the medium term, is key to the question of whether a UK social citizenship will continue to exist.

For one group of participants, the fundamentals of a shared UK system remain in place, albeit that the system has taken on a devolutionary flavour. In some cases, this was regarded as desirable:

> The welfare state and the health service are two elements of public policy that the UK can be rightly proud of … [The] framework is right, how we implement it should take into account particular needs of the geographical or devolved administration (W2I03, Northern Ireland politician, unionist).

[11] For further discussion, see N Timmins, *The Four UK Health Systems: Learning from Each Other* (London: King's Fund, 2013); G Bevan, M Karanikolos, J Exley, E Nolte, S Connolly and N Mays, *The Four Health Systems of the United Kingdom: How Do They Compare?* (London: Health Foundation/ Nuffield Trust, 2014).

> I think our systems will stay broadly similar … We can be that little bit more generous if we wish to. I think that probably will suffice to address perhaps the most outrageous problems … these sort of egregious examples of austerity politics … I think the general expectation is a shared one across our country, and I think it will remain so for some time. (W2I15, Scotland politician, unionist).

Other interviewees saw this as less desirable: 'the system that was being forced on Northern Ireland was not of our making, was not what we wanted, but we were stuck with it' (W2I19, Northern Ireland politician, neutral). However, the same interviewees often regarded general conformity with the UK model as unavoidable. This might be due to the cost of full autonomy in – and full responsibility for funding – social protection, or the practical difficulties associated with unravelling common structures:

> The money that pays for pensions is actually the money that the UK as a state gets off its assets and its investment … To understand what [Scotland's] share of that part would be, that's a hugely complicated thing. You would have to do it for independence but that would only follow years of negotiation (W2I08, Scotland politician, unionist).
>
> Who does pay for your social security long term? Those are really difficult – the monies are so large and there's no easy answer … We're a poor region in a country, in a union that's facing major challenges. Nobody else is going to rush in to pay for our pensions or our social security (W2I29, Northern Ireland official).

For a second broad group, almost exclusively Scottish, the idea of a single social security system seemed an anachronism.

> There is no longer a single UK welfare state, that's not the situation. We don't have it with the NHS anymore, we certainly don't have it with social security anymore … All social security provisions will eventually end up in the Scottish Parliament … the only one short of independence that I think parties could argue should stay at a UK level is pensions (W2I07, Scotland politician, nationalist).

While not all participants in this group felt divergence had reached the point where the single system had ceased to be, this was nonetheless seen as the near-inevitable endpoint: 'Unless there is a significant change in Government on both sides of the border then policy will continue to diverge' (W2I10, Scotland official). This did not necessarily imply the disappearance of *a* UK system in the medium term; even if uniformity were largely maintained in the core low income and retirement benefits, this could sit alongside devolved systems with a more limited remit, but a 'drastically different' philosophy (W2I13, Scotland politician, unionist).

One point of agreement was that, at this early stage of the devolved social security journey, the situation remains dynamic. Northern Ireland unionists remained reluctant to be seen 'hammering the [UK] welfare system', while welcoming the potential for the devolved legislatures to protect citizens from the 'terrible' consequences of some recent policy decisions (W2I01, Northern Ireland politician, unionist). If the disproportionate impact of current UK policies on the devolved countries or a philosophical divide between current UK and devolved elites have driven divergence, future reconvergence cannot be ruled out. Some research participants hoped this could occur through the power of example:

> [Politician] was listing all of the things that were different in Scotland that he was not happy about. Some of them were things like free health and free prescriptions and free education and no bedroom tax … they don't talk about what Scotland's done as being good, why can't we have that. You *could* have that. You could have that tomorrow, vote for it (W1I24, Scotland politician, nationalist).

Whether the Scottish and Northern Irish experiments in social security have greatly influenced the UK Government remains to be seen, but certainly parliamentarians have taken note of developments.[12] Other participants thought the coronavirus pandemic might result in popular demand for (at least) the maintenance of the 'temporary transformation' of social security it had brought about:[13]

> One of the things the Covid crisis has shown is that people do look to the state when they're in crisis and there's an expectation there still that there's a kind of cradle to grave level of provision … There's a chance of some hopefulness, that what emerges from this is a rejection of the idea that huge swathes of the economy can be fed on poverty wages with a little bit of social security to top them up if they behave properly (W2I30, Scotland politician, nationalist).

It would be mere speculation to express a view on whether the legacy of coronavirus will include a reversal of recent trajectories in social security. Public opinion on the subject appears to have been shifting even before the pandemic.[14] What the research findings show is that limited increases to the generosity of the current suite of benefits would better match the objectives of elites in Northern Ireland than their counterparts in Scotland. Even in Northern Ireland, desire for a degree of divergence is likely to remain as long as there is a perceived mismatch between support with housing costs and the country's social housing stock.

The Social Union and the Political Union

Questions about the welfare state and constitutional questions have never been far removed in the story of social citizenship this book tells. The devolution movement in Scotland is widely depicted as a movement for a Scottish social citizenship. Developments in social security since 2012 have occurred against the backdrop of

[12] Work and Pensions Committee and Northern Ireland Affairs Committee, *Welfare Policy in Northern Ireland* (HC2100, London: House of Commons, 2019); Scottish Affairs Committee, *Welfare Policy in Scotland* (HC55, London: House of Commons, 2021).

[13] R Machin, 'COVID-19 and the temporary transformation of the UK social security system' (2021) 41(4) *Critical Social Policy* 651; see also J Abey and A Harrop, *Going with the Grain: How to Increase Social Security with Public Support* (London: Fabian Society, 2021).

[14] J Curtice, 'Will Covid-19 change attitudes towards the welfare state?' (2020) 27(1) *Progressive Review* 93.

a referendum on Scottish independence in which questions of social justice again played a key role.[15] Unionists, nationalists, neutrals and officials all embrace divergence, yet differences of enthusiasm remain. These align with, but may or may not be determined by, constitutional outlooks. More obviously, divergence between the UK's constituent countries on social security has only been possible because of constitutional change, in the form of the post-referendum revision of the Scottish devolution settlement and the reimagining of the powerful constitutional convention in favour of parity in Northern Ireland. If constitutional developments, debates and outlooks can influence developments in social citizenship, changes in the nature of social citizenship and the social union may also have implications for the political union.

Devolution is linked with fundamental questions about the nature of the UK, including whether 'the nation' is represented by the UK itself, its four constituent countries or even England, Wales, Scotland and Ireland. Given its nation building role, the organisation of the welfare state has a part to play in answering that question. If social solidarity is the glue that binds citizens to each other and to the state, regionalisation of the sharing community may reflect, cause or perpetuate a shift in solidarity and loyalties from the UK to its constituent countries. The relationship may work in two ways: regionalisation of welfare states might foster a sense of solidarity and co-citizenship at the Scottish or Northern Irish rather than UK level, or people might favour devolved responsibility because they already regard the devolved country as their 'primary political community'.[16] In either case, unionists might be expected to favour the maintenance of 'a United Kingdom built on the pooling and sharing of risks and resources',[17] nationalists to view welfare state regionalisation as a welcome transfer of 'authority-legitimacy' from Westminster to Holyrood or Stormont.[18]

As Chapter 8 emphasised, the relationship between social citizenship and constitutional questions is more complicated than this caricature. There is precedent for an explicitly unionist case for greater autonomy in social security as a means of creating a 'less dysfunctional' UK.[19] Some unionists in the study

[15] G Mooney and G Scott, 'The 2014 Scottish independence debate: questions of social welfare and social justice' (2015) 21(3) *Journal of Poverty and Social Justice* 5.

[16] Henderson and McEwen suggest citizens may be more likely to exercise their political rights at the regional level if that is where their identity and allegiance is located. According to this logic, the same citizens might be expected to prefer regional responsibility for their social rights – A Henderson and N McEwen, 'Regions as primary political communities: a multi-level comparative analysis of turnout in regional elections' (2015) 45(2) *Publius* 189.

[17] D Gayle, 'UK at risk of becoming a failed state, says Gordon Brown' (*Guardian*, 25 January 2021). Available at: www.theguardian.com/politics/2021/jan/25/uk-at-risk-of-becoming-failed-state-says-gordon-brown; Office of Gordon and Sarah Brown, 'Scotland' (Office of Gordon and Sarah Brown, nd). Available at: https://gordonandsarahbrown.com/campaign/scotland/.

[18] M Evans, 'New Labour and the rise of the new constitutionalism', M Beech and S Lee (eds), *Ten years of New Labour* (Basingstoke: Palgrave Macmillan, 2008) 79.

[19] G Lodge and A Trench, *Devo More and Welfare: Devolving Benefits and Policy for a Stronger Union* (London: IPPR, 2014) 5.

echoed this view, arguing that successful devolution of social security 'shows the UK system working' (W2I13, Scotland politician, unionist). Others advocated divergence from UK policy developments they disliked, despite fears that doing so might 'erode the constitutional settlement' (W1I25, Scotland politician, unionist). Nationalists had no need for soul-searching on the rights and wrongs of divergence in social security; their constitutional and social policy objectives have largely been complementary since 2010. 'Political opportunities' have arisen as 'the imposition of austerity fed an anti-Tory political culture in Scotland and weakened the case for the union as a means of securing and distributing resources to promote the common good'.[20] In Northern Ireland, too, nationalists' anti-austerity position has sat relatively comfortably with an anti-Westminster constitutional position.

Whether or not divergence in social security is pursued for consciously constitutional ends, the enduring position of the constitutional question as the main fault line in Northern Ireland politics, and its increasing centrality to Scottish politics in the era of the independence 'neverendum', means the constitutional implications of such divergence were seldom far from participants' minds. This applies to devolution in general:

> Federalism can provide national minorities with the jurisdictional, fiscal and bureaucratic resources with which to mount more effective secessionist claims. It can create a political and institutional identity that politicises and mobilises simple cultural difference … 'While [federalism] provides national minorities with a workable alternative to secession, it also helps to make secession a more realistic alternative to federalism.'[21]

From this perspective, every step towards greater divergence, every demonstration of administrative (in)competence or political (im)maturity, every assumption of additional powers and every political desire achieved or thwarted at devolved level potentially forms part of a 'constitutional chain reaction'.[22] This particularly evident in Scotland, where it was noted that debates around the use and sufficiency of the new social security competences 'will always be framed around that context [of the constitutional debate]' (W1I09a, Scotland official). Northern Ireland's constitutional debate is no more likely to lose currency. However, despite the convention of parity with Great Britain in social security having its roots (in

[20] J Wiggan, 'Contesting the austerity and "welfare reform" narrative of the UK Government: forging a social democratic imaginary in Scotland' (2017) 37(11–12) *International Journal of Sociology and Social Policy* 639, 640.

[21] R Simeon, 'Federalism and social justice: thinking through the tangle', SL Greer, *Territory, Democracy and Justice: Regionalism and Federalism in Western Democracies* (Basingstoke: Palgrave Macmillan, 2006) 31, citing W Kymlicka, *Politics in the Vernacular: Nationalism, Multiculturalism and Citizenship* (Oxford: Oxford University Press, 2001) 118; see also J Bradbury, *Constitutional Politics and Territorial Politics in the UK, Volume 1: Union and Devolution 1997–2007* (Bristol: Bristol University Press, 2021).

[22] C Jeffery, 'Constitutional change – without end?' (2015) 86(2) *Political Quarterly* 275, 275.

part) in the constitutional objectives of previous Unionist governments,[23] there was less of a feeling there that social policy divergence has a direct bearing on the country's constitutional future:

> In Scotland obviously there's a sense of asserting your own independence in as many ways as possible. Some people would say Sinn Féin here are trying to make Northern Ireland much like the Republic of Ireland so they'll get unification by a thousand cuts … I suppose a break in parity could be seen as a constitutional impact … But you've seen that with the DUP on abortion and marriage equality so … I personally don't view it through a constitutional lens (W2I02, Northern Ireland politician, neutral).

Questions of social citizenship, then, have a role to play in future constitutional debates, particularly in Scotland, but will not, on their own, be decisive.[24] Among current controversies, they almost certainly lag behind the ongoing fallout from the UK's withdrawal from the European Union as a source of 'anxiety around … the constitutional position' (W2I20, Northern Ireland politician, nationalist).[25] Identity politics have a particular salience in Northern Ireland, but may also play a role in Scotland – neither nationalism nor unionism there can claim a monopoly on 'Scottishness',[26] but British, European and social democratic identities, and the constitutional arrangement most capable of accommodating or reconciling them, also matter. Nor should the importance of personality be dismissed. A journalist recounts: 'It is the norm on the Scottish National Party campaign trail to have to fight one's way towards [First Minister] Nicola Sturgeon through streets packed with admirers and selfie-hunters, some even brought to tears by her proximity.'[27] The quote tends towards hyperbole, but captures the importance of a charismatic, popular advocate for independence – in this case an explicitly social democratic independence – or continued union. Some research participants ascribed similar importance to former Prime Minister Gordon Brown as a standard bearer for the union – but a reformed union, possibly involving an enhanced role for the Scottish Parliament as guarantor of the social rights of citizenship:

> Researcher: How important did you feel David Cameron's promises regarding devolution were to the no vote [in the referendum]?
>
> Interviewee: I don't think it was David Cameron. I think it was Gordon Brown plus the Daily Record … That probably made a difference … People myself that I know who

[23] M Simpson, 'Developing constitutional principles through firefighting: social security parity in Northern Ireland' (2015) 22(1) *Journal of Social Security Law* 31.

[24] For a similar perspective on the relationship between constitutional and welfare state competition in Spain, see B Suárez Corujo, 'Devolution and decentralisation in social security: the situation in Spain' in G Vonk and P Schoukens (eds), *Devolution and Decentralisation in Social Security: A European Comparative Perspective* (The Hague: Eleven, 2019).

[25] M Kenny, P Rycroft and J Sheldon, *Union at the Crossroads: Can the British State Handle the Challenges of Devolution?* (London: Constitution Society, 2021).

[26] M Keating and N McEwen, 'The Scottish independence debate', M Keating (ed), *Debating Scotland: Issues of Independence and Union in the 2014 Referendum* (Oxford: Oxford University Press, 2017) 18.

[27] L Brooks, 'Nicola Sturgeon: No 10 cannot stand in the way of independence' (*Guardian*, 11 April 2021). Available at: www.theguardian.com/politics/2021/apr/11/nicola-sturgeon-independence-uk-government-cannot-stand-in-way.

> had intended voting yes who changed to no because we were gonnae get extra things [devolved] anyway (W1I23, Scotland politician, nationalist).

Conversely, a 'more assertive and muscular style of unionism' that denies Scottish claims of popular sovereignty and is seen to tread on the toes of the devolved institutions could itself be a boon to nationalism.[28]

In Northern Ireland, the relationship between the social and political unions is still more complex. 'Doing social security right' might 'demonstrate Scotland's capability to be an independent country' (W2I16, Scotland official), but independence is not a credible option for Northern Ireland at present. Nor did any interviewee suggest its social security system should converge with that of the Republic of Ireland in anticipation of unification. Despite occasional expressions of unionist trepidation, divergence in social citizenship, in its current, tentative form, was not regarded as a serious threat to the political union. A small number of participants suggested that if Brexit or other issues do create a sense that the political union is inexorably 'break[ing] down', then implications for the welfare state will become an increasingly important dimension of the constitutional debate, as in Scotland:[29]

> As questions arise about whether it is union or unity … then more and more people decide well, what is the cost benefits analysis or what is the financial risk and welfare is going to be more and more part of that equation. So, given that the spend is so huge, and disproportionately huge here compared to Britain, then it is going to become just one of those issues that is going to be profiled as people talk about the economics and the viability of … Irish independence through unity (W2I04, NI politician, nationalist).

Important as the welfare state is to the union, it would be an exaggeration to describe it as *the* terrain on which the battle for the future of the UK will be fought. The literature and both waves of fieldwork largely agree that social security and underlying conceptions of social justice were (and are) a vital component of debates on the desirability of Scottish independence. However, this is just one of a range of important policy areas where devolved legislatures and governments have made different choices or sought the freedom to make different choices to those the UK Parliament and Government makes. No single policy issue is likely to be decisive on its own. However, any future constitutional reform – federalisation, continued incremental development of individual devolution settlements or secession by one or more countries – will have to consider the role of the different countries and regions as guarantors of economic welfare.

[28] Kenny and others, above n 25 at 4; A Ramsay, 'It's not enough to vote for an independence referendum, you need to campaign for it' (Open Democracy, 11 May 2021). Available at: www.opendemocracy.net/en/opendemocracyuk/its-not-enough-to-vote-for-an-independence-referendum-you-need-to-campaign-for-it/.

[29] For a tentative academic consideration of this question, see C Fitzpatrick and C O'Sullivan, 'Comparing social security provision in the North and South of Ireland: past developments and future challenges' (2021) 32(2) *Irish Studies in International Affairs* 283.

Marshall's Theory of Citizenship in a Regionalised Welfare State

The ink on the National Assistance Act 1948 had barely dried when Marshall presented his empirical and normative account of citizenship in a modern welfare state in his lecture on 'Citizenship and social class'. Fewer than 20 years had passed between the 1948 Act and the publication of 'The right to welfare'. More than 55 years separate that essay from this book, in which period the UK and its welfare state have undergone considerable change, in ways that can appear at odds with mainstream interpretations of Marshall. His own speculation that, in tempering the excesses of capitalism and eliminating the need for socialism, the arrival of the welfare state had brought about the 'end of ideology' looks no more credible than the notion that the end of the Cold War represented the 'end of history'[30] – although both Fukuyama (explicitly) and Marshall (implicitly) would later deny that these were meant as statements of empirical fact. For Marshall, if the Beveridge report was a 'masterly plan [whose] message had the force of a new Gospel', in practice its promise was never fully realised.[31] Shifting ideological, economic and fiscal considerations, and changing conceptions of poverty, meant the proper function, generosity and conditionality of the welfare state continued and continues to be contested.

This means that normative and empirical perspectives on social citizenship are closely linked. The empirical status of citizenship changes because the dominant normative view of what rights and responsibilities citizenship ought to confer changes. Marshall's observation in 1981, at the start of a previous Conservative-dominated era, that 'welfare appear[s] to be suffering a loss of status'[32] is equally apt as a description of the views of the UK elite, much of the popular media and a sizeable section of the public in 2010. Indeed, Baumberg Geiger suggests that periods of greater generosity *cause* loss of faith in redistribution, while periods of austerity produce demand for greater redistribution.[33] However, Marshall himself offers a powerful normative statement of what the social rights of citizenship ought to involve: as a minimum, the right to 'a modicum of economic welfare and security'.[34] This lacks the legal status of, for example, a right to an adequate standard of living (article 11 ICESCR), but the frequency

[30] TH Marshall, 'Value problems of welfare-capitalism' in *The Right to Welfare and Other Essays* (New York: Free Press, 1981) 105; F Fukuyama, 'The end of history?' (1989) 16 *The National Interest* 3.

[31] TH Marshall, 'Afterthought: the hyphenated society' in *The Right to Welfare and Other Essays* (New York: Free Press, 1981) 130; F Fukuyama, 'Reflections on the end of history, five years later' (1995) 34(2) *History and Theory* 27.

[32] Marshall, above n 31 at 131.

[33] B Baumberg Geiger, 'The elephant in the room of social security reform' (Inequalities, 31 May 2021). Available at: https://inequalitiesblog.wordpress.com/2021/05/31/the-elephant-in-the-room-of-social-security-reform/.

[34] TH Marshall, 'Citizenship and social class' in TH Marshall and T Bottomore, *Citizenship and Social Class* (London: Pluto, 1992) 8.

with which it recurs in academic writing on social protection shows that it remains a compelling manifesto for the citizen's right to welfare. As well as providing a baseline for a minimum acceptable standard of living, 'Citizenship and social class' provides a convenient continuum to track the ebb and flow of social entitlements between that baseline and the more ambitious vision of a society in which everyone can access the resources to 'share to the full in the social heritage and … live the life of a civilised being'.[35]

Changes in the level of working age social security in the UK between 2010 and the onset of the coronavirus pandemic steered the citizen's social rights towards the less generous end of that continuum. For those on the receiving end of some of the system's more punitive features or otherwise excluded from support, it is impossible to credibly claim that even the minimum standard of a modicum of economic welfare is achieved.[36] However, pressures on the welfare state flowing from economic change, austerity, growing conditionality and welfare chauvinism are not unique to this period.[37] In 1981, Marshall noted the 'precarious and somewhat battered condition' of the welfare state,[38] and presumably would have realised that this trajectory could continue absent a further change in the political context.

Devolution brings a new challenge to the Marshallian view of citizenship as an equal status. The above sections emphasise the need for caution about the extent of divergence in vision or in practice. Nonetheless, decisions about the nature of the citizen's social rights are now being taken by devolved as well as UK institutions. Those institutions to some extent base their decisions on different values, socio-economic contexts and policy objectives. As a result, they sometimes reach different decisions, so that the social rights of citizenship do look subtly different in different parts of the UK. Marshall appears to have entirely failed to predict this development and probably would not have welcomed it, given that his account of the modernisation of citizenship is in part an account of movement from local to national welfare systems (see Chapter 3). Nonetheless, in the case of regionalism as much as the cases of austerity and conditionality, Marshallian theory predicts the process by which change has occurred, even if not the nature of the changes. In the UK, accession to and incorporation of human rights treaties has not transformed the essentially political nature of social rights.[39] The welfare state has evolved in a way that reflects voter preference for parties who embrace austerity and conditionality and is evolving in a way that reflects the regionalisation of democratic processes.

[35] Ibid.

[36] C Fitzpatrick, G McKeever and M Simpson, 'Conditionality, discretion and TH Marshall's "right to welfare"' (2019) 41(4) *Journal of Social Welfare and Family Law* 445.

[37] See T Bottomore, 'Citizenship and social class, forty years on', TH Marshall and T Bottomore, *Citizenship and Social Class* (London: Pluto, 1992).

[38] Marshall, above n 31 at 129.

[39] M Simpson, G McKeever and C Fitzpatrick, 'Legal protection against destitution in the UK: restoring a right to a subsistence minimum' (under review).

Marshall might well have shared what Greer and Mätzke suggest is the widely held presumption that such developments are bad news for the citizen's social rights: 'Federalism slows welfare state development, and more federalism slows it more', largely by 'multiplying veto points'. This thesis, they argue, breaks down in the UK context as it ignores the 'much greater elite consensus on the value and structure of the welfare state in Scotland and Wales than … in England'.[40] Jeffery agrees:

> The examples of Scotland [and] Wales … directly contradict the idea of a race to the bottom. There, decentralised government has provided possibilities for reinstating earlier social policy commitments, insuring against their future erosion by central government, or more generally developing new ways of pursuing established policy aims [and] to express a popular preference for territorial community over statewide values.[41]

Northern Ireland is absent from these assessments. In recent years it, too, fails to conform with the orthodoxy Greer, Mätzke and Jeffery critique – albeit for different reasons. Here, decentralisation does create a veto point, but it is retrogression rather than welfare state development that is resisted. Devolution is less likely to act as a brake on welfare state expansion because the parity convention in social security means Northern Ireland has nothing to gain in fiscal terms from being less generous. Resistance to the erosion of certain entitlements was a key driver of demand for social security devolution in Scotland, as the wave one interview data reflect, but following the transfer of competences there has been a greater effort to move from mitigation to innovation. Whether this reflects a 'preference for territorial community' over UK citizenship depends on constitutional aspirations and party allegiances, but the objective of advancing Scottish values over 'statewide values' seems more widely shared.

These developments are not routinely described in Marshallian terms, but it is no great leap to conclude that Scottish and Northern Irish elites no longer believe the UK social security system sufficiently guarantees a modicum of economic welfare. Equally, Scotland's adoption of dignity and the other social security principles as the rhetorical foundation of a devolved system can be interpreted as a promise to underwrite an acceptable minimum standard of living and to treat claimants as citizens with rights, not beneficiaries of taxpayers' goodwill. At the same time, such devolved social citizenships as exist have not diverged sufficiently to describe them as anything other than variants of the UK model. If social citizenship is becoming tiered, the nation (or, in the UK, multi-national) state continues to occupy the top tier. The more apt multi-level governance metaphor might be that the devolved social citizenships are nested within, and therefore continue to

[40] SL Greer and M Mätzke, 'Introduction: devolution and citizenship rights' in SL Greer (ed), *Devolution and Social Citizenship in the UK* (Bristol: Policy Press, 2009) 9.

[41] C Jeffery, 'Devolution and social citizenship: which society, whose citizenship?' in SL Greer (ed), *Territory, Democracy and Justice: Regionalism and Federalism in Western Democracies* (Basingstoke: Palgrave Macmillan, 2006) 90–91.

greatly resemble, the UK model.[42] In the recent political climate, such differences as have emerged may undermine Marshall's vision for an equal citizenship while supporting his vision for a social minimum – but only to a limited extent.

Reflections

The language of social citizenship does not come naturally to policymakers. Nonetheless, it is not difficult to gauge their views on the subject from the views they express on social protection. By the second wave of fieldwork a broad consensus had emerged among participants that elements of the model of social citizenship being constructed at UK level conflict with the needs and/or preferences of the devolved countries, and that the devolved countries should control some of the levers of the welfare state. How much divergence was envisaged varied, but the view that some divergence is welcome and necessary spanned both the unionist-nationalist and left-right spectrums of mainstream political opinion and was embraced by those officials who were prepared to express a view. Clearly, the regionalisation of social citizenship has not reached its endpoint. At the very least, there is work to be done on the construction of a Scottish social security system within the confines of the current devolved competences. However, there was a reasonably widespread expectation among participants that more areas of social security will be devolved in time, assuming Scotland remains in the UK, and that the status quo is unsatisfactory regardless of constitutional objectives. Of course, devolving powers does not guarantee divergence, as Northern Ireland shows. There, the question is whether the post-2015 'mitigations' represent a fundamental change to thinking on parity or simply ease in a fairly painful set of reforms. Whatever the answer to this question proves to be, the principle that social citizenship can, should and does have a regional dimension is unequivocally established, in law and in the minds of Scottish and Northern Irish elites.

With legal and political developments still unfolding, it is fitting to offer some observations on a future research agenda for social citizenship in the devolved context. First, this has been a top-down study, focusing on social citizenship as seen through the eyes of elite actors. A bottom-up perspective is equally important. Some work has been published on experiences of social security in the devolved countries[43] and on which tier of government should be responsible for certain issues,[44] but there is a knowledge gap around citizens' qualitative perspectives on

[42] T Faist, 'Social citizenship in the European Union: nested membership' (2001) 39(1) *Journal of Common Market Studies* 37.

[43] R Patrick and M Simpson, *Universal Credit Could Be a Lifeline in Northern Ireland, but It Must Be Designed with People Who Use It* (York: JRF, 2020); L Robertson, S Wright and ABR Stewart, *How Well is Universal Credit Supporting People in Glasgow?* (York: JRF, 2020).

[44] A Henderson, C Jeffery, D Wincott and R Wyn Jones, 'Reflections on the "devolution paradox": a comparative examination of multilevel citizenship' (2013) 47(3) *Regional Studies* 303.

the desirability of devolutionary divergence in the social rights of citizenship. In light of the claims made in the research about challenges relating to the administrative delivery of devolved social security and the importance of organisational culture, the voice of frontline staff is also an important one – one that researchers with a focus on the UK level have struggled to access.[45] Mindful of the construction of social security as a 'shared space' (W2I07, Scotland politician, nationalist) in which the roles of different tiers of government may be complementary or competitive, supportive or obstructive, but certainly overlap, a further need exists for consideration of the intergovernmental dimension of welfare state regionalisation. Indeed, McEwen and Petersohn suggest neglect of institutions to support 'shared rule' has been a failing of the UK's devolution experiment more broadly.[46]

Should a third wave of fieldwork follow, the omission of Wales will no longer be defensible, given the awakening of interest in devolution of certain social security functions among parliamentarians there.[47] More tentatively, there is currently governmental, parliamentary and/or local government support for universal basic income pilots in all three devolved countries.[48] Endorsement of UBI might represent a repudiation of the liberal approach to social security and the constraints imposed by the current devolution settlement, something that would clearly merit exploration in a later wave. From a more conventionally legal point of view, the implications for social security of the incorporation of social and economic rights into Scottish law will be watched with interest. How respect for dignity is operationalised in Scottish social security may also provide further insights into the interpretation of that contested term.

All this emphasises that devolution remains 'a process not an event',[49] in terms of its impact on social citizenship as in other respects. An opportunity exists for the social rights of citizenship to diverge between the UK countries as never before, yet constraints on their ability to do so remain. Developments in Northern Ireland challenge characterisations of devolution as a 'lost opportunity' for social policy,[50] but also challenge deeply ingrained habits and assumptions about policy development, the legislative process, administration and funding in the field of

[45] Welfare Conditionality, *Final Findings Report: Welfare Conditionality Project 2013–2018* (York: Welfare Conditionality, 2018).

[46] N McEwen and B Petersohn, 'Between Autonomy and Interdependence: The Challenges of Shared Rule after the Scottish Referendum' (2015) 86(2) *Political Quarterly* 192.

[47] Equality, Local Government and Communities Committee, *Benefits in Wales: Options for Better Delivery* (Cardiff: National Assembly, 2019).

[48] See Citizens' Basic Income Feasibility Study Steering Group, *Assessing the feasibility of citizens' basic income pilots in Scotland* (Basic Income Scotland, 2020); P Brown with J Barry, C Donaghy, J Hoey and B Elliott, *Testing A Real Peace Dividend For Northern Ireland: A Proposal for UBI* (Belfast: UBI Lab NI, 2020); G Thomas, L Morgan and P Worthington, 'What might a universal basic income mean for Wales?' (Cardiff: Senedd Research, 2021).

[49] R Davies cited by N Johnson, 'The Government of Wales Act 2006: Welsh devolution still a process and not an event?' (2007) 4 *Web Journal of Current Legal Issues*. Available at: www.bailii.org/uk/other/journals/WebJCLI/2007/issue4/johnson4.html.

[50] G Horgan and AM Gray, 'Devolution in Northern Ireland: a lost opportunity?' (2012) 32(3) *Critical Social Policy* 467.

social security. Those in Scotland promise a new world built on a human rights-based approach to social security and respect for dignity, but with only limited devolved competences and some constraints on their exercise a small number of research participants implicitly or explicitly warned that a form of parity could take root there, that another opportunity could be lost. As one participant opined:

> The only purpose of having devolution is to do things to meet the needs of the people that you represent. So I think there's a contradiction if you're saying that you want devolution, but you want to be the same as everywhere else. (W1I15, Northern Ireland politician, nationalist).

If the age of welfare regionalism has truly arrived for the UK, this remains as good a statement as any of its philosophy.

BIBLIOGRAPHY

Abey, J and Harrop, A, *Going with The Grain: How to Increase Social Security with Public Support* (London: Fabian Society, 2021).

Abou-Chadi, T and Immergut, EM, 'Recalibrating social protection: electoral competition and the new partisan politics of the welfare state' (2019) 58(2) *European Journal of Political Research* 697.

Adamson, B and White, B, 'Making it possible: realising children's rights in Scotland in a changing world' (2021) 2 *European Human Rights Law Review* 133.

Ad-Hoc Committee, *Report on whether the provisions of the Welfare Reform Bill are in conformity with the requirements for equality and observance of human rights* (NIA92/11-15, Belfast: NI Assembly, 2013).

Adler, M, 'Decision-making and appeals in social security: in need of reform?' (1997) 68(4) *Political Quarterly* 388.

Adler, M 'Understanding and analysing administrative justice' in Adler, M (ed), *Administrative Justice in Context* (Oxford: Oxford University Press, 2010).

Advice NI, Housing Rights and Law Centre NI, *Welfare reform: mitigations on a cliff edge* (Belfast: Advice NI, Housing Rights and Law Centre NI, 2018).

Alldridge, P, 'On being able to walk twenty metres: the introduction of personal independence payments' (2019) 46(3) *Journal of Law and Society* 448.

Alston, P, *Digital technology, social protection and human rights* (A/74/493, New York: United Nations, 2019).

Alviar García, H, Klare, K and Williams, LA (eds), *Social and Economic Rights in Theory and Practice: Critical Inquiries* (Abingdon: Routledge, 2015).

Andrew, HM 'The organisation of secondary education' (circular 10/65, London: Department of Education and Science, 1965).

Arendt, H, *The Origins of Totalitarianism* (London: George Allen and Unwin, 1967).

Argar, E, letter to Lord Boswell, 4 January 2019. Available at: www.parliament.uk/globalassets/documents/lords-committees/eu-justice-subcommittee/CWM/EAtoLB-PolDeclationReferencetoECHR040119.pdf.

Ashcroft, E, 'Has Scotland already spent its oil fund?' (Scottish Economy Watch, 10 July 2013). Available at: www.scottisheconomywatch.com/beth-ashcrofts-scottish/2013/07/.

Aughey, A, 'Unionism and self-determination' in Roche, PJ and Barton, B (eds), *The Northern Ireland Question: Myth and Reality* (Aldershot: Avebury, 1991).

Aughey, A and McIlheney, C, 'The Ulster Defence Association: paramilitaries and politics' (1981) 2(2) *Journal of Conflict Studies* 32.

Baldwin, J, Young, R and Wikeley, N, *Judging Social Security: The Adjudication of Claims for Benefit in Britain* (Oxford: Clarendon Press, 1992).

Banting, KG, 'Social citizenship and federalism: is a federal welfare state a contradiction in terms?' in Greer, SL (ed), *Territory, Democracy and Justice: Regionalism and Federalism in Western Democracies* (Basingstoke: Palgrave Macmillan, 2006).

Bauman, Z, 'Freedom from, in and through the state: TH Marshall's trinity of rights revisited' (2005). 44 *Theoria* 13.

Baumberg Geiger, B, 'The elephant in the room of social security reform' (Inequalities, 31 May 2021). Available at: https://inequalitiesblog.wordpress.com/2021/05/31/the-elephant-in-the-room-of-social-security-reform/.

BBC News, 'Scottish independence: Brown sets out more powers timetable' (BBC News, 8 September 2014). Available at: www.bbc.co.uk/news/uk-scotland-scotland-politics-29115556.

Beatty, C and Fothergill, S, *The Impact of Welfare Reform on Northern Ireland* (Sheffield: Centre for Economic Empowerment, 2013).

Beatty, C and Fothergill, S, 'The local and regional impact of the UK's welfare reforms' (2014) 7(1) *Cambridge Journal of Regions, Economy and Society* 63.

Beatty, C and Fothergill, S, *The cumulative impact of welfare reform on households in Scotland* (SP paper 657, Edinburgh: Scottish Parliament, 2015).

Bebayev, R, 'Re-shaping the paradigm of social solidarity in the EU: on the UK's welfare reforms and pre- and post-EU referendum developments' (2016) 18(4) *European Journal of Social Security* 356.

Beblavý, M, Marconi, G and Maselli, I, *A European Unemployment Benefit Scheme: The Rationale and the Challenges Ahead* (Luxembourg: Publications Office of the European Union, 2017).

Béland, D and Lecours, A, 'The politics of territorial solidarity: nationalism and social policy reform in Canada, the United Kingdom and Belgium' (2005) 38(6) *Comparative Political Studies* 676.

Béland, D and Lecours, A, *Nationalism and Social Policy: The Politics of Territorial Solidarity* (Oxford University Press, 2008).

Béland, D and Lecours, A, 'Does nationalism trigger welfare-state disintegration? Social policy and territorial mobilization in Belgium and Canada' (2010) 28(3) *Environment and Planning C: Government and Policy* 420.

Berry, K, *Discretionary housing payments* (SPICe briefing 14/17, Edinburgh: Scottish Parliament, 2014).

Bevan, G, Karanikolos, M, Exley, J, Nolte, E, Connolly, S and Mays, N, *The Four Health Systems of the United Kingdom: How Do They Compare?* (London: Health Foundation/Nuffield Trust, 2014).

Bevan Foundation, *Making Welfare Work for Wales: Should Benefits for People of Working Age be Devolved?* (Merthyr Tydfil: Bevan Foundation, 2016).

Beveridge, W, *Social Insurance and Allied Services* (Cmd 6404, London: HMSO, 1942).

Birrell, D, *The Impact of Devolution on Social Policy* (Bristol: Policy Press, 2009).

Birrell, D, *Comparing Devolved Governance* (Basingstoke: Palgrave Macmillan, 2012).

Birrell, D and Gray, AM, 'The devolved administrations and welfare delivery', *Delivering Social Welfare: Governance and Service Provision in the UK* (Bristol: Policy Press, 2017).

Birrell, D and Heenan, D, 'Devolution and social security: the anomaly of Northern Ireland' (2010) 18 *Journal of Poverty and Social Justice* 281.

Birrell, D and Heenan, D, 'The continuing volatility of devolution in Northern Ireland: the shadow of direct rule' (2017) 88(3) *Political Quarterly* 473.

Birrell, D and Murie, A, 'Ideology, conflict and social policy' (1975) 4(3) *Journal of Social Policy* 243.

Birt, C and Milne, B, 'Turning the tide on child poverty in Scotland' (York: JRF, 2021).

Blair, T, 'Beveridge revisited: a welfare state for the 21st century' in Walker, R (ed), *Ending Child Poverty: Popular Welfare for the 21st Century?* (Bristol: Policy Press, 1999).

Blythyn, H, MS, Letter to John Griffiths AM, 20 May 2020.

Bochel, H and Defty, A, 'MPs' attitudes to welfare: a new consensus?' (2007) 36(1) *Journal of Social Policy* 1.

Bogdanor, V, 'Post-Brexit Britain may need a constitution – or face disintegration' (*Guardian*, 18 January 2019). Available at: www.theGuardian.com/commentisfree/2019/jan/18/brexit-britain-constitution-disintegration-eu-uk-devolution-good-friday-agreement.

Boland, V, 'Stakes high in Northern Ireland welfare reform crisis' (*Financial Times*, 27 May 2015). Available at: www.ft.com/cms/s/0/1172b9c8-0478-11e5-a5c3-00144feabdc0.html.

Bottomore, T, 'Citizenship and social class, forty years on' in TH Marshall and T Bottomore, *Citizenship and Social Class* (London: Pluto, 1992).

Bounds, A, 'Andy Burnham sees more devolution as "best answer" to Brexit' (*Financial Times*, 9 May 2018). Available at: www.ft.com/content/7a6aa9c0-52ce-11e8-b3ee-41e0209208ec.

Boyle, K, *Economic and social rights law: incorporation, justiciability and principles of adjudication* (Abingdon: Routledge, 2020).

Bradbury, J, *Constitutional policy and territorial politics in the UK, vol 1: union and devolution 1997–2007* (Bristol: Bristol University Press, 2021).

Bradshaw, J, *Social security parity in Northern Ireland* (Belfast: Policy Research Institute, 1989).
Brewer, M, 'The new tax credits' (BN35, London: Institute for Fiscal Studies, 2003).
Brodkin, EZ and Marston, G (eds), *Work and the welfare state: street level organisations and workfare policies* (Washington DC: Georgetown University Press, 2013).
Brooks, L, 'Nicola Sturgeon: No 10 cannot stand in the way of independence' (*Guardian*, 11 April 2021). Available at: www.theGuardian.com/politics/2021/apr/11/nicola-sturgeon-independence-uk-government-cannot-stand-in-way.
Brown, P with Barry, J, Donaghy, C, Hoey, J and Elliott, B, *Testing a real peace dividend for Northern Ireland: a proposal for UBI* (Belfast: UBI Lab NI, 2020).
Browne, J, Hood, A and Joyce, R, 'The (changing) effects of universal credit' in Emmerson, C, Johnson, P and Joyce, R (eds), *IFS Green Budget 2016* (London: Institute for Fiscal Studies, 2016).
Bryson, A and Berthoud, R, 'Social security appeals: what do the claimants want?' (1997) 4(1) *Journal of Social Security Law* 17.
Bubeck, D, 'Democratic, gender-neutral citizenship' in Gardner, JP, *Citizenship: the white paper* (London: British Institute of International and Comparative Law, 1999).
Bueren, G van, 'Including the excluded: the case for an economic, social and cultural Human Rights Act' (2002) *Aut Public Law* 456.
Cairney, P, 'Has devolution changed the "British policy style?"' (2008) 3(3) *British Politics* 350.
Cairney, P, Russell, S and St Denny, E, 'The 'Scottish approach' to policy and policymaking: what issues are territorial and what are universal?' (2016) 44(3) *Policy and Politics* 333.
Cameron, D, 'Scottish independence referendum: statement by prime minister' (London: Scotland Office, 2014). Available at: gov.uk/government/news/scottish-independence-referendum-statement-by-the-prime-minister.
Castles, FG and Mitchell, D, 'Worlds of welfare and families of nations', Castles, FG (ed), *Families of nations: patterns of public policy in western democracies* (Aldershot: Dartmouth, 1993).
Cavanagh, M, *Personal independence payment: a second independent review of the assessment process* (Belfast: DfC, 2020).
Chadwick, O, *The secularisation of the European mind in the 19th century* (Cambridge: Cambridge University Press, 1975).
Charmaz, K, *Constructing grounded theory* (London: Sage, 2014).
Child Poverty Action Group, 'Statement on Supreme Court decision on two-child limit' (news release, 9 July 2021). Available at: https://cpag.org.uk/news-blogs/news-listings/statement-supreme-court-decision-two-child-limit.
Citizens' Basic Income Feasibility Study Steering Group, *Assessing the feasibility of citizens' basic income pilots in Scotland* (Basic Income Scotland, 2020).
Clegg, D, 'David Cameron, Ed Miliband and Nick Clegg sign joint historic promise which guarantees more devolved powers for Scotland and protection of NHS if we vote No' (Daily Record, 15 September 2014). Available at: www.dailyrecord.co.uk/news/politics/david-cameron-ed-miliband-nick-4265992.
Clément, D, 'Human rights or social justice? The problem of rights inflation' (2018) 22(2) *International Journal of Human Rights* 155.
Commission of the European Union, Commission Communication establishing a European Pillar of Social Rights COM(2017) 250 final.
Commission on a Bill of Rights, *A UK Bill of Rights? The choice before us* (London: Commission on a Bill of Rights, 2012).
Commission on Devolution in Wales, *Empowerment and responsibility: legislative powers to strengthen Wales* (Cardiff: Commission on Devolution in Wales, 2013).
Commission on Scottish Devolution, *Serving Scotland better: Scotland and the United Kingdom in the 21st century* (Edinburgh: Commission on Scottish Devolution, 2009).
Committee for Social Development, *Report on the Welfare Reform Bill (NIA Bill 12/11–15)*. (NIA 74/11–15, Belfast: NI Assembly, 2013).
Committee of Independent Experts, *Conclusions VII – United Kingdom – article 13-4* (Strasbourg: Council of Europe, 1978–79).

Committee of Independent Experts, *Conclusions XIII-4* (Strasbourg: Council of Europe, 1996).
Committee on Economic, Social and Cultural Rights, 'General comment no 3: the nature of states parties' obligations' (E/1991/23, Geneva: United Nations, 1991).
Committee on Economic, Social and Cultural Rights, 'General comment no 19: the right to social security' (E/C.12/GC/19, Geneva: United Nations, 2008).
Committee on Economic, Social and Cultural Rights, 'Concluding observations on the sixth periodic report of the United Kingdom of Great Britain and Northern Ireland' (E/C.12/GBR/CO/6, Geneva: United Nations, 2016).
Comptroller and Auditor General, *Rolling out universal credit* (HC1123, London: National Audit Office, 2018).
Comptroller and Auditor General, *Welfare reforms in Northern Ireland* (Belfast: NIAO, 2019).
Comptroller and Auditor General, *The Northern Ireland budget process* (Belfast: NI Audit Office, 2021).
Conservative Party, 'Protecting human rights in the UK: the Conservatives' proposals for changing Britain's human rights laws' (London: Conservative Party, 2014).
Conservative Party, *Strong leadership, a clear economic plan, a brighter, more secure future: the Conservative party manifesto 2015* (London: Conservative Party, 2015).
Constitution Committee, *The Union and devolution* (HL149, London: House of Lords, 2016).
Cook, JI 'Financial relations between the Exchequers of the United Kingdom and Northern Ireland' in Newark, FH, Cook, JI, Harkness, DAE, Preer, LGP and Neill, DG, *Devolution of Government: The Experiment in Northern* Ireland (London: George Allen and Unwin, 1953).
Coulter, C and Shirlow, P, 'From the "long war" to the "long peace": introduction to the special edition' (2019) 43(1) *Capital and Class* 3.
Cowan, D, Dymond, A, Halliday, S and Hunter, C, 'Reconsidering mandatory reconsideration' (2017) *Apr Public Law* 215.
Cowan, D and Mumford, A, *Pandemic Legalities: Wealth, Poverty and the Economic Recovery* (Bristol: Bristol University Press, 2021).
Craven, M, *The International Covenant on Economic, Social and Cultural Rights: A Perspective on its Development* (Oxford: Oxford University Press, 1995).
Curtice, J, 'Is it really all just about economics? Issues of nationhood and welfare' (Edinburgh: ScotCen Social Research, 2013).
Curtice, J, 'The three characteristics of the Scottish Conservative revival' (What Scotland Thinks, 1 October 2017). Available at: https://whatscotlandthinks.org/2017/10/the-three-characteristics-of-the-scottish-conservative-revival/.
Curtice, J, 'Is Scotland more egalitarian than England?' (ScotCen, 29 October 2020). Available at: www.scotcen.org.uk/blog/is-scotland-more-egalitarian-than-england.
Curtice, J, 'Scottish election 2021: how the SNP was denied a majority by tactical voting' (Scotsman, 10 May 2021). Available at: www.scotsman.com/news/opinion/columnists/scottish-election-2021-how-the-snp-was-denied-a-majority-by-tactical-voting-professor-john-curtice-3230002.
Curtice, J, 'Will Covid-19 change attitudes towards the welfare state?' (2020) 27(1) *Progressive Review* 93.
Curtice, J and Ormston, R, 'Is Scotland more left-wing than England?' (Edinburgh: ScotCen Social Research, 2011).
Dahlgreen, W, 'Yes campaign lead at 2 in Scottish referendum' (YouGov blog, 6 September 2014). Available at: https://yougov.co.uk/topics/politics/articles-reports/2014/09/06/latest-scottish-referendum-poll-yes-lead.
Dawkins, R, *The God Delusion* (New York: Bantam, 2006).
Deacon, A and Patrick, R, 'A new welfare settlement? The coalition government and welfare-to-work', Bochel, H (ed), *The Conservative Party and Social Policy* (Bristol: Policy Press, 2011).
Dean, H, 'The translation of needs into rights: reconceptualising social citizenship as a global phenomenon' (2013) 22(S1) *International Journal of Social Welfare* S32.
Dean, H, 'A post-Marshallian conception of global social citizenship' in Isin, E and Nyers, P (eds), *The Routledge Handbook of Global Citizenship Studies* (Abingdon: Routledge, 2014).
Deeming, C, 'Social inequality: is Scotland more Nordic than liberal?' in Clery, E, Curtice, J, Frankenburg, J, Morgan, H and Reid, S (eds), *British Social Attitudes 38* (London: NatCen, 2021).

Delanty, G, *Citizenship in a Global Age: Society, Culture and Politics* (Milton Keynes: Open University Press, 2000).

Dellavalle, S, 'From *imago dei* to mutual recognition: the evolution of the concept of human dignity in the light of the defence of religious freedom' in McCrudden, C (ed), *Understanding Human Dignity* (Oxford: Oxford University Press, 2013).

Denham, J, 'A nation divided? The identities, politics and governance of England' (Open Democracy, 16 August 2018). Available at: www.opendemocracy.net/en/opendemocracyuk/nation-divided-identities-politics-and-governance-of-england/.

Department for Communities, 'Northern Ireland benefit statistics summary at November 2016' (Belfast: DfC, 2017).

Department for Communities, 'Section 75 policy screening form: Universal Credit Contingency Fund (UCCF). (Change to eligibility criteria effective from January 2020).' (Belfast: DfC, 2019).

Department for Communities, 'Make the Call supports over 9000 people claim £43.2million in additional benefits and supports' (news release, 18 November 2019). Available at: www.communities-ni.gov.uk/news/make-call-supports-over-9000-people-claim-ps432million-additional-benefits-and-supports.

Department for Communities, 'Northern Ireland benefit statistics summary at November 2019' (Belfast: DfC, 2020).

Department for Communities, 'Universal credit: Northern Ireland data to February 2020' (Belfast: DfC, 2020).

Department for Communities, 'Benefit cap: Northern Ireland data to February 2021' (Belfast: DfC, 2021).

Department for Communities, 'Communities Minister Hargey addresses Committee on welfare mitigations' (news release, 17 June 2021). Available at: www.communities-ni.gov.uk/news/communities-minister-hargey-addresses-committee-welfare-mitigations.

Department for Communities, 'Communities Minister Hargey and Scottish and Welsh Ministers call for reversal of UC £20 uplift decision' (news release, 27 August 2021). Available at: www.communities-ni.gov.uk/news/communities-minister-hargey-and-scottish-and-welsh-ministers-call-reversal-uc-ps20-uplift-decision.

Department for Communities, 'Universal credit: Northern Ireland – data to November 2020' (Belfast: DfC, 2021).

Department for Communities, 'Communities Minister Hargey announces welfare protections extension' (Belfast: DfC, 2021).

Department for Social Security, *Opportunity for all: tackling poverty and social exclusion* (Cm 4445, London: DSS, 1999).

Department for Work and Pensions, *A New Deal for welfare: empowering people to work* (Cm 6730, London: DWP, 2006).

Department for Work and Pensions, *Disability living allowance reform* (Cm 7984, London: DWP, 2010).

Department for Work and Pensions, *Universal credit: welfare that works* (Cm 7957, London: DWP, 2010).

Department for Work and Pensions, *Measuring child poverty: a consultation on better measures of child poverty* (Cm 8483, London: DWP, 2012).

Department for Work and Pensions, 'Benefit cap: number of households capped to August 2020' (London: DWP, 2020).

Department for Work and Pensions, 'Benefit sanctions statistics to January 2020' (London: DWP, 2020).

Department for Work and Pensions, 'Universal credit statistics, 29 April 2013 to 14 January 2021' (London: DWP, 2021).

Department for Work and Pensions, *Shaping future support: the health and disability green paper* (CP470, London: DWP, 2021).

Department for Work and Pensions, caseload statistics at StatXplore (London: DWP, nd). Available at: https://stat-xplore.dwp.gov.uk/.

Devolution (Further Powers). Committee, *New powers for Scotland: an interim report on the Smith Commission and the UK government's proposals* (SP paper 720, Edinburgh: Scottish Parliament, 2015).

DeYoung, E, 'Lest we forget: observations from Belfast's Twaddell Avenue' (2016) 25 Streetnotes 179.

Dickson, B, 'New human rights protections in Northern Ireland' (1999) 24(supp) *European Law Review* 3.

Dilnot, A and McCrae, J, 'Family credit and the working families' tax credit' (BN3, London: Institute for Fiscal Studies, 1999).

Duncan Smith, I, Speech to the Conservative Party conference (Birmingham, 5 October 2010).

Dunleavy, DA, 'Learning Irish amid controversy: how the Irish Language Act debate has impacted learners of Irish in Belfast' (2021) *Journal of Multilingual and Multicultural Development*. Available at: https://doi.org/10.1080/01434632.2020.1854272.

Dunn, A, 'The "dole or drudgery" dilemma: education, the work ethic and unemployment' (2010) 44(1) *Social Policy and Administration* 1.

Dunn, A, 'Activation workers' perceptions of their long-term unemployed clients' attitudes towards employment' (2013) 42(4) *Journal of Social Policy* 799.

Dwyer, P, *Understanding Social Citizenship: Themes and Perspectives for Policy and Practice* (Bristol: Policy Press, 2010).

Economic Dependency Working Group, *Dynamic Benefits: Towards Welfare that Works* (London: Centre for Social Justice, 2009).

Edwards, A, *A history of the Northern Ireland Labour Party: Democratic Socialism and Sectarianism* (Manchester: Manchester University Press, 2009).

Eleveld, A, Kampen, T and Arts, J (eds), *Welfare to Work in Contemporary European Welfare States: Legal, Sociological and Philosophical Perspectives on Justice and Domination* (Bristol: Policy Press, 2020).

Eleveld, A, Kampen, T and Arts, J, 'Welfare to work, social justice and domination: an introduction to an interdisciplinary normative perspective on welfare policies' in Eleveld, A, Kampen, T and Arts, J (eds), *Welfare to Work in Contemporary European Welfare States: Legal, Sociological and Philosophical Perspectives on Justice and Domination* (Bristol: Policy Press, 2020).

Ellison, N, 'The coalition government, public spending and social policy' in Bochel, H and Powell, M (eds), *The Coalition Government and Social Policy: Restructuring the Welfare State* (Bristol: Policy Press, 2016).

Emmenegger, P, Kvist, J, Marx, P and Petersen, K, 'Three worlds of welfare capitalism: the making of a classic' (2015) 25(1) *Journal of European Social Policy* 3.

Equality, Local Government and Communities Committee, *Benefits in Wales: options for better delivery* (Cardiff: National Assembly for Wales, 2019).

Esping-Andersen, G *The Three Worlds of Welfare Capitalism* (Princeton: Princeton University Press, 1989).

European Committee of Social Rights, *Conclusions XV-1 – United Kingdom – article 13-4* (Strasbourg: Council of Europe, 1997–98).

European Committee of Social Rights, *Conclusions XVIII-1 – United Kingdom – Article 12-1* (Strasbourg: Council of Europe, 2003–04).

Evans, M, 'New Labour and the rise of the new constitutionalism' in Beech, M and Lee, S (eds), *Ten Years of New Labour* (Basingstoke: Palgrave Macmillan, 2008).

Expert Working Group on Welfare, *Re-thinking welfare: fair, personal and simple* (Edinburgh: Scottish Government, 2014).

Faist, T, 'Social citizenship in the European Union: nested membership' (2001) 39(1) *Journal of Common Market Studies* 37.

Featherstone, B, 'Why gender matters in child welfare and protection' (2006) 26(2) *Critical Social Policy* 294.

Ferrera, M, *The Boundaries of Welfare: European Integration and the New Spatial Politics of Social Protection* (Oxford: Oxford University Press, 2005).

Ferrera, M, 'Solidarity in Europe after the crisis' (2014) 21(2) *Constellations* 222.

Finn, D, 'Employment policy' in Ellison, N and Pierson, C (eds), *Developments in British Social Policy* (London: Macmillan, 2003).

Finnis, J, *Natural Law and Natural Rights* (Oxford: Clarendon Press, 1980).

Fitzpatrick, C, McKeever, G and Simpson, M, 'Conditionality, discretion and TH Marshall's "right to welfare"' (2019) 41(4) *Journal of Social Welfare and Family Law* 445.

Fitzpatrick, C and O'Sullivan, C, 'Comparing social security provision in the North and South of Ireland: past developments and future challenges' (2021) 32(2) *Irish Studies in International Affairs* 283.

Fletcher, DR, 'Workfare – a blast from the past? Contemporary workfare conditionality for the unemployed in historical perspective' (2015) 14(3) *Social Policy and Society* 329.

Fredman, S, *Human Rights Transformed: Positive Rights and Positive Duties* (Oxford: Oxford University Press, 2008).

Fredman, S, 'New horizons: incorporating socio-economic rights in a British Bill of Rights' (2010, Apr) *Public Law* 297.

Freud, D, *Reducing dependency, increasing opportunity: options for the future of welfare to work* (London: Department for Work and Pensions, 2007).

Frey, J, *Social housing in Northern Ireland: challenges and options* (Glasgow: UK Collaborative Centre for Housing Evidence, 2018).

Fukuyama, F, 'The end of history?' (1989) 16 *The National Interest* 3.

Fukuyama, F, 'Reflections on the End of History, five years later' (1995) 34(2) *History and Theory* 27.

Galligan, DJ, 'Legal theory and empirical research' in P Cane and HM Kritzer (eds), *The Oxford Handbook of Empirical Legal Research* (Oxford: Oxford University Press, 2010).

Garry, J and McNicholl, K, 'Understanding the "Northern Irish" identity' (Knowledge Exchange Seminar Series, NI Assembly, Belfast, 13 May 2015). Available at: www.niassembly.gov.uk/globalassets/documents/raise/knowledge_exchange/briefing_papers/series4/northern_ireland_identity_garry_mcnicholl_policy_document.pdf.

Gayle, D, 'UK at risk of becoming a failed state, says Gordon Brown' (*Guardian*, 25 January 2021). Available at: www.theGuardian.com/politics/2021/jan/25/uk-at-risk-of-becoming-failed-state-says-gordon-brown.

Gearty, C, 'Against judicial enforcement' in Gearty, C and Mantouvalou, V *Debating Social Rights* (Oxford: Hart, 2011).

Gearty, C, 'Socio-economic rights, basic needs and human dignity: a perspective from law's front line', C McCrudden (ed), *Understanding Human Dignity* (Oxford: Oxford University Press, 2013).

Gerards, R and Welters, R, 'Does eliminating benefit eligibility requirements improve unemployed job search and labour market outcomes?' (2021) *Applied Economics Letter*, latest articles https://doi.org/10.1080/13504851.2021.1927960.

Gibb, K, *The 'bedroom tax' in Scotland* (SP paper 409, Edinburgh: Scottish Parliament, 2013).

Glenister, S, 'How can we shape the way the country is run?' (2020) 85 *Socialist Lawyer* 5.

Gormley-Heenan, C and Aughey, A, 'Northern Ireland and Brexit: three effects on "the border in the mind"' (2017) 19(3) *British Journal of Politics and International Relations* 497.

Gover, D and Kenny, M, 'Answering the West Lothian Question? A critical assessment of "English votes for English laws" in the UK Parliament' (2018) 71(4) *Parliamentary Affairs* 760.

Gow, L, 'Permutations of popular sovereignty before, during and after the Scottish independence referendum' in Heintze, H-J and Thielbörger, P (eds), *From Cold War to Cyber War: The Evolution of the International Law of Peace and Armed Conflict over the Last 25 Years* (Cham: Springer, 2016).

Gray, AM and Birrell, D, 'Coalition government in Northern Ireland: social policy and the lowest common denominator thesis' (2012) 11(1) *Social Policy and Society* 15.

Gray, P, *The second independent review of the personal independence payment assessment* (London: DWP, 2019).

Greater Manchester Poverty Action, 'Devolved approaches to social security in the UK – lessons for Greater Manchester' (Manchester: GMPA, 2020). Available at: www.gmpovertyaction.org/devolved-approaches/.

Greer, SL, 'The territorial bases of health policymaking in the UK after devolution' (2005) 15(4) *Regional and Federal Studies* 501.

Greer, SL (ed), *Devolution and Social Citizenship in the UK* (Bristol: Policy Press, 2009).

Greer, SL and Mätzke, M, 'Introduction: devolution and citizenship rights', SL Greer (ed), *Devolution and Social Citizenship in the UK* (Bristol: Policy Press, 2009).

Griggs, J and Evans, M, *Sanctions within conditional benefit systems: a review of evidence* (York: Joseph Rowntree Foundation, 2010).
Hachez, I, 'Le standstill, ou comment les juges ont permis de mieux protéger les droits fondamentaux en limitant des possibilités de recul' (Justice en ligne, 12 February 2016). Available at: www.justice-en-ligne.be/article821.html.
Hale, B, 'The changing legal landscape' (2019) 19(4) *Legal Information Management* 217.
Handler, JF, *Social citizenship and workfare in the United States and western Europe: the paradox of inclusion* (Cambridge: Cambridge University Press, 2004).
Hansard, HC (NI) Deb 7 May 1925, vol 6 col 468.
Hansard, HC deb 9 March 1926, vol 192 col 2174.
Hansard, HL deb 23 March 1926, vol 63 col 747.
Hansard, HC deb 1 March 1929, vol 225 col 2347, 2360, 2361 2374.
Hansard, HL deb 17 March 1936, vol 100 col 4.
Hansard, HC (NI) Deb 2 March 1949, vol 33 col 37.
Hansard, SP deb 12 May 1999, vol 1 no 1 col 5.
Hansard, Committee for Social Development, Pensions Bill deb 8 November 2007.
Hansard, HC deb 9 Mar 2011, vol 524 cols 921, 922, 925.
Hansard, Committee for Social Development, Pensions Bill: accelerated passage deb 8 September 2011.
Hansard, NIA deb 23 November 2011, vol 58 no 2 p 65.
Hansard, HL deb 12 December 2011, vol 733 col 1090.
Hansard, HL deb 14 December 2011, vol 733 col 1312.
Hansard, SP deb 22 December 2011, session 4 cols 4941, 5097.
Hansard, HL deb 11 January 2012, vol 734 col 123, 206.
Hansard, HL deb 23 January 2012, vol 734 col 820.
Hansard, NIA deb 20 November 2012, vol 79 no 6 p 2.
Hansard, NIA deb 18 November 2015, vol 109 no 7 p 14.
Hansard, SP deb 2 October 2018, col 29.
Hansard, SP deb 6 March 2019, col 19.
Hansard, AQO 29/17–22, NIA deb 3 February 2020, vol 125 no 5 p 42.
Hansard, AQO 1423/17-22, NIA deb 19 January 2021 vol 135 no 2 p 33.
Hansard, AQO 2410/17-22, NIA deb 20 September 2021, vol 142 no 4 p 21.
Hanvey, J, 'Dignity, person and *Imago Trinitatis*', McCrudden, C (ed), *Understanding Human Dignity* (Oxford: Oxford University Press, 2013).
Harris, J, 'Could Wales leave the United Kingdom?' (*Guardian*, 1 February 2012). Available at: www.theGuardian.com/uk/2012/feb/01/could-wales-leave-united-kingdom.
Harris, N, 'European Court of Human Rights confirms that both contributory and non-contributory benefits are covered by Article 1 of Protocol 1' (2006) 13(1) *Journal of Social Security Law* 3.
Harris, N, *Law in a Complex State: Complexity in the Law and Structure of Welfare* (Oxford: Hart, 2013).
Harris, N, 'Welfare reform and the shifting threshold of support for disabled people' (2014) 77(6) *Modern Law Review* 888.
Harris, N, 'Complexity in the law and administration of social security: is it really a problem?' (2015) 37(2) *Journal of Social Welfare and Family Law* 209.
Harris, N, 'Demagnetisation of social security and healthcare for migrants to the UK' (2016) 18(2) *European Journal of Social Security* 130.
Harris, N, Fitzpatrick, C, Meers, J and Simpson, M, 'Coronavirus and social security entitlement in the UK' (2020) 27(2) *Journal of Social Security Law* 55.
Harvey, C (ed), *Human Rights, Equality and Democratic Renewal in Northern Ireland* (Oxford: Hart, 2001).
Harvey, C and Russell, D, 'A new beginning for human rights protection in Northern Ireland?' (2009) 6 *European Human Rights Law Review* 748.
Hearty, K, 'The Great Awakening? The Belfast flag protests and Protestant/Unionist/Loyalist counter-memory in Northern Ireland' (2015) 30(2) *Irish Political Studies* 157.
Heater, D, *What is Citizenship?* (Cambridge: Polity Press, 1999).

Henderson, A, Jeffery, C, Wincott, D and Wyn Jones, R, 'Reflections on the "devolution paradox": a comparative examination of multilevel citizenship' (2013) 47(3) *Regional and Federal Studies* 303.

Henderson, A and McEwen, N, 'Regions as primary political communities: a multi-level comparative analysis of turnout in regional elections' (2015) 45(2) *Publius* 189.

Hillyard, P, Rolston, B and Tomlinson, M, *Poverty and Conflict in Ireland: An International Perspective* (Dublin: Institute of Public Administration/Combat Poverty Agency, 2005).

Himsworth, C, 'Legislating for permanence and a statutory footing' (2016) 24(1) *Irish Political Studies* 361.

Hirsch, D, 'After a decade of austerity, does the UK have an income safety net worth its name?' in Rees, J, Pomati, M and Heins, E (eds), *Social Policy Review 32* (Bristol: Policy Press, 2020).

HM Government, *A new approach to child poverty: tackling the causes of disadvantage and transforming families' lives* (Cm 8061, London: DWP, 2011).

HM Government, *Scotland in the United Kingdom: an enduring settlement* (Cm 8990, Edinburgh: Scotland Office, 2015).

HM Government, *Cornwall Devolution Deal* (London: Ministry of Housing, Communities and Local Government, 2016).

HM Government and Scottish Government, *The agreement between the Scottish Government and the United Kingdom Government on the Scottish Government's fiscal framework* (Edinburgh: Scottish Government, 2016).

HM Treasury, *Statement of funding policy: funding the Scottish Parliament, National Assembly for Wales and Northern Ireland Assembly* (London: HM Treasury, 2015).

Holland, S, Adamson, B and Yiasouma, K, letter to Thérèse Coffey MP, 21 May 2021. Available at: https://cypcs.org.uk/resources/childrens-commissioners-for-scotland-northern-ireland-and-wales-letter-to-secretary-of-state-for-work-and-pensions/.

Hollenbach, D, 'Human dignity: experience and history, practical reason and faith', C McCrudden (ed), *Understanding Human Dignity* (Oxford: Oxford University Press, 2013).

Hooghe, L and Marks, G, *Multi-level Governance and European Integration* (Rowman and Littlefield, 2001).

Hooghe, L, Marks, G and Schakel, A (eds), *Measuring Regional Authority* (2008) 18(2/3) Regional and Federal Studies, special issue.

Hooton, V, 'COVID-19, unemployment and social solidarity in EU law' (2021) 28(1) *Journal of Social Security Law* 16.

Hopkin, J, 'Party matters: devolution and party politics in Britain and Spain' (2009) 15(2) *Party Politics* 179.

Horgan, G, 'Devolution, direct rule and neo-liberal reconstruction in Northern Ireland' (2006) 26(3) *Critical Social Policy* 656.

Horgan, G and Gray, AM, 'Devolution in Northern Ireland: a lost opportunity?' (2012) 32(3) *Critical Social Policy* 467.

House of Commons, EDM 591 Commencement and enforcement of the socio-economic duty (tabled 23 November 2017).

Hoxsey, D, 'Debating the ghost of Marshall: a critique of citizenship' (2011) 15(6–7) *Citizenship Studies* 915.

Hunt, M, 'Enhancing Parliament's role in relation to economic and social rights' (2010) 3 *European Human Rights Law Review* 242.

Iversen, T, 'Democracy and capitalism' in Castles, FG, Leibfried, S, Lewis, J, Obinger, H and Pierson, C (eds), *The Oxford Handbook of the Welfare State* (Oxford: Oxford University Press, 2010).

Jeffery, C, 'German federalism from cooperation to competition' in Umbach, M (ed), *German Federalism: Past, Present and Future* (Palgrave, 2002).

Jeffery, C, 'Devolution and social citizenship: which society, whose citizenship?' in Greer, SL (ed), *Territory, Democracy and Justice: Regionalism and Federalism in Western Democracies* (Basingstoke: Palgrave Macmillan, 2006).

Jeffery, C, 'Constitutional change – without end?' (2015) 86(2) *Political Quarterly* 275.

Jensen, T and Tyler, I, '"Benefits broods": the cultural and political crafting of anti-welfare commonsense' (2015) 35(4) *Critical Social Policy* 470.

Johnson, N, 'The Government of Wales Act 2006: Welsh devolution still a process and not an event?' (2007) 4 *Web Journal of Current Legal Issues*. Available at: www.bailii.org/uk/other/journals/WebJCLI/2007/issue4/johnson4.html.

Johnston, R and Miller, A, 'Interview with Professor Alan Miller' (2016) 75 *Scottish Human Rights Journal* 2.

Joint Committee on Human Rights, *Legislative scrutiny: Welfare Reform Bill* (HC233/HL1704, London: Houses of Parliament, 2011).

Jones, DA, 'Is dignity language useful in bioethical discussion of assisted suicide and abortion?', McCrudden, C (ed), *Understanding Human Dignity* (Oxford: Oxford University Press, 2013).

Jönsson, JH and Kojan, BH, 'Social justice beyond neoliberal welfare nationalism: challenges of increasing immigration to Sweden and Norway' (2017) 5(3) *Critical and Radical Social Work* 301.

Joyce, R, 'Child poverty in Britain: recent trends and future prospects' (W15/07, London: IFS, 2014).

Keating, M, 'Social citizenship, solidarity and welfare in regionalised and plurinational states' (2009) 13(5) *Citizenship Studies* 501.

Keating, M and McEwen, N, 'The Scottish independence debate' in M Keating (ed), *Debating Scotland: Issues of Independence and Union in the 2014 Referendum* (Oxford: Oxford University Press, 2017).

Keep, M, *Scotland: public spending and revenue* (BP06625, London: House of Commons, 2020).

Kenny, M, Rycroft, P and Sheldon, J, *Union at the Crossroads: Can the British State Handle the Challenges of Devolution?* (London: Constitution Society, 2021).

Keskinen, S, 'From welfare nationalism to welfare chauvinism: economic rhetoric, the welfare state and changing asylum policies in Finland' (2016) 36(3) *Critical Social Policy* 352.

King, DS and Waldron, J, 'Citizenship, social citizenship and the defence of welfare provision' (1988) 18(4) *British Journal of Political Science* 415.

King, J, *Judging Social Rights* (Cambridge: Cambridge University Press, 2012).

Kymlicka, W, *Politics in the Vernacular: Nationalism, Multiculturalism and Citizenship* (Oxford: Oxford University Press, 2001).

Langford, M (ed), *Social Rights Jurisprudence: Emerging Trends in International and Comparative Law* (Cambridge: Cambridge University Press, 2008).

Laparra, M and Aguilar, M, 'Social exclusion and minimum income programmes in Spain' in Rhodes, M (ed), *Southern European Welfare States: Between Crisis and Reform* (London: Frank Cass, 1997).

Larkin, PM, 'Incapacity, the labour market and social security: coercion into "positive" citizenship' (2011) 74(3) *Modern Law Review* 385.

Larkin, PM, 'Delineating the gulf between human rights jurisprudence and legislative austerity: the judicial entrenchment of "less-eligibility"' (2016) 23(1) *Journal of Social Security Law* 42.

Law, A and Mooney, G, 'Devolution in a "stateless nation": nation-building and social policy in Scotland' (2012) 46(2) *Social Policy and Administration* 161.

Leijten, I, 'From *Stec* to *Valkov*: possessions and margins in the social security case law of the European Court of Human Rights' (2013) 13 *European Human Rights Law Review* 309.

Leith, MS, 'The view from above: Scottish national identity as an elite concept' (2012) 14(1) *National Identities* 39.

Lister, M, '"Marshall-ing" social and political citizenship: towards a unified conception of citizenship' (2005) 40(4) *Government and Opposition* 471.

Lister, R, *The Exclusive Society: Citizenship and the Poor* (London: Child Poverty Action Group, 1990).

Lister, R, 'Doing good by stealth: the politics of poverty and inequality under New Labour' (2001) 8(2) *New Economy* 65.

Lister, R, *Citizenship: Feminist Perspectives* (Basingstoke: Palgrave Mamillan, 2003).

Lister, R, 'Children (but not women) first: New Labour, child welfare and gender' (2006) 26(2) *Critical Social Policy* 315.

Lister, R, 'Power not pity: poverty and human rights' (2013) 7(2) *Ethics and Social Welfare* 109.

Lister, R, 'To count for nothing: poverty beyond the statistics' (2015) 3 *Journal of the British Academy* 139.

Lister, R, *Poverty* (Cambridge: Polity Press, 2021).

Lister, R, 'Defining poverty' in *Poverty* (Cambridge: Polity Press, 2021).
Lister, R, Williams, F, Anttonen, A, Bussemaker, J, Gerhard, U, Heinen, J, Johansson, S, Leira, A, Siim, B and Tobio, C with Gavanes, A, *Gendering Citizenship in Western Europe: New Challenges for Citizenship Research in a Cross-national Context* (Bristol: Policy Press, 2007).
Lodge, G and Trench, A, 'Devo more and welfare: devolving benefits and policy for a stronger union' (London: IPPR, 2014).
Lowe, R, *The Welfare State in Britain since 1945* (London: Macmillan, 1999).
Lundy, L, 'Parity, parrotry or plagiarism? Legislating for the unemployed poor in Northern Ireland 1838–1995' in Dawson, N, Greer, D and Ingram, P (eds), *One Hundred and Fifty Years of Irish Law* (Belfast: SLS Legal Publications, 1996).
Maas, W, 'Migrants, states, and EU citizenship's unfulfilled promise' (2008) 12(6) *Citizenship Studies* 583.
Machin, R, 'COVID-19 and the temporary transformation of the UK social security system' (2021) 41(4) *Critical Social Policy* 651.
Machin, S 'Childhood disadvantage and intergenerational transmissions of economic status', Centre for Analysis of Social Exclusion, *Persistent poverty and lifetime inequality: the evidence* (occasional paper no 10, London: HM Treasury, 1999).
MacGregor, M, 'Citizenship in name only: constructing meaningful citizenship through a recalibration of the values attached to waged labour' (2012) 32(3) *Disability Studies Quarterly*. Available at: http://dx.doi.org/10.18061/dsq.v32i3.
Mackinnon, D, 'Devolution, state restructuring and policy divergence in the UK' (2015) 181(1) *The Geographical Journal* 47.
Mackley, A, *Coronavirus: universal credit during the crisis* (BP8999, London: House of Commons, 2021).
Mann, M, 'Ruling class strategies and citizenship', Bulmer, M and Rees, AM, *Citizenship Today: The Contemporary Relevance of TH Marshall* (London: UCL Press, 1996).
Mantouvalou, V, 'In support of legalisation' in Gearty, C and Mantouvalou, V, *Debating Social Rights* (Oxford: Hart, 2011).
Marshall, TH, 'Social selection in the welfare state' in *Class, Citizenship and Social Development* (New York: Doubleday, 1964).
Marshall, TH, 'The welfare state and the affluent society' in *Class, Citizenship and Social Development* (New York: Doubleday, 1964).
Marshall, TH, 'Work and wealth' in *Class, Citizenship and Social Development* (New York: Doubleday, 1964).
Marshall, TH, *Social Policy in the Twentieth Century* (London: Hutchinson, 1975).
Marshall, TH, 'Afterthought: the hyphenated society' in *The Right to Welfare and Other Essays* (New York: Free Press, 1981).
Marshall, TH, 'The right to welfare' in *The Right to Welfare and Other Essays* (London: Heinemann, 1981).
Marshall, TH, 'Value problems of welfare-capitalism' in *The Right to Welfare and Other Essays* (New York: Free Press, 1981).
Marshall, TH, 'Citizenship and social class' in Marshall, TH and Bottomore, T, *Citizenship and Social Class* (London: Pluto, 1992).
Mashaw, JL, *Bureaucratic Justice: Managing Social Security Disability Claims* (Newhaven: Yale University Press, 2009).
Matchett, C, 'Fact check: Labour peer's claim Scottish cross-border ban unlawful mostly false' (The Scotsman, 23 December 2020). Available at: www.scotsman.com/health/coronavirus/fact-check-labour-peers-claim-scottish-cross-border-ban-unlawful-mostly-false-3076779.
McCrone, D, *Understanding Scotland: the Sociology of a Nation* (London: Routledge, 2001).
McCrudden, C, 'Human dignity and judicial interpretation of human rights' (2008) 19(4) *European Journal of International Law* 655.
McCrudden, C (ed), *Understanding Human Dignity* (Oxford: Oxford University Press, 2013).
McCrudden, C, 'In pursuit of human dignity: an introduction to current debates' in C McCrudden (ed), *Understanding Human Dignity* (Oxford: Oxford University Press, 2013).

McEwen, N, 'State welfare nationalism: the territorial impact of welfare state development in Scotland' (2002) 12(1) *Regional and Federal Studies* 66.
McEwen, N, 'The territorial politics of social policy development in multilevel states' (2005) 15(4) *Regional and Federal Studies* 537.
McEwen, N, 'Welfare: contesting communities of solidarity' in Keating, M (ed), *Debating Scotland: Issues of Independence and Union in the 2014 Referendum* (Oxford: Oxford University Press, 2017).
McEwen, N, 'Brexit and Scotland: between two Unions' (2018) 13(1) *British Politics* 65.
McEwen, N and Petersohn, B, 'Between autonomy and interdependence: the challenges of shared rule after the Scottish referendum' (2015) 86(2) *Political Quarterly* 192.
McKay, S and Rowlingson, K, 'Social security and welfare reform' in Powell, M (ed), *Modernising the Welfare State: The Blair Legacy* (Bristol: Policy Press, 2008).
McKeever, G, 'Reforming social security appeal tribunals in Northern Ireland: parity whether we Leggatt or not' (2010) 17(2) *Journal of Social Security Law* 71.
McKeever, G, 'A ladder of legal participation for tribunal users' (2013) (Win) *Public Law* 575.
McKeever, G, 'Accessing social citizenship' (PhD thesis, University of Ulster, 2013).
McKeever, G, 'Improving decision making in employment and support allowance' (2014) 21(1) *Journal of Social Security Law* 13.
McKeever, G, 'Legislative scrutiny, co-ordination and the Social Security Advisory Committee: from system coherence to Scottish devolution' (2016) 23(3) *Journal of Social Security Law* 126.
McKeever, G, 'Scrutinising social security law and protecting social rights: Lord Kerr and the benefit cap' in Dickson, B and McCormick, C (eds), *The Judicial Mind: A Festschrift for Lord Kerr of Tonaghmore* (Oxford: Hart, 2022).
McKeever, G and Simpson, M, 'Worlds of welfare collide: implementing a European unemployment benefit scheme in the UK' (2017) 19(1) *European Journal of Social Security* 21.
McKeever, G, Simpson, M and Fitzpatrick, C, *Destitution and Paths to Justice* (London: Legal Education Foundation/York: Joseph Rowntree Foundation, 2018).
McLean, I, Gallagher, J and Lodge, G, *Scotland's Choices: The Referendum and What Happens Afterwards* (Edinburgh: Edinburgh University Press, 2013).
McNicholl, K, Stevenson, C and Garry, J, 'How the "Northern Irish" national identity is understood and used by young people and politicians' (2019) 40(3) *Political Psychology* 487.
Mead, LM, 'The new politics of the new poverty' (1991) 103 *Public Interest* 3.
Mead, LM, 'Citizenship and social policy: TH Marshall and poverty' (1997) 14(2) *Social Philosophy and Policy* 197.
Meers, J, 'Discretion as blame avoidance: passing the buck to local authorities in "welfare reform"' (2019) 27(1) *Journal of Poverty and Social Justice* 41.
Meers, J, 'Problems with the "manifestly without reasonable foundation" test' (2020) 27(1) *Journal of Social Security Law* 12.
Milligan, A and Hughes, J, *Attitudes to Social Welfare and Reform* (Belfast: Department for Communities, 2018).
Mitchell, J, *Devolution in the UK* (Manchester: Manchester University Press, 2009).
Mooney, G, 'Scotland, the CSR and public sector cuts' in Yeates, N, Haux, T, Jawad, R and Kilkey, M (eds), *In defence of welfare: the impacts of the spending review* (York: Social Policy Association, 2011).
Mooney, G and Poole, L, '"A land of milk and honey"? Social policy in Scotland after devolution' (2004) 24(4) *Critical Social Policy* 458.
Mooney, G and Scott, G, 'The 2014 Scottish independence debate: questions of social welfare and social justice' (2015) 23(1) *Journal of Poverty and Social Justice* 5.
Moreira, A and Hick, R, 'COVID-19, the Great Recession and social policy: Is this time different?' (2021) 55(2) *Social Policy and Administration* 261.
Moreno, L, 'Multilevel citizens, new social risks, and regional welfare' in Suszycki, AM and Karolewski, IP (eds), *Citizenship and Identity in the Welfare State* (Baden-Baden: Nomos, 2013).
Moyn, S, 'The secret history of constitutional dignity' in McCrudden, C (ed), *Understanding Human Dignity* (Oxford: Oxford University Press, 2013).

Mullard, M and Swaray, R, 'New Labour legacy: comparing the Labour governments of Blair and Brown to Labour governments since 1945' (2010) 81(4) *Political Quarterly* 511.
New Statesman, 'The welfare conundrum' (2021) 150 (5603) *New Statesman* 3.
NI Direct, 'How much universal credit you will get' (Belfast: NI Direct, nd). Available at: www.nidirect.gov.uk/articles/how-much-universal-credit-you-will-get.
Nolan, A (ed), *Economic and Social Rights after the Global Financial Crisis* (Cambridge: Cambridge University Press, 2014).
Nolan, A, O'Connell, R and Harvey, C (eds), *Human Rights and Public Finance: Budgets and the Promotion of Economic and Social Rights* (Oxford: Hart, 2013).
Northern Ireland Affairs Committee, 'A Bill of Rights for Northern Ireland: an interim statement' (HC236 incorporating HC360, London: House of Commons, 2010).
Northern Ireland Housing Executive, 'Current LHA rent levels' (Belfast: NIHE, 2021). https://www.nihe.gov.uk/Housing-Help/Local-Housing-Allowance/Current-LHA-rent-levels.
Northern Ireland Human Rights Commission, *A Bill of Rights for Northern Ireland: advice to the Secretary of State for Northern Ireland* (Belfast: NIHRC 2008).
Northern Ireland Office, *Agreement reached in the multi-party negotiations* (Cm 3883, Belfast: NIO, 1998).
Northern Ireland Office, *A Bill of Rights for Northern Ireland: next steps* (Belfast: NIO, 2009).
Northern Ireland Office, *New decade, new approach* (Belfast: NIO, 2020).
Northern Ireland Public Services Ombudsman, *PIP and the value of further evidence* (Belfast: NIPSO, 2021).
Northern Ireland Welfare Reform Group, *Social Development Committee: Welfare Reform Bill (Northern Ireland) 2012* (Belfast: Law Centre NI, 2012).
O'Brien, C, 'Real links, abstract rights and false alarms: the relationship between the ECJ's "real link" case law and national solidarity' (2008) 33(5) *European Law Review* 643.
O'Brien, C, '"Done because we are too menny": the two-child rule promotes poverty, invokes a narrative of welfare decadence, and abandons children's rights' (2018) 26(4) *International Journal of Children's Rights* 700.
O'Cinneide, C, 'A modest proposal: destitution, state responsibility and the European Convention on Human Rights' (2008) 5 *European Human Rights Law Review* 583.
Offer, J, '"Desert," "need," the social theory of the Poor Law report of 1834 and John Stuart Mill' (1989) 9(1) *International Journal of Sociology and Social Policy* 63.
Office for Budget Responsibility, *Welfare trends report* (CP02, London: HM Treasury, 2019).
Office for National Statistics, *Annual survey of hours and earnings, 2014 provisional results* (Newport: ONS, 2014).
Office of Gordon and Sarah Brown, 'Scotland' (Office of Gordon and Sarah Brown, nd). Available at: https://gordonandsarahbrown.com/campaign/scotland/.
O'Dowd, L and Komarova, M, 'Contesting territorial fixity? A case study of regeneration in Belfast' (2011) 48(10) *Urban Studies* 2013.
O'Mahony, C, 'There is no such thing as a right to dignity' (2012) 10(2) *International Journal of Constitutional Law* 551.
Opinium, 'UK: national identity in Britain' (Opinium, 9 March 2020). Available at: www.opinium.com/resource-center/national-identity-in-britain/.
Osborne, G, Speech to Conservative Party conference (Birmingham, 8 October 2012).
Paine, T, *Rights of Man* (Harmondsworth: Penguin, 1971).
Palmer, E, 'The Child Poverty Act 2010: holding government to account for promises in a recessionary climate?' (2010) 3 *European Human Rights Law Review* 305.
Partington, M, 'Empirical legal research and policy-making' in P Cane and HM Kritzer (eds), *The Oxford Handbook of Empirical Legal Research* (Oxford: Oxford University Press, 2010).
Pateman, C, *The Disorder of Women* (Cambridge: Polity Press, 1989).
Patrick, R, *For Whose Benefit: The Everyday Realities of Welfare Reform* (Bristol: Policy Press, 2017).
Patrick, R, 'Unsettling the anti-welfare commonsense: the potential in participatory research with people living in poverty' (2020) 49(2) *Journal of Social Policy* 251.
Patrick, R and Brewer, M, *Pandemic Pressures: Why Families on a Low Income are Spending More during Covid-19* (London: Resolution Foundation, 2021).

Patrick, R, Power, M, Garthwaite, K, Page, G and Pybus, K, *A Year Like No Other: Family Life on a Low Income in Covid-19* (Bristol: Policy Press, 2022).

Patrick, R and Simpson, M, 'Conceptualising dignity in the context of social security: bottom-up and top-down perspectives' (2020) 54(3) *Social Policy and Administration* 475.

Patrick, R and Simpson, M, *Universal credit could be a lifeline in Northern Ireland, but it must be designed with people who use it* (York: JRF, 2020).

Paun, A, Rutter, J and Nicholl, A, *Devolution as a policy laboratory: evidence sharing and learning between the UK's four governments* (London: Alliance for Useful Evidence, 2016).

Paun, A, Sargent, J and Nice, A, *A four-nation exit strategy: how the UK and devolved governments should approach coronavirus* (London: Institute for Government, 2020).

Paun, A and Sargeant, J, 'Explainer: Scottish independence' (London, Institute for Government, 2021). Available at: www.instituteforgovernment.org.uk/explainers/scottish-independence.

Pearce, N and Taylor, E, 'Government spending and welfare: changing attitudes towards the role of the state' in Park, A, Bryson, C, Clery, E, Curtice, J and Phillips, M (eds), *British Social Attitudes 30* (London: NatCen Social Research, 2013).

Peterson, PE, *The Price of Federalism* (Washington DC: Brookings Institution, 1995).

Piachaud, D, 'The New Right and New Labour' in Walker, R (ed), *Ending Child Poverty: Popular Welfare for the 21st Century?* (Bristol: Policy Press, 1999).

Piachaud, D and Sutherland, H, 'Child poverty in Britain and the New Labour government' (2001) 30(1) *Journal of Social Policy* 95.

Piattoni, S, 'Multi-level governance: a historical and conceptual analysis' (2009) 31(2) *Journal of European Integration* 163.

Pierson, P, *Dismantling the welfare state? Regan, Thatcher and the Politics of Retrenchment* (Cambridge: Cambridge University Press, 1994).

Plant, R, 'Supply side citizenship?' (1999) 6(3) *Journal of Social Security Law* 124.

Polomarkakis, KA, 'The European Pillar of Social Rights and the quest for EU social sustainability' (2020) 29(2) *Social and Legal Studies* 183.

Porter, I, *Nowhere to Turn: Strengthening the Safety Net for Children and Families Facing Crisis* (London: Children's Society, 2019).

Portes, J and Reed, H, *The Cumulative Impact of Tax and Welfare Reforms* (London: Equality and Human Rights Commission, 2018).

Powell, M, 'The hidden history of social citizenship' (2002) 6(3) *Citizenship Studies* 229.

Prosser, DT, 'Poverty, ideology and legality: supplementary benefit appeals tribunals and their predecessors' (1977) 4 *British Journal of Law and Society* 39.

Purnell, J, 'We need a welfare state that secures Beveridge's legacy' (*Financial Times*, 2 March 2012). Available at: www.ft.com/content/6c8aa290-639e-11e1-b85b-00144feabdc0.

Ramsay, A, 'It's not enough to vote for an independence referendum, you need to campaign for it' (Open Democracy, 11 May 2021). Available at: www.opendemocracy.net/en/opendemocracyuk/its-not-enough-to-vote-for-an-independence-referendum-you-need-to-campaign-for-it/.

Reed, H and Portes, J, *Cumulative impact assessment of tax and social security reforms in Northern Ireland* (Belfast: Northern Ireland Human Rights Commission, 2019).

Rees, AM, 'TH Marshall and the progress of citizenship' in M Bulmer and AM Rees (eds), *Citizenship Today: The Contemporary Relevance of TH Marshall* (London: Routledge, 1996).

Research and Library Services, 'A background paper on the Barnett Formula' (RP12/01, Belfast: Northern Ireland Assembly, 2001).

Revi, B, 'TH Marshall and his critics: reappraising "social citizenship" in the twenty-first century' (2014) 18(3–4) *Citizenship Studies* 452.

Ritchie, DG, *Natural rights: a criticism of some political and ethical conceptions* (London: Allen & Unwin, 1924).

Rixen, S, 'Devolution and decentralisation in social security: the situation in Germany' in Vonk, G and Schoukens, P (eds), *Devolution and Decentralisation in Social Security: A European Comparative Perspective* (The Hague: Eleven, 2019).

Robertson, L, Wright, S and Stewart, ABR, *How well is universal credit supporting people in Glasgow?* (York: JRF, 2020).
Royal Commission on the Constitution, *Report of the Commission* (Cmnd 5460, London: HMSO, 1973).
Ruiz Jiménez, AM, Romero Portillo, D and Navarro Adoy, L, 'Social patriotism: populist glue for a multinational democracy' (2021) 23(2) *National Identities* 127.
Russell, R, 'Census 2011: key statistics at Northern Ireland and LGD level' (NIAR005-13, Belfast: NI Assembly, 2013).
Salmond, A, interview on Andrew Marr show (BBC One, 14 September 2014).
Sassen, S, 'The repositioning of citizenship: emergent subjects and spaces for politics' (2002) 46 *Berkeley Journal of Sociology* 13.
Schall, CE, 'Is the problem of European citizenship a problem of social citizenship? Social policy, federalism and democracy in the EU and United States' (2012) 82(1) *Sociological Inquiry* 123.
Schlink, B, 'The concept of human dignity: current uses, future discourse', McCrudden, C (ed), *Understanding human dignity* (Oxford: Oxford University Press, 2013).
Scholes, A, 'The changing role of identity and values in Scotland's politics' (What Scotland Thinks, 28 April 2021). Available at: https://whatscotlandthinks.org/2021/04/the-changing-role-of-identity-and-values-in-scotlands-politics/.
Schoukens, P and Vonk, G, 'The state of devolution and decentralisation in social security, a comparative European analysis: an introduction' in Vonk, G and Schoukens, P, (eds), *Devolution and decentralisation in social security: a European comparative perspective* (The Hague: Eleven, 2019).
ScotCen Social Research, 'Do you agree or disagree that Government should redistribute income from better-off to less well off?' *What Scotland thinks: non-partisan information on attitudes to how Scotland should be governed* (Edinburgh: ScotCen Social Research, 2013). Available at: http://whatscotlandthinks.org/questions/do-you-agree-or-disagree-that-government-should-redistribute-income-from-better#line.
Scottish Affairs Committee, *Welfare policy in Scotland* (HC55, London: House of Commons, 2021).
Scottish Campaign on Rights to Social Security, *Beyond a safe and secure transition – a long term vision for disability assistance in Scotland* (Glasgow: SCoRSS, 2020).
Scottish Commission on Social Security, *Scrutiny report on draft Regulations: Disability Assistance for Working Age People (Scotland). Regulations* (Edinburgh: SCoSS, 2021).
Scottish Government, *Creating a fairer Scotland: social security – the story so far … and the next steps* (Edinburgh: Scottish Government, 2015).
Scottish Government, 'Further devolution beyond the Smith Commission' (Edinburgh: Scottish Government, 2015).
Scottish Government, *A new future for social security: consultation on social security in Scotland* (Edinburgh: Scottish Government, 2016).
Scottish Government, *Creating a fairer Scotland: a new future for social security in Scotland* (Edinburgh: Scottish Government 2016).
Scottish Government, *It takes all of us to build a fairer Scotland: Fairer Scotland action plan* (Edinburgh: Scottish Government, 2016).
Scottish Government, *Welfare Reform (Further Provision) (Scotland) Act 2012: annual report 2016* (Edinburgh: Scottish Government, 2016).
Scottish Government, *Consultation on Funeral Expense Assistance Regulations* (Edinburgh: Scottish Government, 2018).
Scottish Government, *Every child, every chance: the tackling child poverty delivery plan 2018–22* (Edinburgh: Scottish Government, 2018).
Scottish Government, *Social security experience panels: about your benefits and you* (Edinburgh: Scottish Government, 2018).
Scottish Government, *The fairer Scotland duty: interim guidance for public bodies* (Edinburgh: Scottish Government, 2018).

Scottish Government, 'Cold spell and winter heating assistance: policy position paper' (Edinburgh: Scottish Government, 2019).
Scottish Government, *Disability assistance in Scotland: consultation* (Edinburgh: Scottish Government, 2019).
Scottish Government, 'Funeral expense assistance: Fairer Scotland duty assessment' (Edinburgh: Scottish Government, 2019).
Scottish Government, 'Scottish child payment: position paper' (Edinburgh: Scottish Government, 2019).
Scottish Government, *Scottish Government response to consultation on the draft regulations of the Young Carer Grant* (Edinburgh: Scottish Government, 2019).
Scottish Government, *Social security experience panels: personal independence payment health assessments* (Edinburgh: Scottish Government, 2019).
Scottish Government, *The Scottish approach to service design* (Edinburgh: Scottish Government, 2019).
Scottish Government, *Social security experience panels: personal independence payment health assessments – part two* (Edinburgh: Scottish Government, 2020).
Scottish Government, 'Social Security policy position paper – disability benefit applications: extra support options' (Edinburgh: Scottish Government, 2020).
Scottish Government, 'Social Security policy position paper – disability benefit applications: how decisions are made' (Edinburgh: Scottish Government, 2020).
Scottish Government, 'Social security policy position paper – disability benefit applications: making applications' (Edinburgh: Scottish Government, 2020).
Scottish Government, *A Scotland for the future: opportunities and challenges of Scotland's changing population* (Edinburgh: Scottish Government, 2021).
Scottish Government, *Adult disability payment: consultation analysis* (Edinburgh: Scottish Government, 2021).
Scottish Government, *Consultation on adult disability payment* (Edinburgh: Scottish Government, 2021).
Scottish Government, 'Local Housing Allowance Rates: 2021–2022' (Edinburgh: Scottish Government, 2021). Available at: www.gov.scot/publications/local-housing-allowance-rates-2021-2022/.
Scottish Government, 'New Human Rights Bill' (news release, 20 March 2021). Available at: www.gov.scot/news/new-human-rights-bill/.
Scottish Government, 'Pledge on children's rights' (news release, 6 October 2021). Available at: www.gov.scot/news/pledge-on-childrens-rights/.
Scottish Government, *Scottish carer's assistance – discussion paper* (Edinburgh: Scottish Government, 2021).
Scottish Government, *Scottish welfare fund statutory guidance update* (Edinburgh: Scottish Government, 2021).
Scottish Government, Social security experience panels publications (Edinburgh: Scottish Government, nd). Available at: www.gov.scot/collections/social-security-experience-panels-publications/.
Seawright, D, 'The Scottish Conservative and Unionist Party: "the lesser spotted Tory"?' in Hassan, G and Warhurst, C (eds), *Tomorrow's Scotland* (London: Lawrence and Wishart, 2002).
Sépulchre, M, 'This is not citizenship: analysing the claims of disability activists in Sweden' (PhD thesis, Uppsala University, 2019).
Shaw, J and Stiks, I (eds), *Citizenship Rights* (Farnham: Ashgate, 2013).
Simeon, R, 'Federalism and social justice: thinking through the tangle' in Greer, SL (ed), *Territory, democracy and Justice: Regionalism and Federalism in Western Democracies* (Basingstoke: Palgrave Macmillan, 2006).
Simpson, M, 'Developing constitutional principles through firefighting: social security parity in Northern Ireland' (2015) 22(1) *Journal of Social Security Law* 31.
Simpson, M, 'The Agreement and devolved social security: a missed opportunity for socio-economic rights in Northern Ireland?' (2015) 66(2) *Northern Ireland Legal Quarterly* 105.
Simpson, M, 'The social union after the coalition: devolution, divergence and convergence' (2017) 46(2) *Journal of Social Policy* 251.

Simpson, M, 'Renegotiating social citizenship in an age of devolution' (2017) 44(4) *Journal of Law and Society* 646.

Simpson, M, 'Assessing the compliance of the United Kingdom's social security system with its obligations under the European Social Charter' (2018) 18(4) *Human Rights Law Review* 745.

Simpson, M, 'Brexit and devolved social security in Scotland: a tale of two referenda' 25(1) (2018) *Journal of Social Security Law* 56.

Simpson, M, 'Social rights, child rights, discrimination and devolution: untangling the web' (2018) 40(1) *Journal of Social Welfare and Family Law* 3.

Simpson, M, McKeever, G and Fitzpatrick, C, 'Legal protection against destitution in the UK: restoring a right to a subsistence minimum' (under review).

Simpson, M, McKeever, G and Gray, AM, 'From principles to practice: social security in the Scottish laboratory of democracy' (2019) 26(1) *Journal of Social Security Law* 13.

Smith, A, 'Internationalisation and constitutional borrowing in drafting Bills of Rights' (2011) 60(4) *International and Comparative Law Quarterly* 867.

Smith, A, McWilliams, M and Yarnell, P, *Political capacity building: advancing a Bill of Rights for Northern Ireland* (Newtownabbey: Transitional Justice Institute, 2014).

Smith Commission, *Report of the Smith Commission for further devolution of powers to the Scottish Parliament* (Edinburgh: Smith Commission, 2014).

Social Security Advisory Committee, *Young people living independently* (OP20, London: SSAC, 2018).

Social Security Advisory Committee, *How DWP involves disabled people when developing or evaluating programmes that affect them* (OP25, London: SSAC, 2021).

Social Security Committee, *The contributory principle* (HC51-I, London: House of Commons, 2000).

Social Security Committee, *Benefit take-up* (SP696, Edinburgh: Scottish Parliament, 2020).

Social Security Scotland, *Our Charter* (Dundee: Social Security Scotland, 2019).

Social Security Scotland, *Client survey: 2018–20* (Dundee: Social Security Scotland, 2021).

Soskice, J, 'Human dignity and the image of God', McCrudden, C (ed), *Understanding human dignity* (Oxford: Oxford University Press, 2013).

Special issue on Positive obligations and the European Court of Human Rights (2010) 61(3) *Northern Ireland Legal Quarterly*.

Special issue on COVID-19 (2021) 28(1) *Journal of Social Security Law*.

Spence, R, 'Local welfare: tips and tactics' (2015) 248 Welfare Rights Bulletin. Available at: https://cpag.org.uk/welfare-rights/resources/article/local-welfare-tips-and-tactics.

Spicker, P, 'The devolution of social security benefits in Scotland: the Smith Commission' (2015) 23(1) *Journal of Poverty and Social Justice* 17.

Sprague, A, Raub, A and Heymann, J, 'Providing a foundation for decent work and adequate income during health and economic crises: constitutional approaches in 193 countries' (2020) 40(9/10). *International Journal of Sociology and Social Policy* 1087.

Sturgeon, N, 'Foreword from the Deputy First Minister' in Scottish Government, *Child poverty strategy for Scotland: our approach 2014–2017* (Edinburgh: Scottish Government, 2014).

Sturgeon, N, speech at Bute House, 13 March 2017.

Suárez Corujo, B, 'Devolution and decentralisation in social security: the situation in Spain' in Vonk, G and Schoukens, P (eds), *Devolution and decentralisation in social security: a European comparative perspective* (The Hague: Eleven, 2019).

Subirats, J, 'Multi-level governance and multi-level discontent: the triumph and tensions of the Spanish model' in Greer, SL (ed), *Territory, Democracy and Justice: Regionalism and federalism in Western Democracies* (Palgrave Macmillan, 2006).

Tamanaha, BZ, 'Law and society' in Patterson, D (ed), *A Companion to Philosophy of Law and Legal Theory* (Hoboken: Wiley-Blackwell, 2010).

Tambakaki, P, *Human Rights or Citizenship?* (Abingdon: Birkbeck Law Press, 2010).

Tange, H and Kirsten, J, 'From Bologna to welfare nationalism: international higher education in Denmark, 2000–2020' (2021) 21(2) *Language and Intercultural Communication* 223.

Taylor-Collins, E and Bristow, D, *Administering social security in Wales: evidence on potential reforms* (Cardiff: Wales Centre for Public Policy, 2020).

Taylor-Gooby, P, *Reframing Social Citizenship* (Oxford: Oxford University Press, 2009).
Teague, P, 'Northern Ireland: the political economy of peace' (Belfast: Mitchell Institute for Global Peace, Security and Justice, 2016).
Thomas, G, Morgan, L and Worthington, P, 'What might a universal basic income mean for Wales?' (Cardiff: Senedd Research, 2021).
Thomas, R, 'Administrative justice, better decision making and organisational learning' (2015) Jan *Public Law* 111.
Thurley, D and McInnes, R, *State pension triple lock* (CBP-07812, London: House of Commons, 2021).
Tickell, A, 'The technical Jekyll and the political Hyde: the constitutional law and politics of Scotland's independence "neverendum"' in McHarg, A, Mullen, T, Page, A and Walker, N (eds), *The Scottish Independence Referendum: Constitutional and Political Implications* (Oxford: Oxford University Press, 2016).
Timmins, N, *The Four UK Health Systems: Learning from Each Other* (London: King's Fund, 2013).
Todd, J, 'Two traditions in unionist political culture' (1987) 2(1) *Irish Political Studies* 1.
Tomlinson, J, 'Remodelling social security appeals (again): the advent of online tribunals' (2018) 25(2) *Journal of Social Security Law* 84.
Tonge, J, *Northern Ireland* (Cambridge: Polity Press, 2006).
Tonge, J and Gomez, R, 'Shared identity and the end of conflict? How far has a common sense of 'Northern Irishness' replaced British or Irish allegiances since the 1998 Good Friday Agreement?' (2015) 30(2) *Irish Political Studies* 276.
Torrance, D, *'A process not an event': Devolution in Wales, 1998–2020* (CBP8318, London: House of Commons, 2020).
Townsend, P, *Poverty in the United Kingdom* (London: Penguin, 1979).
Trench, A, 'Un-joined-up government: intergovernmental relations and citizenship rights', Greer, SL (ed), *Devolution and Social Citizenship in the UK* (Bristol: Policy Press, 2009).
Trevor-Roper, H, *The Invention of Scotland: Myth and History* (New Haven: Yale University Press, 2008).
Trevor-Roper, H, 'The invention of tradition: the Highland tradition of Scotland' in Hobsbawm, E and Ranger, T, *The Invention of Tradition* (Cambridge: Cambridge University Press, 2012).
Trump, DJ, 'Inaugural address' (Washington DC, 20 January 2017).
Trussell Trust, *Dignity or destitution? The case for keeping the universal credit lifeline* (Salisbury: Trussell Trust, 2021).
Turner, BS, 'The erosion of citizenship' (2001) 52(2) *British Journal of Sociology* 189.
Turner, BS, 'In defence of monarchy' (2012) 49 *Society* 84.
Turner, BS and Rojek, C, *Society and Culture: Principles of Scarcity and Solidarity* (London: Sage, 2001).
Twine, F, *Citizenship and Social Rights: The Interdependence of Self and Society* (London: Sage, 1994).
Valuation Office Agency, 'Local Housing Allowance (LHA) rates applicable from April 2021 to March 2022' (London: HM Government, 2021). Available at: www.gov.uk/government/publications/local-housing-allowance-lha-rates-applicable-from-april-2021-to-march-2022.
Vonk, G and Schoukens, P (eds), *Devolution and Decentralisation in Social Security: A European Comparative Perspective* (The Hague: Eleven, 2019).
Waddell, G and Burton, AK, *Is work good for your health and well-being?* (London: TSO, 2006).
Walby, S, 'Is citizenship gendered?' (1994) 28(2) *Sociology* 379.
Waldschmidt, A and Sépulchre, M, 'Citizenship: reflections on a relevant but ambivalent concept for persons with disabilities' (2019) 34(3) *Disability and Society* 421.
Walker, P, 'Amber Rudd condemns UN poverty report in combative return to frontline politics' (*Guardian*, 19 November 2018). Available at: www.theGuardian.com/politics/2018/nov/19/amber-rudd-un-poverty-report-return-frontline-politics.
Warwick, B, 'Socio-economic rights during economic crises: a changed approach to non-retrogression' (2016) 65(1) *International and Comparative Law Quarterly* 249.
Watson, B, 'Labour market in the regions of the UK: September 2020' (Newport: Office for National Statistics, 2020).
Watts, B and Fitzpatrick, S, *Welfare Conditionality* (Abingdon: Routledge, 2018).

Webster, D, 'Tackling Britain's misleading benefit sanctions statistics' (Welfare Conditionality, 21 April 2016). Available at: www.welfareconditionality.ac.uk/2016/04/tackling-britains-misleading-benefit-sanctions-statistics/.

Webster, D, Written evidence (ANC0019). to the Work and Pensions Committee Benefit Sanctions inquiry (London: House of Commons, 2018).

Welfare Conditionality, *Final findings report: Welfare Conditionality project 2013–2018* (York: Welfare Conditionality, 2018).

Welfare Reform Committee, *Stage 1 report on the Welfare Reform (Further Provision) (Scotland) Bill* (SP125, Edinburgh: Scottish Parliament, 2012).

Welfare Reform Committee, *Interim report on the 'bedroom tax'* (SP459, Edinburgh: Scottish Parliament, 2014).

Welfare Reform Mitigations Working Group, *Welfare Reform Mitigations Working Group report* (Belfast: OFMDFM, 2016).

Wells, I, 'Welsh independence: how worried should Ministers be?' (BBC News, 2 February 2021). Available at: www.bbc.co.uk/news/uk-wales-politics-55890643.

Welsh Government, 'Benefits in Wales: options for better delivery – Welsh Government response' (Cardiff: Welsh Government, 2019).

Welsh Government, 'Local housing allowance rates from April 2021 to March 2022' (Cardiff: Welsh Government, 2021). Available at: https://gov.wales/local-housing-allowance-lha-rates-april-2021-march-2022.

Weyer, J de and Schoukens, P, 'Devolution and decentralisation in social security: the situation in Belgium' in Vonk, G and Schoukens, P (eds), *Devolution and Decentralisation in Social Security: A European Comparative Perspective* (The Hague: Eleven, 2019).

Wheare, KC, *Federal Government* (Westport, CT: Greenwood Press, 1963).

Whyte, J, 'How much discrimination was there under the unionist regime, 1921–68?' in Gallagher, T and O'Connell, J, *Contemporary Irish Studies* (Manchester: Manchester University Press, 1983).

Wiggan, J, 'Contesting the austerity and "welfare reform" narrative of the UK Government: forging a social democratic imaginary in Scotland' (2017) 37(11–12) *International Journal of Sociology and Social Policy* 639.

Wilson, B, 'Labour market in the regions of the UK: April 2021' (Newport: Office for National Statistics, 2021).

Wincott, D, 'Citizenship in time and space: observations on TH Marshall's *Citizenship and social class*', Greer, SL (ed), *Devolution and Social Citizenship in the UK* (Bristol: Policy Press, 2009).

Wind, M, 'Post-national citizenship in Europe: the EU as a welfare rights generator?' (2009) 15 *Columbia Journal of European Law* 239.

Winkler, IT and Mahler, C, 'Interpreting the right to a dignified minimum existence: a new era in German socio-economic rights jurisprudence?' (2013) 13(2) *Human Rights Law Review* 388.

Work and Pensions Committee *Decision making and appeals in the benefits system* (HC313, London: House of Commons, 2010).

Work and Pensions Committee, *Benefit sanctions: Government response to the Committee's nineteenth report of session 2017–2019* (HC1949, London: House of Commons, 2019).

Work and Pensions Committee, *DWP's response to the coronavirus outbreak* (HC178, London: House of Commons, 2020).

Work and Pensions Committee and Northern Ireland Affairs Committee, *Welfare policy in Northern Ireland* (HC2100, London: House of Commons, 2019).

Yarde, J and Wishart, R 'An unequal Union? Attitudes towards social inequality in England and Scotland' (London: NatCen Social Research, 2020).

YouGov, 'YouGov/Sunday Times survey results' (London: YouGov, 2013).

INDEX

www.ingramcontent.com/pod-product-compliance
Ingram Content Group UK Ltd.
Pitfield, Milton Keynes, MK11 3LW, UK
UKHW020814290926
15470UKWH00003B/1144

9 781509 946419